Computers and People
Essays from *The Profession*

1/08

Computers and People

Essays from *The Profession*

W. Neville Holmes
School of Computing
University of Tasmania

IEEE
COMPUTER
SOCIETY

WILEY-
INTERSCIENCE

A JOHN WILEY & SONS, INC., PUBLICATION

Library of Congress Cataloging-in-Publication Data is available.

ISBN-13: 978-0-470-00859-1
ISBN-10: 0-470-00859-8

Printed in the United States of America.

10 9 8 7 6 5 4 3 2 1

In memory of my parents
without whose patience, generosity and love
in my early years
this book could never have been written
in my late years

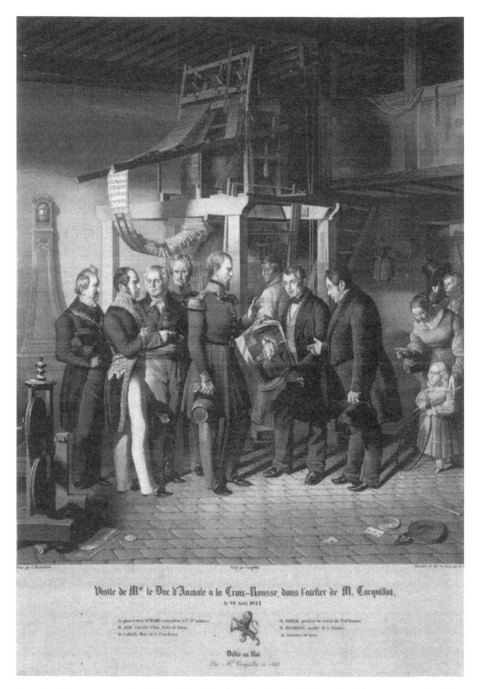

Visite de Mᵍʳ le Duc d'Aumale à la Croix-Rousse, dans l'atelier de M. Carquillat,
le 9? Août 1841

An mid-19th century digital graphic showing the Duke of Aumale being presented with a digital portrait of Joseph-Marie Jacquard, inventor of the digital machine used to produce both pictures and shown here in the background.

Contents

Preface

This book features a selection of my essays published over the last decade in *Computer,* the house journal of the IEEE Computer Society. The treatment is mostly non-technical so as to interest readers of all levels, backgrounds and specialities, and to provoke them to think about broad social and professional aspects and issues in the general area of computing and digital technology.

The very broad coverage of the essays was natural because I have always regarded myself as a generalist. Standing back from small issues to look at broad implications is important to professionalism, and to ordinary social life for that matter, and in my writings I have tried to get more people to do the same.

The essays are grouped in chapters treating different broad areas. In each chapter the essays are preceded by an introduction to put them in context, and followed by some "notions" picked out of the chapter, and by a formal and annotated bibliography.

A book like this may be read in many different ways, but I have had in mind three distinct possibilities.

1. The introductory sections, independently of their essays, are intended to provide an overall discussion of *Computers and People.* Although the text of each introduction is sequenced and tailored to suit the essays, the description should be meaningful and complete in its own right.
2. The individual chapters, read with their essays, are each meant to provide a detailed treatment of a different broad area. The notions and the bibliography have been added to each to help teachers and students focusing on the area. The Table of Contents shows what the areas are, and they are described in the brief introductory chapter following that Table, starting page xv.
3. The individual essays are relatively independent of each other, and were written each to carry its own message. Most of the essays appeared in a monthly

column called *The Profession* and these will be close to 2,000 words long, though essay 3.1 was a formal article and is quite a bit longer. The early essays—the date is given at the head of each—may be quite a bit shorter.

There are also two short secondary chapters and a quite lengthy index. The chapter entitled *The Context* is in the nature of an extended preface for anyone wanting more details about how the essays came about, and why they have been arranged as they are.

The chapter entitled *Technical Details* is really an appendix where some of the more technical aspects are explained or elaborated. Some of the essays are more technical than others, and interested readers may find a few important topics relevant to those essays dealt with in this chapter.

The index at the back of the book is extensive so that readers interested in a particular person or topic or book will be more easily be able to find a relevant essay or page.

The wording of the selected essays is, with very few exceptions, unchanged from that of the original publication. One result of this is that references to "the computing profession" abound and that many of the essays end with a small sermon addressed to "computing professionals." I hope readers outside that profession will understand that my observations are mostly much more widely relevant, and that they may safely ignore the sermons.

The original citations, which were embedded within the text and tended to disrupt reading, have been replaced by superscript indexes to the chapter's bibliography. The citations were often only of what I had been reading about the topic at that time, and many were simply URLs (pointers to Web pages). In making a more formal bibliography, I have checked the URLs, which are notoriously volatile, to update them or to replace them if the material seems to have left the Web altogether.

The notions have been extracted to provide a focus for contemplation or discussion, even for formal debates. Education, and professional education in particular, should include practice in formal presentation and discussion, and my students were required in their first semester to give individual and pair presentations and to take part in a formal debate, all on professional and social aspects of computing, and I recommend this tactic to other educators. Students need to understand that commonly accepted notions are topics for debate; consider, for example, the contradiction between *he who hesitates is lost* and *look before you leap*.

There is one notion which should not be debateable, however, a notion that is central to this book, that is mentioned often, and that is much more a matter of definition than of opinion, as explained in "The Great Term Robbery" (essay 1.3, p. 16):

Only people process information; computers only process data

Prefaces commonly include acknowledgements. Because the content of this book depends so much on a lifetime of practical experience, experience gained from association with very many people, and because its development and production has depended on the encouragement and help of so many people, I prefer to list the areas of indebtedness and imply the people I am thanking.

For my experience in computing I am indebted to my colleagues in the Melbourne Patents Subbranch for impelling me into the industry in the first place, and to colleagues in IBMand its customers, in Australia and overseas, and in the computing industry and profession generally, for an extraordinary variety of personal friendships and professional challenges.

For my experience in education I am indebted to various University people I liaised with during my last decade with IBM, particularly those at the then NSW Institute of Technology where I was seconded for two years, for inspiring me to retire into teaching, and to my colleagues at the Tasmanian State Institute of Technology, now part of the University of Tasmania, for their friendship and support, and to my students for requiring me to try to make my preaching simpler and more coherent.

For the writing behind this book I am indebted to the encouragement and editorial skill of the people at *Computer,* punctilious in their corrections and understanding of my foibles, and to the annual camaraderie of the Editorial Board meetings.

For the production of this book I am indebted to the School of Computing's technical support people in Launceston for their friendly and expert help with my computing and Internet needs, with the reviewers for their evaluations and suggestions, and to my IEEE Computer Society and Wiley Publishing partners for their patience with my delays and for allowing me to submit camera-ready copy. This concession means that I alone am responsible for any dislikes that readers may have about my taste in page composition, such as might come from my reluctance to split lines by hyphenating words.

But above all I am indebted to my wife of nearly fifty years for her patience with the long hours I have spent away from home in professional work and at home at the computer, and for her help with what I write.

NEVILLE HOLMES

May 2006

The Context

The essays brought together in this book were first published in *Computer,* the house journal of the IEEE Computer Society, beginning in May 1997. All have to do with computers, or more generally with digital technology.

To expect the essays to be interesting for general reading, or for people learning how to use computers professionally, might seem unjustified. My experience in the computing industry and in education, however, suggests very strongly that the topics dealt with here are very important both in the workplace and in everyday life, and are interesting to most people.

After taking a degree in electrical engineering, I worked for two years as a patent examiner, during which time I had to study and pass examinations in law.

Starting in 1959,1 worked for thirty years as a systems engineer with IBM Australia Limited, a subsidiary of the largest computer manufacturer in the world. My experience was mostly in Australia but with a few postings to other countries. As I approached early retirement age, IBM supported my studies for a degree in cognitive science.

Turning 55 I took up a teaching position at the Tasmanian State Institute of Technology, where an undergraduate degree in Applied Computing was just starting. In much of my teaching there I tried to give an understanding both of what it would be like to work in computing as a professional, and an appreciation of the very significant social effects of the use of computers.

Some of the ideas expressed in the essays here are ideas I covered in my lecturing. But how I came to write these essays is a story in itself.

The Background

After the TSIT was taken over by the University of Tasmania the emphasis shifted from simple undergraduate teaching to research and teaching, and staff were required to get academic papers published.

I had long felt that the arithmetic within digital computers was much less reliable numerically than it should be, so I wrote a paper explaining what was wrong and how this could be fixed. Getting a refereed academic paper accepted and published is a rather long and tedious process, but eventually mine went through. As a reward, the people at Computer sent me by air mail six copies of the issue my paper was in.

Although I had been reading Computer for many years, normally each issue took three months getting to Tasmania (it now takes only a few weeks). So, after admiring my own article, I did my usual browse through the rest of the journal. As sometimes happened, there was a column that I disagreed with quite a bit.

Normally, I would have just disagreed mentally and left it at that, but the recentness in this case prompted me to put my disagreement in writing and send it off. It was published straight away ("What Can Computers Do?" essay 1.1, p.8).

Again I was sent a copy (an essay was deemed to deserve only one) of Computer by air mail. Straight after it came the radio news reporting that a computer had beaten Carry Kasparov at chess and this worried me, so I wrote an essay about my worry and sent it off. Again it was published promptly ("The Myth of the Intelligent Computer," essay 1.4, p. 21).

Such clear encouragement could not be resisted, so I wrote several further and longer pieces on social issues, which were accepted, and some of which are in this book ("The Myth of the Computer Revolution," essay 2.1, p. 50, "The Myth of the Educational Computer," essay 3.1, p. 99).

Then I was offered and accepted the role of editor of a column to be called *The Profession* to start mid-2000, for which I was to write about half the essays myself. The nature of this column, as explained in "Fashioning a Foundation for the Computing Profession" (essay 4.1, p. 152), meant that essays for the column had to be about various issues from the point of view of professionals who help others get the best out of computing technology.

The Chapters

The column, monthly after 2000, has covered a great variety of topics, both on technical issues and, as is appropriate to a profession, social issues. The social issues are very relevant to the community at large, so I have selected for this book mostly the less technical essays which, although they are addressed directly to professional readers of *The Profession* column, should nevertheless convey much of significance to other readers. Some technical matters have been broadly covered in Chapter 5, but a detailed explanation of a few of them will be found in the Appendix.

Largely to keep the style consistent I have chosen only my own essays, though volunteers have over the years written some excellent contributions to *The Profession* on a wonderful variety of topics.

The six chapters have distinct themes.

1   The Basis of Computing

Fundamental aspects of computers, and of digital technology generally, are not well understood even within the computing profession.

Perhaps the greatest cause of this misunderstanding is a failure to think of digital technology in its historical and social contexts.

Popular writing portrays digital technology as a wonder, a miracle even, which has sprung out of almost nowhere to astonish and transform the world. This portrayal is a gross exaggeration, but one that has marketing advantages.

Popular writing portrays computers as wonders that rival humans. Such portrayal is a woeful confusion of people and machinery.

To understand the basis of computing, what is needed is

- knowledge of the history and nature of technology generally, which is in effect the history and nature of our civilization,
- a proper basic terminology of computing, both for the profession and for the public,
- a proper appreciation of the nature of digital technology, including that of digital computers, •
- a clear idea of why computers are not at all like people, and
- some idea of how special interest groups in society might seek to control digital technology and the data that technology uses.

2   Computers So Far

Such an understanding of the basis of computing in turn makes possible an understanding of the history of computing and a consideration of the role of computers and digital technology in contemporary society.

Perhaps the key point to be kept in mind here is the distinction between machinery and people—people use machines, and they can use them to great effect. But the proper use of digital technology is a social choice, a choice that can be made selfishly or unselfishly. However, the choosing is at present dominated by the manufacturers of computers and of the programs that run on the computers.

Many important uses and misuses of computers are not well understood, nor have computers always been used as well as they might have been.

Some of the issues relevant to the present use of computers are

- how computers and their uses have evolved,
- what the use of digital technology has achieved, and what it might have achieved,
- the importance of computation to the development of society,
- how computers are used by people, and
- how computing systems are used to get work done in organizations.

3   Computers and Education

How we use computers is governed by what kind of people we are. What kind of people we are is determined by our education, a process administered by our family, our community, our society, and our government.

Education is intended to keep our community together, to empower us to improve society, and to enable us to wisely influence our government. In many ways this process is failing, at least partly because digital technology is not being properly used in schools.

What we are able to do with computers is governed by what we are taught about them, and by what technicians and professionals are able to develop to make the enormous potential benefits of digital technology available, and able to be used well, in education.

What technicians and professionals can do is governed by their training and education, its breadth and its depth. This training and education could be greatly extended and enhanced by proper use of digital technology, but, by and large, it isn't.

Some of the educational aspects of computers and other digital technology that need to be considered are

- the nature of education and how computers can best be used in this process,
- the bias that commercial and recreational uses of digital technology are now imposing on society and the need for countering that bias,
- the influence that computers and networks now have on intellectual life,
- the people who design and implement the uses of digital technology and how they they are trained and educated, and
- the nature of the Internet and its World Wide Web and its potential support of education and intellectual life.

Education constructs our future, industry exploits our future. Education is essential to make it possible for digital technology, the basis of civilization, to be used to harness our past experience so that our civilization can grow into the future. Nothing is more important socially than a good education for all.

4   Computing and Professions

There are two components of society that most affect the uses to which digital technology is put.

The first component, and by far the most effective strategically, is made up of the suppliers and marketers of equipment using digital technology—the computer and telecommunications industries.

The second component, of very little effect other than tactical, comprises the designers and builders of the equipment—the hardware, the software, and the allied services.

Some years ago there was an emergent third component—the computing profession.

Ideally, a computing profession would grow in strength in parallel with the enterprises based on digital technologies, exerting a balancing pressure on the commercial agents. This has not happened.

Certainly, professional bodies were formed in the early days of electronic digital computing, but they have been rather static in membership numbers for much more than a decade now, and are having difficulty in attracting new young members at anything like the rate at which new graduates are finding employment in the related industries and businesses. The reasons for this are debateable.

The reality of this languor in the computing profession is undeniable and its effects are arguably adverse.

My column, *The Profession,* was intended to address professional issues of this kind, and has persistently done so. Many volunteered essays have been very concerned with professional directions and education.

However, change of the kind that is needed to balance commercial and social interests in digital technology cannot come merely from the bleating of a column or two in the digital wilderness. Society itself needs to address these issues. That is the justification for including essays on professional issues in a book intended for general readership.

The six essays in this chapter of the book give my view of the changes needed in the structure of the technological endeavors and in the education of digital technologists of various kinds. Quite a few of the issues are pertinent to other professions and vocations.

It seems that if there is to be substantial change in the putative professions and occupations that focus on the use of digital technology, that change will only come about through external pressure. This external pressure can only arise if public consideration is given to the issues involved, issues such as those considered in the essays selected for the fourth chapter.

The essays cover a variety of complementary topics:

- the nature of a profession,
- the professional structure appropriate to digital and system technologists, and
- the attitudes of workers in computing and related fields.

There is quite a bit of overlap between the essays, but this is needed so that an outsider can acquire a better appreciation of the professional issues involved. My hope is that exposing these issues here might support a public discussion of what is happening in what is from some points of view the most fundamental area of work in our society.

5   The Potential of Computing

Once the social issues marking the uses of digital technology are at least sketched out, particularly in the field of education, some of the more general and valuable possibilities of that technology can be understood more clearly and evaluated more effectively.

The most interesting and least explored possibilities in the social sphere are related to the way life can be enriched beyond mundane considerations of employment and productivity, and domestic occupation with recreation and entertainment. Two approaches can be taken to speculation about, and the analysis of, ways to get such enrichment.

The first approach looks at broad cultural areas and the possible use of digital technology in those areas. The three examples in the fifth chapter of this book are

- how digital technology could be used to translate text, and even speech, from one language to another to widen interpersonal communication,
- how text could be coded in different writing systems to enhance retrieval and cultural exchange, and
- how people might better be able to get at the enormous amount of text stored on computers around the world.

The second approach looks at the culture of digital technology itself, and of the people supporting its use, considering why computers are seen by many as hard to use, and how the expertise of computing professionals might be used to improve various social institutions. The three essays chosen of this kind consider

- the nature of programs that people use for day-to-day activities, and how these programs could be made more comprehensible,
- how digital technology might make it possible for government by elected representatives to be more democratic, and
- how a system engineering approach could bring the Olympic Games back towards their earlier ideals.

These essays only begin to suggest the possibilities for social and cultural enhancement through use of digital technology. There are many possibilities beyond those examples.

6 Facing the Future

People fill various roles in the societies of our civilization, our communities. Some roles are hierarchical, some are vocational, and there are some of various other kinds. One important role is that of members of the learned professions, who have benefited from an advanced education and training given to them on the understanding that their profession will work to the benefit of society as a whole.

The argument is made in various parts of this book that, because digital technology is now being used in all professions, the computing profession should be seen a secondary profession, ideally one that should work with other professions helping them exploit digital technology within their areas of expertise and in fulfilling their duty to improve the workings of society.

These are glossy ideals at present. Looking beyond the near future, and beyond our individual communities, there are immense problems both present and looming that all professions, indeed all educated people, should be facing up to. And digital technology is, in a fundamental sense, both behind these problems and central to their eventual solution.

The essays in this chapter therefore examine the context and nature of these big problems not only from the point of view of the computing profession and its expertise and technology, but also as it relates to professionalism in general. The specific topics are

- the responsibility of professionals of all kinds to be aware of the problems of our civilization as a whole, and to be active in promoting its health,
- the growing divisions in our civilization and the need for a concerted effort, directed through the United Nations, to heal those divisions,
- the need to act against the causes of terrorism, and similar major problems, rather than against their symptoms, so that the action will be effective, and
- the urgent need to consider the long term effects of our global activities that threaten the very survival of our civilization.

So much for the background and the context of the essays that are in the rest of this book. There remains the main theme to explain.

Modern society is simply ancient society evolved. The evolution is based on our developing ability to communicate and cooperate, with setbacks when the communication and cooperation break down.

There seem to be many threats and dangers in modem society. These threats and dangers will need to be countered and avoided by those members of society with the resources and knowledge to do so.

What seems certain to me is that successful use of those resources and that knowledge will depend on the exploitation of the digital technology that is both the quintessence of our society and the ultimate cause of our perils.

Chapter 1

The Basis of Computing

The computer is both a product and a tool of technology, so an understanding of computers and their uses can only follow from an understanding of what technology is.

Technology in its broad sense means "the scientific study of the practical or industrial arts" but may be applied to "[a] particular practical or industrial art" (*The Oxford English Dictionary*, second edition, 1989). The word is related to the word *technique*, which means "*loosely*, a skilful or efficient means of achieving a purpose" (*ibidem*).

These definitions make plain several important points. Firstly, technology is something people do or use. Secondly, technology is used practically or industrially. Thirdly, technology is used by people to achieve their purposes.

The distinction between people and machines is thus a very basic one, and very important. Computers are tools that people use. A failure to make this distinction provoked the first essay in this chapter, "What Can Computers Do?" (essay 1.1, p. 8).

Technology

Many animals have techniques and use tools. Birds build nests, dolphins use sponges to protect their snouts, platypuses dig burrows, orcas bait birds with regurgitated fish, otters use rocks to break shellfish open, beavers build dams, gorillas use walking sticks, and so on, and so on.

Humans are different only in degree, in their accumulation of techniques that has produced technologies. In prehistoric societies, before *homo sapiens* even, people were using tools and techniques for providing food, clothing and shelter. In later societies, technologies were used to exploit and develop plants and animals to support human activities and supply human needs.

1

The degree to which the human race has developed its technology is way beyond that of other species, however. Why is this?

The basic reason is that humans have developed a metatechnology, that is, a technology for passing on and improving tools and techniques.

What is easy to overlook is that *metatechnology* is simply a fancy way of referring to the essence of modern society itself. Without technology there would be no society as we know it, and the development of technologies by our society is what has made a society like ours possible. And this is not just true today, but has been true for many millennia.

Another reason, one that follows from the first, is that the development of technologies has made possible the enlargement of world society through higher food production and lower death rates. More people means technology can be developed faster, provided social conditions allow this.

Our appreciation of technology is quite subjective. Simply by talking about it in isolation from its social context, particularly when we use terms such as *hi-tech* and *nanotechnology*, we put it on a pedestal as something to be admired if not worshipped. A proper appreciation of technology is often blocked by its jargon, and by those who jabber about it unthinkingly.

But in a quite fundamental way, human society is what it is because of technology, and technology in turn is what it is because of human society. The two are inseparable.

Some of the general social aspects of technology are brought out in the second essay of this chapter, "Revising the Principles of Technorealism" (essay 1.2, p. 10).

Digital Technology

What is this metatechnology that enables humans to exploit and systematically improve their technologies? It's simply our language.

What is language? Early language was a system of signals, perhaps both vocal and gestural, used to convey ideas. More recently relatively permanent symbols have been used to represent spoken language visibly or magnetically.

Signalling, by voice or gesture, is not peculiar to humans. Many creatures practise systematic signalling: bees by dancing, birds by whistling, whales by singing. Many primates use signalling systems, vervet monkeys having more than a dozen distinct signals, for instance.

What makes human language, and maybe dolphin and some other animal languages, different is its combinatoriality. Whereas vervet monkeys can only signal as many ideas as they have different signals, we can put sounds together to make words, words together to make phrases, phrases to make sentences, and sentences to make poems and speeches, laws and plays, and essays and books. Our words and sentences and books can be used to instruct beginners in the use of technologies and engineers and scientists in the development of technologies.

Having only a finite number of distinct signals, or symbols, is the basis of digital technology. With just twelve different signals—ten digits plus a decimal point and a negative sign—we can write down any decimal number we can think of. Internally, modern digital computers use only two symbols, zero and one, but combinations of these *binary* symbols can be used to represent any numbers or words we need to have processed.

Digital computers can process our language in various ways because of the digitality of language, but its own digitality limits what the machinery can do. We use language for a special mode of communication and thought that we have built on top of the richness of the perceptions and feelings that make up our daily life.

When language is represented digitally, we call that representation *data*. When people extract facts and ideas from data, we call those facts and ideas *information*. Or we SHOULD do so, which is why "The Great Term Robbery" (essay 1.3, p.16) explains that the definitions of these two terms come from the formally accepted international standard vocabulary of the computing world.

The point to be emphasized is that computers can only process data, while only people can process information. Only people have knowledge and ideas, computers only have representations of them.

People and Computers

The definitions of the standard vocabulary do not by themselves justify the very important principle that computers only process data while only people process information. To compare the basic nature of people and computers is much more revealing.

Digital computers and their associated equipment encode everything they process as binary digits (called *bits* for short) or, rarely nowadays, as digits of other kinds. The glory of bits is that, though they are imperfectly stored and retrieved, and imperfectly sent and received, any particular bit must be very thoroughly imperfect before automatic machinery will fail to distinguish which of the only two possible values is encoded.

Furthermore, if a digital storage or transmission medium is known to be unreliable in particular ways, then extra bits can be added systematically to every record or message to allow automatic machinery to detect and even to correct errors. In this way a medium can be made as reliable as it is worthwhile to make it.

The corollary to this is that what goes in, and only what goes in or can be computed therefrom, can come out. Two compatible computers running the same program on the same data will give exactly the same result, unless there is a malfunction. Digital computers are determinate.

In contrast, anything anyone says can convey many kinds of information to a listener beyond, and to a degree independently of, the specific words used, information about the speaker's feelings and intentions, for example, or about the speaker's age, gender and background.

Further, although a listener can memorize a speech and even mimic its pronunciation, the information got out of the actual words themselves will depend on the listener's background and state of mind. The information got from speech equates to the thoughts provoked in the listener's mind by that speech, and the associations triggered by those thoughts. Those associations depend on the peculiarities of mind working on memories imperfectly laid down.

No two listeners are identical in background and state of mind, not even identical twins. Thus the information conveyed by the spoken word will not be identical for any two listeners, and will typically be quite different. Similarly, though to a lesser degree, different readers will acquire different information from reading the same text.

In this variety lies the richness of society, a richness that only fades when a person's perceptions fade, as for example in sleep or starvation, or are so swamped that background and personality become largely irrelevant, as for example when watching television.

Thus any conflating of people and machines is totally unjustified, a point examined further in "The Myth of the Intelligent Computer" (essay 1.4, p. 21).

Computers and People

Our society is based on our metatechnology of language. Our language is a social construct. We learn it from our parents and other companions, and our community maintains and develops the language we use.

Although our bodies and our brains have changed little over hundreds of millennia, our societies have changed enormously. We have changed our physical environment through farming and industry, and we have changed our systems of interpersonal relationships through wars and laws.

All these changes have been made possible by our social development of language, firstly spoken language, then written language, and most recently by the application of machinery to language.

The changes seem to be accelerating, partly and importantly because we have begun using complex machinery to process our language, going from printing machinery to electronic computers in only a few centuries. Indeed for several decades now we have been completely dependent on the use of digital computers to develop cheaper and more capable digital computers and telecommunications, a kind of positive feedback.

However, our society is developing digital computers of ever-increasing complexity while we, the individual members of society, are not developing at all, in the sense that a baby born today has the same innate potentiality as a baby born millennia ago.

Utopians see this contrast in development rates as leading to a society where all the work is done by machinery and everyone lives a life of leisure and luxury. Luddites see this contrast as foreshadowing a takeover of our world by "silicon-based lifeforms," such as extremely capable androids able to manufacture and develop their own kind.

Obviously, utopians are either extremely naïve or inhabit another world. Anyone who follows, however intermittently, the sequence of annual reports from the United Nations Development Programme[23] will understand this, as will anyone who has any familiarity with the history of the industrial world.

Luddites are in turn extremely naïve about the nature of the human mind and of human society.

Digital computers are a very long way from having a consciousness or a mind like ours. In the first place they are fundamentally different in kind, and in the second place they are still much less complex and adaptable, as explored in "Having a Mind to Computing" (essay 1.5, p. 23).

Digital computers, even when linked by the Internet, have nothing like our sociality and mobility and little prospect of ever attaining these. Even collectively, they are simply and fundamentally different. They are inanimate tools, we are their users.

The Law and Property

One of the most obvious differences between people and machinery is in the way they function, in their behavior.

When we blithely talk of machines such as cars or digital computers as behaving or misbehaving, we are referring to what they do as we use them. What we can get them to do depends firstly on what they were designed to be able to do, and secondly on the knowledge and skill we can apply to our use of the machinery. If we cannot get them to carry out some task then it is either because they can't do it (from design or malfunction) or because we don't know how to get them to do it.

When we talk about people behaving or misbehaving then we are talking about the effect of what they are doing on themselves and on other people. People behave or misbehave in that they cause emotions in each other.

Machines "behave" or "misbehave" in that they cause emotions in *us* by their mechanistic operation.

What machinery does is mechanical and functional. What people do is social and intentional.

Much social interaction is linguistic, and is typically activity intended to affect or control other people's behavior. Of course humans are not the only social animals. By developing our language we have simply extended social behavior like the grooming of monkeys, and indeed some linguists see our language as having a gestural origin.

Behavioral control is of two kinds, though the kinds overlap.

People use language to control interpersonal relationships, typically in a hierarchy of some kind. Hierarchies exist in other animal communities and signalling of various kinds is used to uphold the structure and control its lower members. But the complexity of human communities, even of entirely oral communities, is arguably made possible only by the use of language.

As language is developed social hierarchies become more complex and more extensive. The use of written language coincides with, and is certainly related to, the growth in the size of human hierarchies, witness the historical importance of documents in religion and the law. Today digital technology has become the basis of the global community.

People also use language to control the behavior of other people in respect of objects and entities other than humans.

Within a community of hunters or gatherers the provision of shelter, food and clothing involves negotiation or command, in particular when children are concerned, so that the community can survive or prosper. Commodities are owned by the community insofar as their possession and use is controlled by the community.

The combination of ownership and hierarchy has led to the development of the formal idea of property. Interestingly, since its first use well over five thousand years ago, written language beyond isolated symbols has been used primarily for the administration of society and property. Literature and science have been very minor sideshows, and universal literacy is a very recent ideal.

Property is about ownership and its rights, and has, at least in the British tradition of law, been of two kinds—realty and personalty.

Realty is land, and structures fixed to the land, and ownership is asserted either by battle or title. Title is established by documentation. Ownership is not quite the same as possession because a leaseholder can have rights of possession, again established by documentation.

Personalty is of three kinds——leasehold interests, tangible property, and intangible property. Leasehold interests relate closely to realty.

Ownership of tangible property has to do with the possession of material objects. These are often physically marked to identify their real owner in case of disputes. Interestingly, the seals used to identify sometimes the owner and sometimes the maker (like a modern trademark) of goods in the Middle East well over five millennia ago were possibly the very first examples of a printing technique used for language.

The ownership of intangible property (formally *choses in action*) such as shareholdings, debts and trademarks, is more complex. Rights in intangible property can only be claimed or enforced by legal action, action that depends almost entirely on documentation.

As society and its various uses of language have been developing, so too have the significance and the use of intangible property. For example, money was once valuable in its own right and thus relatively free of inflation, but now it is purely symbolic almost everywhere in the world.

The development of intangible property has become very rapid indeed with recent advances in digital technology. Digital machinery processes data, and data are intangible. Further, programs for computers are also intangible, and both programs and digital recordings have come to the forefront as items of commerce.

Some of the implications of this are discussed in "Data and Information as Property" (essay 1.6, p. 28).

1.1   What Can Computers Do?

(1997 May)

Marty Leisner answers his own question "Do Computers Make Us Fools?,"[13] with the statement:"It seems that computers make people incapable of independent thought." On the other hand, he concludes that "reliance on them ... might make us fools," and this, together with many of his other comments, answers quite a different question and answers it well. But it seems to me that neither question is the real question—the basic question.

So what is the real question? What is the basic problem? The context is that computers are seen as underpinning social change. The mistake is that computers are seen as causing social change. Let me illustrate one relevant social change.

Computer as Scapegoat

In 1970 I returned to Australia after living for awhile in the Hudson River Valley, where there was fairly widespread use of computers and punched cards. The state of New York had a very simple and effective drivers' license system based on stub cards, which required only that you send back the stub with your payment each year; the remainder of the card was your license.

When I went to get a license in Canberra, I was given a three-part form. The form not only asked for many more personal details than New York ever required, it required them to be written three times. When I mildly criticized the form design at the counter, I was solemnly informed that the design was as it was because of The Computer. I left it at that, but my later inquiries revealed that the department had neither a computer nor any plans to get one.

This incident alerted me to the most important social role of the computer, then as now: universal scapegoat. I have seen nothing since to change my mind on this, and indeed I have seen much to confirm it. The social change here is that people seem to be eager to use computers to avoid personal responsibility. Computers are being used to replace personal values with impersonal ones, like the ultimate abstraction—money.

Computer as Tool

Computers are merely tools. They are not members of society; they are not even pseudomembers, like corporations and governments. They are not independent agents. Like cars and telephones, they only do things if and when someone uses them. They can neither be blamed for what they do (are used for), nor given credit for what they do (are used for). If there is blame or credit then it belongs to the users, or to the owners, or to the designers, or to the manufacturers, or to the researchers, or to the financiers, never to the computer itself.

Computers cannot make us fools—they can only allow us to be foolish faster. And they can be used by others to make fools of us, for profit or power.

This is not understood by everyone because the computer industry and the computing profession seem to be saying otherwise. We seem to be saying that computers are like people; that they have memory, intelligence, understanding, and knowledge; that they are even friendly. How foolish! How ignorant! How impressive! How profitable!

Attitudes to Computers

Those in the industry who warned against anthropomorphic language have been ignored. The people who put together the first standard vocabularies for the industry urged people to call the devices where data are put "stores" or "storage", not "memories". To suggest there is any likeness between the computer storage and the memories a human might reconstruct is farcical, if not insulting.

Those in the industry who urged that people be distinguished from machines have been ignored. The people who put together the first standard vocabulary for the industry installed such a distinction in its very first two definitions. In brief, they defined "data" as representations of facts or ideas, and they defined "information" as the meaning that people give to data. Only people can process information; machines can process only data. Embodying this fundamental distinction in the definition of the two most basic computing terms was a complete waste of ink.

As long as we allow people to think of computers as anything else than machines to be owned and used, powerful people and institutions will be able to use computers as scapegoats and avoid blame for the social inequities they are able to bring about for their own benefit by using computers.

An endnote referred readers with concerns about computers and social inequities, in particular through the global financial market, to George Soros, "The Capitalist Threat."[20]

1.2   Revising the Principles of Technorealism

(2003 January)

While preparing a talk for the Victorian Section of IEEE, I stumbled on the home page of the technorealists.[19] The overview proclaims that technorealists "seek to expand the fertile middle ground between techno-utopianism and neo-Luddism." Their goal is "neither to champion nor dismiss technology, but rather to understand it and apply it in a manner more consistent with basic human values." Although these statements show the technorealists' hearts to be in the right place, the eight principles that follow suggest that their minds have drifted way off course. The principles smack more of popular journalism than realism.

My misgivings grew stronger when further Web wandering brought me to Harvey Blume's comment in *Atlantic Unbound* that the technorealist movement seemed by 2000 "to have faded away . . . because the initial statement of technorealistic principles was simply too noncontroversial."[3]

That the technorealists little understand technology is unfortunate; that their mistaken ideas should be deemed uncontroversial is a revelation of the prevalent misunderstanding of technology that makes us tragically prone to be its slaves instead of its masters. These thoughts prompted me to suggest in my talk that engineers have a professional responsibility to bring realism to technorealism.

Technologies

The first technorealist principle asserts that

Technologies are not neutral.

This principle derives from the statement that "Technologies come loaded with both intended and unintended social, political, and economic leanings." Yet technologies do not simply come—loaded or otherwise—technologists develop them. Further, technologists—not the technology itself—supply any intended or unintended leanings these technologies might have.

In digital technology's case, technologists do not yet know themselves. The workers in more traditional technological areas distinguish between technicians, who know a trade and build and repair things, and professional engineers, who exercise professional judgment to develop and design the things the technicians use, build, and repair. By nature, technicians must answer to their employers and customers. Professionals, theoretically at least, hold a privileged place in the community because their education and experience qualify them to exercise judgment in their use of technology—which the public assumes will be exercised for the community's benefit. People expect professionals to be beyond the command of employers and clients in matters that concern the public good.

Digital technologists, at least in the computing field, seem mostly to be technicians who do their own designing and who seek distinction in arcane specialties. As technicians, they have little incentive or inclination to look past their employer's interests and leanings. The first principle should be that

Technology is neutral.

The Internet

The second technorealist principle maintains that

The Internet is revolutionary, but not Utopian.

All the technorealist principles suffer from a misplaced preoccupation with digital technology, but it's especially strong here. Digital technology provides only a secondary tool, one that supports primary technologies such as genetic manipulation, medical imaging, and integrated-circuit manufacture.

The Internet is thus neither "an extraordinary communications tool" nor "revolutionary." It simply represents the current stage in the development of human capabilities through written language, which itself derived from the spoken form. Europe had an Internet two centuries ago: a semaphore system connecting Spain, Italy, France, Germany, and the Low Countries. Internets have developed in fits and starts since then, and will go on doing so.

So far, the main impersonal uses of the Internet and other digital technologies have been conservative, reinforcing and extending the existing social structure. This process has been good for some, bad for many, not because of the technology but because of how people use it.

The personal use of the Internet represents nothing more than a continuing evolution that has taken us from post to telegraph to telephone and beyond. The second principle should be that

The Internet is the present stage in
   the evolution of the technology that underpins human civilization.

Cyberspace

The third technorealist principle observes that

Government has an important role to play on the electronic frontier.

In their explanation, the technorealists equate the electronic frontier to "cyberspace [which] is not formally a place or jurisdiction separate from Earth."   For them, "the state has the right and the responsibility to help integrate cyberspace and conventional society."

Cyberspace, one of technobabble's more ludicrous coinings, seems to be anything but a place or jurisdiction. Margaret Wertheim sees it as "a repackaging of the old idea of Heaven but in a secular, technologically sanctioned format."[24]

If cyberspace refers to anything, it refers to the ubiquitous storage and transmission of digital data. The third principle should be that

Government has an important role to play in bringing
the benefits of digital technology to the community.

Information

The fourth technorealist principle states that

Information is not knowledge.

The technorealists explain their reasoning with a welter of pompous banality for which, unfortunately, the computing profession must bear responsibility.

Nearly 50 years ago, wise pioneers persuaded the profession to officially adopt clear and unambiguous definitions for the two most important words in our professional vocabulary: *data* and *information*. In brief, *data* refers to the conventional representation of facts or ideas, while *information* refers to the meaning people give to data. The profession has ignored this vitally important distinction, allowing the two terms to become almost synonymous, and has thus supported confusion and obfuscation in public discussion of digital technology [see also essay 1.3, p. 16].

If the profession would only re-adopt these two standard definitions and promote them to the public, the difference between machines and people would always be clearly visible. The fourth principle should be that

Only people process information, machines only process data.

Schools Versus Education

The fifth technorealist principle states that

Wiring the schools will not save them.

Two assertions underpin this principle:
- "The problems with ... public schools ... have almost nothing to do with [digital] technology," and
- "The art of teaching cannot be replicated by computers, the Net, or by 'distance learning.'"

Despite the truth of these assertions, the resulting principle is much too weak. Its weakness lies in aiming at *schooling* rather than *education*, for only through education can children become full participants in society. Anything less than education for all children perpetrates a gross injustice.

Why is schooling secondary to education? Because the other members of a child's family constitute the child's first society and thus provide his or her main educators. If the family fails, the community must step in. If a family or community cannot educate its children, school will be unlikely to succeed where they have not. A misfit in the family usually becomes a misfit everywhere else.

Therefore, before they worry about schools, professional technologists should be concerned with the effect their technology has on families and communities. So should the government. The fifth principle should be that

Education is a basic human right, but it must come
    from the family and the community, not from schools or machines.

Intellectual Property

The sixth technorealist principle claims that

Information wants to be protected.

The motivation behind this absurdly worded principle is "that cyberspace ... [is] challenging our copyright laws and frameworks for intellectual property." The technorealists' solution to this perceived problem calls for updating the old laws in pursuit of an old goal: "to give authors ... an incentive to create."

They have their background wrong. Intellectual property rights are monopoly rights and as such have been regarded with extreme disfavor by democratic legislators. Coming late on the intellectual property scene, the drafters of the US Constitution—wary of the bad effects such property law had caused in Europe—stood strongly against monopolies of any kind.[21] Only with great reluctance did they give to Congress, in Article I Section 8, "the Power ...

To promote the Progress of Science and useful Arts, by securing for limited Times to Authors and Inventors the exclusive Right to their respective Writings and Discoveries."

Viewed in this light, much intellectual property law has run off the rails and could even be viewed as unconstitutional in the US. Lawmakers stretch copyright to allow commercial profit from any expression of any idea and for its each and every use. Patent holders use their rights to aggressively discourage innovation and competition.

Jefferson and Madison would regard what is happening as a contemptible perversion of their work. Both copyrights and patents should be dropped, and only intellectual property monopolies such as trademarks and industrial designs should be granted—and then only to promote fair trade [more in essay 1.6, p. 28]. The sixth principle should be that

Facts and ideas must be used for the public good.

Controlling the Airwaves

The seventh technorealist principle argues that

The public owns the airwaves; the public should benefit from their use.

This strangely worded principle springs from the Gilbertian antics of governments and telecommunications companies during the feeding frenzy that third-generation mobile-telephone technology prompted. Although the frenzy seems to have subsided, some points remain to be made.

The radio spectrum cannot be owned. Clearly, a government can grant or deny the right to emit electromagnetic radiation, just as it can grant or deny the right to fly or otherwise drive vehicles. The point of a democratic government is that it should use its power over rights to serve the greatest public good. In matters of public good, the community's welfare, not the economy's, provides the main criterion. The seventh principle should be that

Electromagnetic radiation cannot be owned,
   but the community must control its use for the public good.

Understanding

Curiously, the eighth technorealist principle proclaims that

Understanding technology should be an essential component of global citizenship.

The technorealists pin this requirement's necessity on "a world driven by the flow of information," as though the world of humans hasn't always been thus. They define *global citizenship* as involvement in understanding "interfaces" and creating better tools.

Citizenship is more a matter of understanding society than of understanding digital technology. Further, the only understanding we need of any particular technology is how to control and exploit it. I need to know how to drive my car, but I get a mechanic to maintain it. Trying to make a technologist out of everyone is silly.

The idea of global citizenship does raise the important issue of public good on a global scale. Simply getting everyone to use digital technology is tragically impractical in a world where two billion people exist on less than one or two dollars a day. Surely, we should marshal technologies of all kinds to reduce this shameful inequality. The eighth principle should be that

Using technology to reduce inequity should be an aim of global citizenship.

Techno-utopianism, the belief that advancing technology will automatically bring global prosperity, is as ridiculous as neo-Luddism, the belief that global prosperity can be achieved only by rejecting technology. Although technology is inherent in all human civilizations, *people* develop it.

Yet the nature of any civilization depends on how it uses technology. Low technology used well might better serve a community than high technology used poorly. To prosper, any community must include professionals who use their expert judgment to guide the development and use of technology to the community's greater benefit. In today's world, digital technology clearly holds great importance, not only for its role in supporting human interactions and everyday activities, but for supporting the development and use of other technologies as well.

Technorealism should be based on the idea that people are more important than technologies. Before we can properly develop and use technology, we must first understand how people interact and coexist. Computing professionals can play an important role in guiding the future development of our global civilization, but their view of digital technology and the people they help must be realistic.

1.3   The Great Term Robbery

(2001 May)

In *Computer*'s January Letters to the Editor column, a reader responding to my November 2000 column (appendix, p. 285) described my suggestion that the phrase "coding scheme" would be less misleading than "programming language" as the onset of a Newspeak campaign aimed at undermining the computing profession.[10] His concerns about a real-life Newspeak are only too well founded, but computing Newspeak is long established rather than a mere threat, despite the computing profession's official adoption decades ago of a standard terminology.

As George Orwell saw and foresaw it, Newspeak aims to reduce if not remove meaning from language, thereby making political control of the masses easier. Although Orwell coined the term and wrote much on the topic, the slogans of *1984*'s Inner Party display Newspeak's character most clearly: "War Is Peace," "Freedom Is Slavery," "Ignorance Is Strength."

Although the régimes Orwell depicted have yet to appear in their full glory, at least in the world's advanced nations, Newspeak is with us nevertheless. Orwell's scornful bluntness prompted him to depict a blunt Newspeak, but a subtle version harbors more subtle dangers.

Modern Newspeak

That we already have a form of Newspeak became clear to me last December when I wandered into a bookshop dominated by several tables of books on sale, labeled bestsellers, at what the signs declared to be "lowest prices." Most of these "bestsellers" simply bore a sticker declaring that status, although others received further qualification, such as "best-selling horror story" or "bestselling war story."

The hovering sales assistant noticed my bemusement and offered her help. When I told her I somehow expected a bestseller to be unique, she brightly reassured me that they all were. My pedantry received a further jolt when I got home and noticed that the front cover of my current favorite, *The Surgeon of Crowthorne*,[25] bore the phrase "The Number One Bestseller."

Modern Newspeak hastens the decline of literacy in countries where, until a few decades ago, government schools had sustained universal literacy for most of the twentieth century. Now, the inability and disinclination to read have reached proportions that hark back to the nineteenth century. Present-day marketing does not need literate consumers—it needs an unthinking, unquestioning audience, able to be swayed by image and assertion, by repetition and hyperbole. Our ignorance is their strength.

The Computing Industry

The computing industry has also suffered from marketing hyperbole—christening data diskettes "floppy disks" provides but one example. Clothes flop, dough flops, dot-coms flop, but diskettes don't. Even the earliest versions, which lacked rigid covers, merely flexed. So why call them floppies?

To better distribute microprogram code, IBM developed the diskette drive in the late 1960s. In the 1970s, when this storage medium became widely used, marketers must have found the sober name "diskette" too bland, and so coined "floppy" to jazz it up.

Why not "flexy"? Well, by the 1970s marketers within the computing industry had drained all meaning from the word "flexible" by dubbing *everything* flexible: programs, computers, controllers, tape drives, card readers, printers, application programs, suppliers, even customers. Marketers routinely suffer from such naming exuberance. In the 1980s, "user friendly" dominated; in the 1990s, "intelligent" took pride of place; and in the 2000s, "e–" appears to lead the pack.

The computing industry and its profession require a certain amount of jargon. Our use of mnemonic initialisms and acronyms for the many transient technicalities makes technical discussion and education easier, although the practice bewilders neophytes and the public.

A responsible profession can less easily justify jargon that distorts ordinary language, either in meaning or grammar. The computing profession, for instance, uses the verb *to sort* to mean *to order* or *to sequence*. The dictionary defines *sort* as "to arrange according to sort, kind, or class"—a meaning too useful to lose, surely.

This distortion has an historical foundation, however: When data processors kept data on punched cards, they used repetitive sorting—in the true sense of the word—to put a card file in any desired sequence. Thus, sequencing on a five-digit ID number would take five passes of the card file through a sorter, moving from low-order digit tor high-order digit. Unfortunately, when magnetic tape replaced punched cards, the term "sorting" assumed the meaning "sequencing," even though the process no longer involved sorting, but rather progressive merging of subsequences. When using four tape drives, a tape "sort" would typically halve the number of subsequences with each merge pass, then stop when it arrived at a single sequence.

Grammatical distortion has its comical aspects. Computing profession-als who would never think of inputting sugar into their coffee, or outputting their dog at night, unashamedly commit these grammatical atrocities on data. When jargon distorts ordinary language, it becomes harmful. A profession has a responsibility to the public to use ordinary language whenever it's possible and convenient to do so.

Terminology Standards

A profession also has a responsibility, both to the public and its members, to develop and employ a vocabulary for expressing the fundamental concepts on which its discipline is based. The example of the American Psychiatric Association shows that such a standard vocabulary can greatly hasten a profession's maturity. The APA's *Diagnostic and Statistical Manual*[1] has been of enormous benefit, as its adoption internationally attests.

Computing professionals, too, have a standard vocabulary. In 1961, the International Federation for Information Processing set up a Terminology Committee in conjunction, later, with the International Computation Centre. The committee published an international standard vocabulary in 1966[22] that remains, with some modifications, an ISO/IEC standard.[12]

This heroic and noble work deserved a better fate than oblivion. Yet dictionary makers and—far worse—most computing professionals have largely ignored the international standard vocabulary. No computing text-books seem to adhere to the standard, nor do the multitude of specialist computing dictionaries that flood bookstores and the Web.

The common neglect of the standard's two most fundamental definitions, which are listed first in that work, best reveal this lack of observance. In their original form, these definitions read as follows:

• **Data.** A representation of facts or ideas in a formalized manner capable of being communicated or manipulated by some process.
• **Information.** In automatic data processing the meaning that a human assigns to data by means of the known conventions used in its representation.

These two clear and distinctive definitions conform reasonably with traditional usage. Contrast them with the corresponding definitions from *The New International Webster's Pocket Computer Dictionary of the English Language*[17]:

• **Data.** (*sing.* datum) Information, as that processed by a computer.
• **Information.** Any data that can be stored, retrieved, and manipulated by a computer.

These latter definitions are even murkier than the book's title. Completely confused, they conflict with the words' traditional usage. Although the worse dictionaries typically maul these definitions, the better dictionaries treat them almost as roughly.

We cannot really blame the dictionary makers for this nonsense, however. The confusion of specialist dictionaries and textbooks mirrors the terminological confusion and irresponsibility of our so very immature profession.

The Robbery

Professionals carefully and thoughtfully drew up the definitions of *data* and *information* in the standard, giving them pride of place as words that describe the computing professional's two most important concepts. Thus, the profession's dismissal of these definitions implies a profound dereliction of duty.

This neglect leaves us with two terms used more or less interchangeably for meanings so wide and indefinite as to surpass "flexible" and "intelligent" in uselessness to the profession and the public at large. Further, the profession and the public have been robbed of computing's two most important concepts, as defined and contrasted by some of the profession's wiser pioneers.

Specifically, we have been robbed of the ability to simply and consistently distinguish between people and machines. What do these two standard definitions tell us? That only people can process information, while machines can only process data. No more important distinction can be made in the field of computing.

By not making this distinction strongly, we hide from people their natural status and rights in respect to computers and their users, allow unscrupulous people to bewilder and confuse the public as to the proper role of digital technology in our society and its government, and allow our fellows to drift unconsciously from being citizens of our nations to being subjects of our economies. In effect, we support a fourth Inner Party slogan: "People Are Machines."

By not making this distinction strongly, we also rob ourselves of an important classification within digital technology. If people serve an important role in a given digital system, it is an *information* system and must be based on *information technology*. If people do not play such a role, it is a *data* system and must be based on *data technology*. Information technology should be based on cognitive science, data technology on computer and communications sciences.

The Restitution

The computing profession must review and extend the standard vocabulary in the spirit of the pioneers who did the original work, as Ian Gould described in "In Pursuit of Terminology."[9] We must pay particular attention to arriving at definitions of phrasal terms that contain either *data* or *information* to ensure that we preserve and even reinforce the humanistic distinction.

This restitution cannot happen speedily, as the linguistic habits of the community change only slowly. But we must bring the distinction between people and machines into everyday conversation. The profession must press both specialist and general dictionary makers to adopt the standard vocabulary and must persuade editors and authors of technical articles and texts to conform to the standard.

Further, the Computer Society, jointly with other professional computing societies, must make the standard vocabulary conveniently and prominently available online, for public use and for professional comment regarding the standard's concepts and their definitions.

The computing profession's most important responsibility is to plainly and consistently define the role that digital technology plays in its community. To accomplish this task, the community must distinguish between itself and its machines, and our terminology must support, not hinder, this distinction.

1.4 The Myth of the Intelligent Computer

(1997 July)

When I awoke to the radio announcement that Deep Blue had beaten world chess champion Garry Kasparov, I was at first bemused and then dismayed. I was bemused because I had just written a column (essay 1.1, p. 8) that clearly explained why it would actually be Deep Blue's designers, programmers, and builders who had beaten Kasparov, not the machine itself.

I was dismayed because—as surely as night follows day—the radio, television, and newspapers would unleash a torrent of utter claptrap about the Intelligent Computer, and some would even forecast the imminent takeover of the world by silicon-based life forms.

That this is complete twaddle is easily demonstrated. That it will be widely believed is a condemnation of our education system, which should be giving our children truth and self-respect, and of our own industry, which actively promotes the myth of intelligent machinery.

Intelligence is social

To imagine that intelligence can be equated with skill at chess playing is to completely misunderstand what intelligence is. Chess playing is to logic and calculation what intelligence is to relationships and negotiation. Chess is abstract; intelligence is social.

Intelligence is not only displayed socially, it is induced socially. Not only intelligence, but the ability to become intelligent, comes from social stimulation and interaction. People exhibit their intelligence as they learn it, entirely by the richness and versatility of their behavior with others. Did you see Deep Blue on television? Any behavior at all was only implied, and even this implied behavior was anything but rich and versatile.

Intelligence is multidimensional

In *Frames of Mind*[8] the celebrated and respected Howard Gardner distinguished seven dimensions of intelligence: linguistic, logico-mathematical, spatial, musical, kinesthetic, intrapersonal, and interpersonal. Even more have been identified since then.

To hold that a written test that takes 30 minutes or so to complete can be used to measure intelligence must be the greatest educational con job of all time. Although individuals will differ from one another (and from themselves from time to time) in their skills in these various dimensions, all normal individuals will have a modicum of skills in each—otherwise they are subnormal.

In how many of these dimensions does the Deep Blue program have any capability at all? Only one, logico-mathematical, and here its capability is quite inhuman, both in kind and degree.

Who needs androids?

Of course, in 50 or 100 years' time we may be able to build machines that can simulate, even perhaps possess, skills in all these dimensions. But by then these machines will no longer be computers. Science fiction writers have long called such machines androids. Isaac Asimov, in particular, wrote many of his stories about the problems of fitting androids into human society. Asimov's stories raised many moral and philosophical issues, most memorably *"The Caves of Steel,"*[2] which featured an android detective called Daneel Olivaw.

It may be that we will eventually make such machines. But it is hard to see why. The people who are able to own such special-purpose machines as Deep Blue will get much more benefit, at least in the short term, from their very special-purposeness.

Consider the effectiveness of the highly specialized network of computers that runs the international financial market. Many eminent economists consider that this machine is so effective that national governments no longer have any control over the economies of their countries. As one scholar put it, "The policy role of government has ... been reduced to one of obedience to financial and foreign exchange markets."[15]

The result is an accelerating gap between rich and poor people and between rich and poor nations. As one observer sardonically points out, there are more than six million people in the world worth more than $1 million and more than 1,000 people who die every day of diseases that would cost at most $1 a day to treat.

With special-purpose machines as effective as the world's financial engine, who needs androids?

This essay appeared in the column Open Channel, *edited by Will Tracz.*

1.5   Having a Mind to Computing

Originally *Would a Digital Brain Have a Mind ?*

(2002 May)

Certain recent events caused me to doubt whether I know my own mind or not. Let me explain.

Last week, the first of our academic year, all first-year students in our degree program underwent a supervised test in which they pull an old computer to pieces and put it back together again. We give this test to put a healthy disrespect for digital circuitry—which is, at heart, only carefully polluted sand—into each student's mind as early as possible. We intend this disrespect to counter the superstition, held both by naïve students and by members of the public susceptible to media persuasion, that digital machinery has much in common with the human brain.

Yesterday, I went to a lunchtime philosophy club lecture titled "Why the Body Is the Mind." Because some of the discussion related to consciousness, I recalled Giorgio Buttazzo's article, "Artificial Consciousness: Utopia or Real Possibility?."[5] The juxtaposition suggested a strange contrast between computing people, who see mental capabilities in machines because they do not appreciate how complex the human brain is, and philosophers, who see complexities in the human mind because they do not appreciate that the brain and the computer share some simple and fundamental properties.

However, not being a philosopher, I find it difficult to be confident that I understand them when they discuss the mind. This uncertainty leaves at least three possibilities:

- either I understand the basic nature of my mind and the philosophers don't,
- vice versa, or
- we share the same understanding
                but express it in mutually incomprehensible language.

Later, I read Bob Colwell's provocative essay "Engineering, Science, and Quantum Mechanics."[6] Toward his essay's end, Colwell reported of entanglement theory that "the [photon's] wave function's actual point of collapse is when a conscious mind perceives the results" and that the collapse was caused by "the synapses of our brains, acting in concert to form our minds, at the instant we detected the photon."

Suddenly, I felt alone, isolated, out of my depth, and fearfully vulnerable. What follows is meant to enlist your sympathy and rebuild my confidence.

The Mind as Process

According to my *Macquarie Dictionary*, the principal meaning of *mind* is "that which thinks, feels, and wills, exercises perception, judgment, reflection, etc., as in a human or other conscious being: *the processes of the mind*." The principal definition of *process* is "a systematic series of actions directed to some end."

An action requires an actor, presumably the mind in this case. Why not the brain? The Macquarie defines the *brain* as "the . . . nerve substance that fills the cranium of man and other vertebrates; centre of sensation, body coordination, thought, emotion, etc." Why so coy? Where is the mind in this brain?

The computer works like the mind–as–actor in that it functions as a device that processes data—conventional representations of facts or ideas. The circuits carry out the computer's processing by copying, transmitting, and transforming these data.

The mind, given the Macquarie definition, processes thoughts, feelings, intentions, perceptions, judgments, reflections, and so on. Neurons and glial cells process neural and hormonal representations of sensations past and present.

Although the idea of the mind as distinct from the brain has a natural appeal, defining the mind as an actor distinct from the brain invokes an unnecessary, even deceptive, dualism. Our mind thinks, feels, perceives, and so on, whereas our brain merely exists between our ears. The distinction can be useful and productive.

The problem lies in defining the mind as an *actor* rather than an *action*. If we regard the mind as the thinking *process*, it becomes distinct from the brain and becomes the systematic series of actions the brain takes as it processes sensations and reconstructs memories.

We can thus view the brain as substance, the mind as process. Likewise, we can view the computer as substance and its computations as process. The brain exists materially, while the mind arises as a property of changes within the brain. Similarly, the computer exists materially, while computation occurs as a property of changes within the computer. So far, so simple.

Source of Confusion

Consciousness seems to be the confusing factor. We associate self–awareness and identity with consciousness. Buttazzo writes, "Because we cannot enter another being's mind, we cannot be sure about its consciousness." This theme recurs in writings on the philosophy of the mind. But if a mind *is* a process, it's meaningless to talk about anything entering it.

Processes can only be perceived, thus inferring the operation of another mind from such perception must surely be sufficient. If anyone argues that we need certainty, we can counter that no one can be certain of anything, as the "brain in a vat" argument shows.[4]

Cycle time versus data rate

In speculating about the effect of cycle time on artificial consciousness, Buttazzo poses a curious question, "If consciousness emerges in an artificial machine, what will time perception be like to a simulated brain that thinks millions of times faster than a human brain?" What does "be like" mean here? In any case, the question confuses cycle time with data rate—the stupendous parallelism of the brain makes the cycle time of our present digital computers irrelevant.

However, Buttazzo speculates that the world might seem to slow down for a simulated brain as perhaps it does for a fly, "thus giving the fly plenty of time to glide out of the way" of a swatting hand.

The fly and I have much the same kind of neural signaling system. The average local fly measures about 10mm, and I am roughly 200 times that length. My reaction time is about one-tenth of a second. A submillisecond reaction time for a fly is thus not at all mysterious, nor would much shorter reaction times in a digital computer be in any way puzzling. Where then is consciousness in all this?

Whence consciousness?

Is a fly conscious? Well, it's aware to the extent it can often dodge a swat—its perceptual neural system alerts it to the swatting hand so that it can dart out of harm's way. But what part of the fly's nervous processing is aware, and thus to some degree conscious?

Awareness must emerge at least from the transformation of perception into the intent or neglect of an action. The transformation of sensation into perception can be unconscious because it can be automatic: We remain, for example, cheerfully oblivious to the dramatic data compression our retinas carry out. The transformation of intention into motion can similarly be unconscious: We do not consciously stimulate each individual muscle in our mouth, throat, and chest as we speak.

For the fly, we might imagine that its nervous system functions like a computer system: Its central processor "consciously" forms intentions on the basis of perceptions that its peripheral sensory system "unconsciously" produces, then its peripheral motor system "unconsciously" puts those intentions into effect.

Cache as cache can

We can transfer this analogy to the human nervous system to explain how consciousness arises from it, except that we have a more complex central processor than does a fly and much more occupies our minds than mere perceptions and intentions. We have extensive memory traces from which neural processes can reconstruct pseudoperceptions that pass through our consciousness. Intentions cannot be based practically on reconstructing all our possible memories at once. Part of our brain processes perceptions together with relevant pseudoperceptions to derive intentions. The processing of this area within the forebrain must be closely allied to our consciousness.

Human consciousness therefore strongly resembles the processing that a digital computer's central processor and its associated main store cache carry out. The cache brings relevant data close to where the current computation can use them. In this sense, then, our present-day computers are conscious, if their CPU has a cache.

Vive la Différence

Observing that "The human brain has about 10^{12} neurons, and ... 10^{15} synapses," Buttazzo calculates that, using artificial neural networks, "Simulating the human brain requires 5 million Gigabytes" of data storage. Moore's law suggests that digital computers will have main stores of that capacity by 2029, although Buttazzo carefully qualifies this observation by adding that it "refers only to a necessary but not sufficient condition for the development of an artificial consciousness."

Using a digital computer to simulate an artificial neural network that simulates the human brain does not seem the best approach. Given the neural parallelism to be modeled, using analog circuits to directly implement neural networks would seem a better alternative, one that might bring the feasibility date well forward, if research could divert the circuit manufacturing industry to this cause. But this begs the question of whether artificial neural networks can be made comparable with real ones.

In an artificial neural network, each node, or neuron, has an activation value that the network passes forward to other nodes through connections, or synapses. The synapse to each forward node has an associated weight that modulates the incoming activation value's effect on the forward node's activation. The weights can be adjusted in various ways likened to "learning." An artificial neural network's nodes mimic the classical neuron—but very roughly—with an axon down which the repetition rate of an action potential, the *spike*, passes an analog value, dependent on the activation of the neuron's main body.

Disregarding as a mere production problem attaining 10^{12} neurons and 10^{15} synapses in analog circuitry, where do artificial neural networks fall short of the real thing?

• The activation of a classical neuron is not an arithmetic sum of the synaptic effects. Rather, a complex process involving the intervals between action potentials at individual synapses and their relative timings between synapses determines the activation. The more neurons are studied the more such complexity is revealed.

• The human nervous system contains many different kinds of neurons and many kinds of glial cells. The glial cells provide more than support because they signal and have synapses just as neurons do.

• Action potentials alone do not control nervous signaling. Graded potentials and hormonal signaling also play a part, as does the great variety of different neurotransmitters and hormones.

Creating an artificial consciousness does not require simulating these complexities. But human consciousness lies far beyond any presently contemplated artificial one. We have, for example, developed a highly complex and utterly human consciousness of our physical bodies. Likewise, we have a highly developed consciousness of other people and of our society, whose collective consciousness shapes our development as humans.

Obvious parallels exist between the brain and digital computers. To fulfill their responsibility to themselves, and to others who might be misled by journalistic hyperbole, computing professionals should have well-founded opinions about the extent of these parallels. The profession should refrain from applying humanistic names to its mechanistic endeavors, and it must be conscious always of the essential differences between people and computers.

Perhaps in 50 or 100 years, our machines will acquire a humanlike consciousness and intelligence. But such machines will be utterly different from the puerile imitations we now have or can realistically design. Getting to such machines will raise professional and philosophical issues quite different from those that reflect on the nature of what human and machine consciousness can generate.

And what about the mind and entanglement theory? If a CPU and its cache possess consciousness, we could leave looking at photons to them. In any case, I've now put entanglement theory into the back of my mind under the shade of the tree in Bishop Berkeley's quad![6]

1.6 Data and Information as Property

(2004 May)

Digital technologists concern themselves with data—conventional representations of facts or ideas–and with machines for storing, transforming, and
transmitting it. Although computing professionals also concern themselves
with digital technology, they focus primarily on people and information—the
meaning that people give to data.

The use of data to convey information is vitally important to our social
systems. This is underlined by recent research showing that dogs are much
more able to get meaning from data than chimpanzees, which probably
explains why dogs make better pets.

The sharing of meaning has been the foundation of social development.
The different data technologies have been used both to empower and to constrain members of our society as technology and society have evolved together.
Computing professionals should thus always be sensitive to the social uses of
data and information. They should also be alert to legal developments related
to using data and to digital technology's role in producing data.

Data's Evolution

Spoken language was the first digital technology. Many oral societies were
quite extensive and persistent, although oral data is short-lived and only
persists through memory. The rulers of successful oral societies depended on
respect for oral tradition as reflecting acceptable past behavior.

Written language was the second digital technology. Writing gave a permanent and copyable *aide memoire* to the institutions in control of literate societies,
making the written word law. Literacy remained the exclusive province of the
élite until late in the development of printing.

Electromagnetic media underpin the third digital technology. Not only has
the capture, storage, manipulation, transmission, and display of electromagnetic data gone far beyond that possible with the old kinds of written language
that developed and developing societies use, it has also given the leaders of
those societies much greater scope for controlling and exploiting the people
under their leadership.

The use of digital technology now encompasses and facilitates not only
written and spoken language, but also the production and delivery of goods

and services. Abstract goods and services such as pictures, speech, and music—which have in the past been relatively awkward to deal with as analog data—have, through digital technology, become easy to produce and reproduce.

Intellectual Property

In the affluent fraction of the world at least, digital data has become more bureaucratically and commercially significant than any other product. In particular, its commercial significance has led to the rapid expansion and extension of so-called intellectual property (IP) law. The World Intellectual Property Organization (WIPO) and the international Trade Related Aspects of Intellectual Property Rights Agreement have extended such laws around the globe.

IP rights figure importantly, but remain almost unnoticed publicly, in so-called free-trade agreements such as the recently negotiated but not yet [but since] ratified agreement between Australia and the US.

The 1967 WIPO convention[26] defines intellectual property to include those rights relating to:
• literary, artistic, and scientific works;
• performances of performing artists, phonograms, and broadcasts;
• inventions in all fields of human endeavor;
• scientific discoveries;
• industrial designs;
• trademarks, service marks, and commercial names and designations; and
• protection against unfair competition.

WIPO's definition of IP also includes all other rights resulting from intellectual activity in the industrial, scientific, literary, or artistic fields.

Calling such rights *intellectual* property is a misnomer, and the definition is both a chimera and a hydra. The misnomer is because many of the rights do not result primarily from intellectual activity, especially when computers are used. The chimera is because it cobbles together quite different kinds of rights with quite independent and distinct histories. The hydra is because the definition's specific items go far beyond precedent, and a rapacious ambit claim follows them.

There are, or were, three kinds of property covered here: commercial identifications intended to provide for fair competition, novel ideas of use to industry, and original creations of interest to the public at large. Until recently, the first two kinds were usually called industrial property, for obvious reasons. Digital technology has great significance for all three kinds of property, which is why all computing professionals should take an active interest in IP law.

Commercial identification

The rights relating to industrial designs—and to trademarks, service marks, commercial names, and designations—are rights to produce goods with an appearance or with labeling or markings that identify the goods' origin.

Industrial design rights relate only to the visual appearance of goods. First introduced in England in 1787 in support of the textile industry, these rights provide a distinct industrial form of copyright. There has been much discussion of the overlap between appearance and function, but patents of invention rightly cover novel function. Provided this separation remains, using a computer to produce a design should not affect rights that a registration process ensuring distinctness of design establishes.

Trademark registration granted a monopoly that extended the protection of the tort of passing off, and it is nowadays supplemented legislatively by various trade practices, laws, and regulations intended to prevent unfair trading. However, the use of trademarks to identify the origin of goods is disappearing as they increasingly become the lynchpin of modern marketing, which uses them to condition purchasing behavior through advertising.

Information as property

The second kind of IP rights, monopoly in information, involves ideas as ideas, such as the rights established under patent law.

Nations began granting monopolies for inventions in Europe in the 15th century. England's Queen Elizabeth enthusiastically adopted the idea of such grants in the 16th century for a variety of monopolies, the official document of grant being called a letter patent.

Gross overuse of letters patent in England led to legislation in the 17th century that rendered all patent monopolies invalid except for patents that protected the "sole working or making of any manner of new manufacture." Governments granted these to inventors, a term which then included importers of technology.

The English tradition of patent law developed from this legislation. Several aspects of this tradition are important:

• Patents sought to encourage innovation for the good of the nation. An exception to the rule against monopolies, they were not primarily granted to reward the inventor, but to discourage the use of trade secrets that hamper innovation.

• Rights targeted innovation in manufacturing and excluded a "mere scheme or plan." The present extension into business processes and beyond is questionable.

• Novelty, a requirement, excludes any development that would be obvious to one skilled in the prior art. The plethora of patents being granted currently implies the scarcity of true novelty.

• Innovation excludes scientific discoveries. In the English tradition, such discoveries belong in the public domain—invention relates solely to the industrial exploitation of discoveries. Thus, while a new substance is not patentable, processes for making or exploiting that substance are.

Some indirect aspects are also important. For example, patent holders all too often use their rights to prevent innovation, which they do easily by blocking any innovation that extends their invention. Also, modern inventions typically have a much shorter useful life than a patent, denying the public any residual benefit.

Software patents are indefensible in principle.[11] Most importantly, disputes over patents incur great expense and have notoriously unpredictable outcomes. Patent holders can thus easily use litigation to discourage competition.

These aspects of the patent system are particularly relevant to computing professionals now that so many patents involve digital technology.

Data as property

The third kind of IP rights confers a monopoly in data—representations of facts or ideas, such as rights established under copyright law. In England, the Stationers' Company established a monopoly in printing, and its members held exclusive control over the importation and publication of books. Because copyright holders came to use the monopoly extortionately, Parliament passed the Statute of Anne, an "Act for the Encouragement of Learning ...," in 1709. After an immense legal and political battle, it replaced the earlier and much wider monopoly. Originally covering books only, rights were gradually extended to artistic, dramatic, and musical works.

In general, copyright lets the owner control the copying of works, although extensions over the past few decades to cover modern works such as broadcasts and computer programs have made copyrights much more complicated. In essence, copyright pertains to the representation of a fact or idea, not the fact or idea itself. The work need not be novel, but it must be original, and until recently it had to be in material form.

The idea of copyright monopoly arose with the introduction of printing, but technology has made copyright grotesque.[18] The first stage of the copyright farce came when photocopiers replaced spirit duplicators and Roneo machines, which led to absurd fee-collection systems. The farce continues today in the recorded music industry.

The Future

Digital technology has been universally adopted in the commercial world, so data is becoming the main and often only source of revenue for many enterprises. The importance of data to business enterprises has led to the extension of IP rights in scope, duration, and severity—and geographically through WIPO. Extension of existing legislation and legislation for entirely new rights—such as those for circuit layouts and software patents—widens the scope of rights even further. The duration of both copyrights and patents of invention is being greatly extended. Large companies, unable to protect their own intellectual property through the traditional civil courts, are persuading legislators to make crimes of what have always been torts, so that governments must enforce commercial property rights. Extended IP rights are being propagated internationally by, for example, so-called free trade agreements.

Because IP rights are of tremendous significance to computing professionals, we must be well informed about them. We have a clear duty to counter the persistently uttered falsehood that they are intended to reward the inventor or author who is, in fact, rarely the main beneficiary. Indeed, it seems likely that in the future, inventors and authors will often be computers.

Personal views on IP rights range widely. Identification rights are in principle necessary as a basis for fair trading in goods, but data and information have become goods in themselves. Given that capitalism is based on extending property rights to artificial entities, it would seem logical to extend the property rights themselves as far as capitalism requires. In contrast, since property rights are monopolies, and monopolies act in restraint of trade, free-market principles would outlaw copyright, patent, and related rights.

I believe that the expansion in scope and duration of these rights should be greatly and promptly reversed. Eliminating copyright and patents altogether would be interesting and certainly different, possibly more beneficial, but impractical.

As computing professionals, our views should be well founded, wherever in the spectrum they might lie. We should also be prompt to speak out against obvious absurdities, such as the push to bring deep linking under copyright law. If this push were to succeed, its logic would make it illegal for someone to cite this essay other than by giving its title, my name, and the name of this publication. Giving the date, volume and issue, and pages would be illegal and possibly criminal.

Much of the background information in this essay was gleaned from Intellectual Property in Australia.[14]

1.7 Notions

The notions are given here partly as a rough summary, but more particularly as topics and issues for students to study and debate. They are in the sequence of their *key word* or *phrase*. The page number to the right of each notion points to its context.

1. Machines *"behave"* or "misbehave" only
   in that they cause emotions in us by their mechanistic operation   5

2. That digital machinery has much in common
   with the human *brain* is a superstition   23

3. The Internet is the present stage in the evolution
   of the technology that underpins human *civilization*   11

4. Electromagnetic radiation cannot be owned,
   but the *community* must control its use for the public good   14

5. Only what goes into a computer,
   or can be *computed* therefrom, can come out   3

6. Digital computers are a very long way
   from having a *consciousness* or a mind like ours   5

7. Human *consciousness* lies far beyond
   any presently contemplated artificial one   27

8. *Copyright* monopoly arose with the introduction of printing,
   but technology has made copyright grotesque   31

9. *Cyberspace* is a repackaging of the old idea of Heaven
   but in a secular, technologically sanctioned format   12

10. *Education* is a basic human right, but it should come first
    from the family and the community, not from schools or machines   13

11. To hold that a written test that takes 30 minutes or so
    to complete can be used to measure intelligence must be
    the greatest *educational* con job of all time   22

12. A misfit in a proper *family* is usually a misfit everywhere else   13

13. With special-purpose machines as effective
    as the world's *financial* engine, who needs androids?   22

14. Computers cannot make us *fools*—
    they can only allow us to be foolish faster   9

34. Facts and ideas must be used for the *public good*   14

35. The computing profession's most important *responsibility*
         is to plainly and consistently define the role
                that digital technology plays in its community   20

36. Intellectual property is a chimera is because
       it cobbles together quite different kinds of *rights*
           with quite independent and distinct histories   29

37. As long as we think of computers
       as anything else than machines to be owned and used,
          people will be able to use computers as *scapegoats*   9

38. The prevalent misunderstanding of technology
       makes us tragically prone to be its *slaves* instead of its masters   10

39. The development of technologies by our *society*
         is what has made a society like ours possible   2

40. *Software patents* are indefensible in principle   31

41. *Spoken language* was the first digital technology   28

42. Trying to make a *technologist* out of everyone is silly   15

43. *Technorealism* should be based on the idea
       that people are more important than technologies   15

44. Computers are *tools* that people use   1

45. An *understanding* of computers and their uses
       can only follow from an understanding of what technology is   1

46. *Written language* was the second digital technology   28

1.8   Bibliography

The entries are in order of the first or only author's name. Where no personal author is known, as for popular news items, an indicative name is used. Where there is a page number or two in *italics* at the beginning of the annotation, they point back to where the item was cited. Where some of the annotation is given in quotes it has been taken from the item itself or from some of its publicity.

1. *APA* (1994). *Diagnostic and Statistical Manual of Mental Disorders DSM-IV-TR: Text Revision*. Washington, D.C.: American Psychiatric Association, 2005, ISBN 0-89042-024-6, xxxvii+943 pp. (*p. 18*; the APA is at psych.org and they "feature" DSM-IV-TR at psychiatryonline.com).

2. Isaac Asimov (1954). *The Caves of Steel*. St. Albans, Hertfordshire: Granada Publishing, 1958, ISBN 0 586 00835 7, 206 pp. (*p. 22*; only one of his many books and stories about positronic robots, his term for androids; see also en.wikipedia.org/wiki/The_Caves_of_Steel and en.wikipedia.org/wiki/Android).

3. Harvey Blume (2000, January 13). "Alternate Realities," *Atlantic Unbound* (*p. 10*; in the quondam *Digital Culture* series; online for subscribers at theatlantic.com/unbound/digicult/dc2000-01-13.htm).

4. Tony Brueckner (2004). "Brains in a Vat," *The Stanford Encyclopedia of Philosophy*, Winter 2004 edition, editor Edward N. Zalta (*p. 24*; the other citation went missing, so, as introductory reading at a useful website, see plato.stanford.edu/archives/win2004/entries/brain-vat, although it's simpler and less formal at en.wikipedia.org/wiki/Brain-in-a-vat).

5. Giorgio Buttazzo (2001, July). "Artificial Consciousness: Utopia or Real Possibility?," *Computer*, Vol. 34, No. 7, pp. 24–30 (*p. 23*; "Many researchers believe that artificial consciousness is possible, and that, in the future, it will emerge in complex computing machines.").

6. Robert P. Colwell (2002, March). "Engineering, Science, and Quantum Mechanics," *Computer*, Vol. 35, No. 3, pp. 8–10 (*p. 23*; "Quantum physics is both wildly successful and incredibly weird.").

7. *The Economist* (2004, February 19). "Dog Behaviour: Sensitive Souls," (*p. 28*; "How dogs became man's best friend"; included here because several emails asked for a citation, which wasn't in the original essay; economist.com/printedition/PrinterFriendly.cfm?story_id=2441795).

8. Howard Earl Gardner (1983). *Frames of Mind: The Theory of Multiple Intelligences*. BasicBooks, HarperCollins, with new introduction, 1985,

ISBN 0-465-02509-9, xx+440 pp. (*p.21*; for context, discussion and links, see infed.org/thinkers/gardner.htm).

9. Ian H. Gould (1972, February). "In Pursuit of Terminology," *The Computer Bulletin*, Vol. 16, No. 2, pp. 84–90 (*p.19*; "... the attempt to provide our field with a soundly-based terminology is a fascinating, if frustrating, pastime. This paper examines various problems that face terminologists and discusses some attempts to find solutions.").

10. Michael Grunberg (2001, January). "Letters to the Editor: Is Holmes Out to Get Us?," *Computer*, Vol. 34, No. 1, pp. 10–12 (*p.16*; several letters with my response, but Grunberg's is the one I cite).

11. W. Neville Holmes (2000, March). "The Evitability of Software Patents," *Computer*, Vol. 33, No. 3, pp. 30–34 (*p.31*; a response to an earlier article declaiming that software patents are inevitable).

12. *ISO* (1993). *Information Technology—Vocabulary: Part 1: Fundamental Terms*. Geneva, Switzerland: International Organization for Standardization, 32 pp. (*p.18*; the third edition, ISO/IEC 2382-1:1993, can be bought in PDF or paper form for 120 Swiss francs from www.iso.org/iso/en/CatalogueDetailPage.CatalogueDetail?CSNUMBER=7229).

13. Marty Leisner (1997, March). "Open Channel: Do Computers Make Us Fools?," *Computer*, Vol. 30, No. 3, p. 8 (*p.8*).

14. Jill McKeough and Andrew Stewart (1997). *Intellectual Property in Australia*. Sydney: Butterworths, second edition, ISBN 0-409-30677-0, xlx+525 pp. (*p.32*).

15. Russell Lloyd Mathews (quoted 1996, November 25). "Malign or Benign?: Global Market Mania" by Geoffrey Barker, *The Australian Financial Review*, p. 14 (*p.22*; another quote: "... financial globalisation has 'effectively put an end to the capacity of governments to implement policies which run counter to the beliefs of financial markets.'"; some appreciation of Mathews' stature in accounting and finance can be got from nla.gov.au/nla.ms-ms6594).

16. Francis Oakley (1996). "Scholarship and Teaching: A Matter of Mutual Support," *American Council of Learned Societies*. Occasional Paper No. 32 (*p.27*; cited for the Ronald Knox limericks early in the paper—they are often mis-quoted–though the paper is interesting in its own right; acls.org/op32.htm, but the limericks appear more in more direct context in en.wikipedia.org/wiki/George_Berkeley).

17. J. Radcliffe (1997). *The New International Webster's Pocket Computer Dictionary of the English Language*. Naples, Florida: Trident Press International, new revised edition 1998, ISBN 1-888777-54-0, 318 pp. (*p.18*).

18. Simone Santini (2003, August). "The Profession: Bringing Copyright into the Information Age," *Computer*, Vol. 36, No. 8, pp. 104, 102–103

(*p.31*; "Current copyright statutes promote an outdated, Industrial Age approach to intellectual property.").

19. Andrew Shapiro, David Shenk and Steven Johnson (1998, March 12). *Technorealism: Home Page* (*p.10*; technorealism.org; the authors and the date were those and when responsible for the draft principles; the final version was from "a collaboration of twelve technology writers," which makes the wording of Principle 7 unaccountable).

20. George Soros (1997, February). "The Capitalist Threat," *The Atlantic Monthly*, Vol. 279, No. 2, pp. 45–48   (*p.9*; "The main threat to social justice and economic stability now comes from the uninhibited pursuit of laissez-faire economics ... the very ideal of an 'open society' is at stake."; the table of contents is at theatlantic.com/issues/97feb and the essay, for subscribers only, is capital.htm).

21. Robert Thibadeau (2004, August 28). *Thomas Jefferson and Intellectual Property including Copyright and Patents.* (*p.13*; the URL that I cited originally has become restricted to UPenn people, but this interesting website also links to it: rack1.ul.cs.cmu.edu/jefferson but simpler is users.vnet.net/alight/jefferson.html).

22. Geoffrey C. Tootill (Ch. 1966).   *IFIP-ICC Vocabulary of Information Processing.*   Amsterdam: North-Holland Publishing Company, 1968, xii+208 pp. (*p.18*; by the Joint Technical Committee on Terminology of the International Federation for Information Processing and the International Computation Centre).

23. *UNDP* (2006).   *United Nations Development Programme: Home Page.* (*p.5*; undp.org, and the various Human Development Reports are at hdr.undp.org).

24. Margaret Wertheim (1999). *The Pearly Gates of Cyberspace: A History of Space From Dante to the Internet.* Sydney: Doubleday, ISBN 1 86471 0187, 336 pp. (*p.12*; "Seeking to understand this mapping of spiritual desire onto digitised space, Wertheim takes us on an astonishing historical journey, tracing the evolution of our conception of space from the Middle Ages to today."; the cited quote is on page 24 there).

25. Simon Winchester (1998). *The Surgeon of Crowthorne: A Tale of Murder, Madness and the* Oxford English Dictionary. Harmondsworth, Middlesex: Penguin Books, ISBN 0 14 0271287, x+207 pp. (*p.16*).

26. *WIPO* (1967, July 14). *Convention establishing the World Intellectual Property Organization.* WIPO, Geneva, Switzerland, a specialized agency of the United Nations (*p.29*; the quoted definition is from Article 2, unaffected by the amendments of 1979; both PDF and HTML copies are free online, the latter at wipo.int/treaties/en/convention/trtdocs_wo029en.html).

Chapter 2

Computing So Far

In the 1960s, the computing industry, at least the commercial part of it, saw itself as having suddenly and dramatically changed the way government and business processed their data.

What previously had been done in a large machine room by numerous operators feeding tens, sometimes hundreds, of thousands of punched cards through a succession of electromechanical machinery—sorters, calculators, collators and tabulators—to produce huge stacks of documents and reports, was now, by using magnetic data storage and stored program computers, done on one machine by operators who were more minders than laborers.

The word *revolution* was freely bandied about, We had reached for, and attained, the ultimate. The future could surely hold nothing to match this! Improvements, yes, but revolution, no.

Yet ultimates kept on coming. As new computing technologies went past they were called *generations*: the first generation, the second generation, the third and fourth generations, until the numbering started to look a bit silly. To an old-timer it's rather quaint to see the mobile phone industry going through its generations now.

Then in the 1980s the personal computer "suddenly" appeared, launching the PC Revolution, and now we have the Internet, its World Wide Web, and the Information Society Revolution.

These revolutions are, of course, the way marketing people would like us to see what is actually evolution. As new products appear it's easier to sell them if they can be made to look really different from the old.

Really, what is more important than the technology is what the technology is used for. So it's important to ask whether digital technology has led to quite new activities for its users. One answer to this question is given in "The Myth of the Computer Revolution" (essay 2.1, p.50).

39

The History of Digital Technology

Digital technology is about the use of representations of facts or ideas, that is, about data, encoded digitally. The significance of digital encoding is that it is resistant to error resulting from degradation. We can understand language, because it is digital, even when spoken with a heavy accent or a heavy cold. Before digital telephony international phone conversation could sometimes be impossible because of noisy line conditions.

What is really impressive about digital technology is that its history is in effect the history of human civilization.

The first variety of digital technology, spoken language, made extended communities possible and so started civilization. It has been the only digital technology until relatively recently.

Spoken language is digital at several levels.

At the lowest level we think of spoken words as being composed from only a few distinct sounds, components that linguists call *phonemes*. So we recognize that the first sound in the words *add am and* and *at* is the same in all, and that the last sound in the words *at eat it* and *oat* is the same in all.

At the next higher level we think of utterances as being composed from words. The words a person uses in speech are called their *active* vocabulary; those a person only recognizes in speech are called their *passive* vocabulary.

The first major branch of digital technology, written language, is only a few millennia old, but is likely to have been the main factor in making possible communities much larger than a single village.

Written language comes in many forms. The text you are reading here is encoded using the Latin alphabet. The letters of this alphabet notionally represent the phonemes of spoken English, though English spelling is more historical than systematic.

The main advantage of written language is that it is relatively and reliably permanent. Spoken language only persists through human memory.

Written language is the basis of nations and religions. The development of printing machinery has boosted the power of bureaucracies and priesthoods.

The most recent major branch of digital technology, the technology behind our computers and telecommunication systems, has two important aspects, the first related to encoding of data, the second related to its transmission and storage.

Written language, which is already digitally encoded, simply has a further encoding when text is to be stored or transmitted. Unencoded (analog) data are now also digitally encoded by machinery; speech and music, once recorded as soundwave analogs in grooves on plastic disks, and pictures, until recently recorded chemically in photographic emulsions, are now routinely encoded digitally and stored and transmitted alongside text.

Digitally encoded data are stored and transmitted in a variety of ways, all distinguished by the enormous speed of transmission or capacity of storage. It is this speed and capacity that makes possible, for example, the widespread use of mobile telephones not only for speech and music, but also for both still and moving pictures.

On the surface, this last branch of digital technology seems completely new and profoundly disruptive. Certainly it is significant and very powerful, but questions about the nature of this significance and power can only answered properly in the historical context of digital technology, a context sketched out in "The Profession's Future Lies in its Past" (essay 2.2, p.54), though that essay also holds a message for the computing profession in its conclusion.

The Splendor of Digital Technology

Electromagnetic digital technology has made it possible, often quite easy, to produce, reproduce, process and transmit enormous amounts of data very swiftly and very cheaply, at least for those in our civilization who can afford the equipment.

The benefits of this technology are really quite marvellous, regardless of who gets the benefits. I used a laptop computer to put this book together, keying in the text and using the LaTeX program to set its type and compose it. The book, in its various stages, was backed up on a memory stick much smaller than a domino which I was able to take to another computer and so send copies of the book to editors and reviewers living on the opposite side of the world, copies they might get within minutes.

The memory stick could hold much more data than the typical hard disk of the late 1950s, which held five million six-bit characters and was bigger and heavier than an ordinary car. A plastic disk smaller than my hand can hold, digitally recorded, a movie hours long with a choice of sound-tracks, and the device needed to play it is small and relatively inexpensive. The mostly digital electronic equipment in a new motor car can nowadays cost more than the mechanical equipment, and is used both to control the car and to inform and entertain its passengers.

Electromagnetic digital technology, in short, is splendid and its products wonderful. Through this technology we are able to enlarge our environment and our lives, hearing and seeing much that would be impossible without it.

Although we cannot but admire the technology, that admiration should not block us from looking closely and critically at it. There are several traps in the path of admirers.

The most obvious and perhaps least important trap is to assume that digital technology so far has been faultless, that it has developed along the one true path with the best of engineering design decisions guiding it along that path. The truth is that this path was not chosen by rational technicality, nor, it can be argued, is this path the best that could have been chosen.

In the history of most areas of technology there are occasionally points at which an important choice has to be made between alternatives. There might not be any absolute case for one alternative over the other.

At one stage the automobile industry had a choice between the internal combustion engine and the external combustion engine. It could be argued that, had they chosen the external combustion engine, today's cars would have been much more versatile and economical in their fuel usage (braking can be regenerative), much simpler in their electrical and mechanical control, and much quieter and less stressed in their operation.

If these arguments were valid, then the choice of the internal combustion engine could be described as a blunder. If the choice was a blunder this does not mean that the development of the internal combustion engine has not been highly admirable and extremely beneficial to those societies that depend on automotion. Nor would the committing of a blunder mean that the blunderers should have known better.

It's easy to be wise in hindsight, but crucial decisions often have to be made when no relevant hindsight is available.

Today's digital equipment is based on binary encoding, that is, on signals and fields in which only two states are to be distinguished. It could be, and has been, argued that it would have been better to have based our equipment on ternary encoding, that is, on signals and fields in which three states are to be distinguished? This would reduce the number of basic components and, in particular, of interconnections by one third. Circuit chips with ternary logic would be smaller, cheaper, and cooler than their binary equivalents[14]

To argue, then, that binary encoding is a blunder would not be to invalidate today's digital technology or to denigrate the achievements of the inventors and designers who have given us this technology.

In an endeavor to cast the history of modern computing in a more realistic light than is usual, I wrote the essay "Seven Great Blunders of the Computing World" (essay 2.3, p.59). The blunders I chose for the essay are of fairly general interest, though most are only very briefly described.

When the essay was published I was sent many emails, mostly critical. Some took me to be attacking the pioneers of computing, and were thus quite angry. This is why I have taken some trouble to explain above the implications and context of technical blundering.

Another important point to be made arising from the emails is that pointing out a blunder is not necessarily arguing that it is practical to go back on the arguably wrong decision. Some blunders it is practical to fix, the older ones probably not. Even if binary encoding is a blunder, and in fact I'm not seriously arguing that it was, conversion to ternary is quite impractical, except perhaps in arithmetic units where it has added advantages.

The Importance of Arithmetic

Perhaps the earliest major branch of digital technology came with numerics, the technology of numbers. Numbers must have started very simply.

In spoken language, words for numbers *one two* and *three* seem to have been all that existed until several thousand years ago, and there are still preliterate cultures in which manual signing is used for numbers larger than three.

In written language, using marks like notches to record counts was the earliest and simplest writing technology, and is known to have been used at least 30,000 years ago in Europe. These were used for quite complex tasks, one example of 10,000 years ago, for example, seems to be recording the lunar cycle. Roman numerals are a development of such marks.

The history and nature of numerics is fascinating and intricate, and books like the splendid and detailed *Number Words and Number Symbols*[18] and the more recent and technical *The Number Sense*[3] are quite fascinating to read if you have any interest at all in the topic.

One intriguing aspect is the relationship between ordinary language and numeric language as digital technologies. It seems that the early number words were very few, and used as adjectives like *red* and *sour*, while simple marks were being used for recording counts. Thus numbers could be written for which there were no words. It was ultimately from such counting systems that our complex alphabetic and syllabic writing systems developed.

The peculiarity is that in numerics writing came before speaking, but in other language speaking came before writing.

Language technology is used to represent facts or ideas about beings and things, their nature and their history. Numeric technology is used mainly to represent and manipulate two kinds of property: quantity and indication. These two kinds of numbers are called *cardinal* and *ordinal* in mathematics.

The distinction between quantity and indication is quite fundamental to computing technology.

The most obvious use of numbers is *quantitative*. Commerce started with the recording of quantities by using clay tokens, with different tokens used for different goods.[20] This developed into the cuneiform writing on clay tablets. Early computational techniques and machinery, for example, counting with fingers or pebbles (the word *calculate* comes from the Latin word for pebble, *calculus*), and addition and subtraction with the abacus or with counters on marked tables. Later machinery was able to multiply and divide, at first by repetitive addition and subtraction. Modern computers can do more complex arithmetic still, on numbers stored inside the machine.

Modern computers, however, store many numbers, so the need is for the machinery to be able to fetch the numbers requiring arithmetic to the circuitry that does the arithmetic. To do this, all the quantitative numbers are stored in *indicatively* numbered locations so that the machinery can fetch any number by using its place in the data storage device to identify it. This indicative number is called an *index* or *address*. So in modern computers, every stored number has two numeric values associated with it, its quantitative value for arithmetic and its indicative value for location.

Of course a number can be used both quantitatively and indicatively. Where I live, the house numbers come from dividing by ten the distance in metres of the entrance from the beginning of the road, and selecting as the address the nearest whole number, even for houses on the right and odd for houses on the left. Our number in the road thus indicates which house we live in and quantifies roughly how far we are from the beginning of the road.

In everyday life we, or at least those of us in the consumer society, are surrounded by indicative numbers—street numbers, phone numbers, credit card numbers, part numbers, clock times, dates; and quantitative numbers—account balances, wages, prices, weights, distances, volumes, temperatures, durations, rainfall.

Our consumer society, all of commerce and finance, is based on numerics.

Beyond that, text is stored in computers and transmitted around the world as indicative numbers, numbers that indicate where in the alphabet being used each letter or other symbol occurs. Recorded and transmitted speech, music and images are nowadays usually represented as numbers, in speech and in music as momentary air pressures, in images as pixel colors and intensities.

So our cultural and entertained society now also depends on numerics.

Technology itself is numerically dependent to a much greater degree, not only in its use of digital machinery, but also in technologists' use of complex computation both in their overall design and in their underlying science.

In the world of commerce and finance the numbers and the computations are very simple. Exact numbers, addition and subtraction dominate, and even when multiplication and division are used their results are usually forced into exactness by a process known as rounding. There is even a special "bankers' rounding" used to break ties fairly.

Science and technology are hugely more demanding. Numbers are often inexact, and are left inexact during computation. Multiplication and division are at least as much used as addition and subtraction. A multitude of other arithmetic computations, such as the trigonometric and hyperbolic functions, are necessary as well as a host of special operational combinations used on large collections of numbers.

From these observations two things should be crystal clear. Firstly, basic numeracy is essential for competently functioning membership of a consumer society. Secondly, for technological development to keep going the institutions that train and educate technologists, engineers, scientists, computing people and, especially, teachers, need to be given students with a very high level of numeracy.

Yet numeracy in countries like the United States, the United Kingdom and

Australia is steadily going down. The students starting scientific or technical studies at colleges and universities are becoming less and less able to deal with quantitative ideas and procedures. The result is that such countries are relying more and more on immigrant students and professional workers, and giving preferential treatment for such immigrants, who are needed not just for science and engineering but also areas such as medicine. Raising levels of numeracy in some at least of the "advanced" countries is quite plainly an urgent challenge to their education systems.

The National Academies in the US see this quite clearly. In a detailed report, *Rising Above The Gathering Storm*, the first of only four recommendations is "Increase America's talent pool by *vastly* [my emphasis] improving K-12 science and mathematics education."

Because digital technology could help a lot, because the problem is so large and important, and because it goes way beyond the development of numeracy, I have set aside the following chapter (starting p. 87) to examine the broader issue of computers in education.

There are, however, technical barriers to the development of numeracy. One very significant barrier is the design of the commodity calculator. This design is so greatly flawed that in some countries calculators are banned from use in elementary education. The flaws are discussed below in "Truth and Clarity in Arithmetic" (essay 2.4, p. 64).

The Use of Computers

The digital computer is just a tool. Like a hammer, it comes in various sizes and styles, and it has many uses. As with a hammer, the benefits of using it depend on the skill of the user.

Nowadays the computer is increasingly being used as a component of other machinery, just as hammers are built into pianos, carillons and hammer mills.

Apart from considerations of manufacture and marketing, machinery with built-in computation, such as a modern sewing machine, is expected to be more capable and easier to use. Usually they are more capable, but all too often they are much harder to use, except when the machine is being used for repetitive work.

A computer, when being used as a computer, is not at all like a hammer in that a hammer is used to manipulate physical objects while a computer is used to manipulate data. Another way the computer is different is that its manipulations are done at two or three levels.

At the hardware level, components such as transistors and capacitors are connected in circuits to deal with the individual binary digits of the data.

At the firmware level, functional data called the microprogram is used to control the circuitry of the hardware and to facilitate the software level.

At the software level, operational data called programs are used to cause the computer to manipulate the user's data in the required way.

That is the nature of computation nowadays, or at least a very simple view of it. Computers have evolved through changes in this structure.

Before the stored program computer there was no software. Instead firmware in the form of a plugged panel was used to rewire the machine for it to do its work for the user directly. In effect, the plugged panel (or panels— some machines needed several) was the program, that is, the specification of what was to be done by the machine for the user. New programs were brought into use by by swapping panels.

For a while, around the 1950s, the program was split between plugged panels (firmware) and punched cards or paper tape (software). The part of the program kept in cards or tape was brought into the computer and stored, for example on a magnetic drum, alongside the data being processed for the user.

In the late 1950s and early 1960s, plugged panels fell from favor, at least for use in digital computers. Microprograms became popular as firmware in the mid-'60s, though they were in use earlier. These microprograms were in the heart of the computer and were difficult to change, unlike the plugged panels.

Now the typical computer is an extremely complex structure of hardware, firmware and software, each of which is itself an extremely complex structure. Only specialists deal with the hardware and firmware because programmers and other users of computers are shielded from the complexity of the hardware and firmware by the software.

There are two kinds of software: *system* programs and *application* programs.

System programs are of two kinds. The programs of the *operating system* hide the complexity of the computer from both programmers and ordinary users. Other programs help programmers, particularly those who write the application programs for ordinary users.

The programming aids hide the complexities of the operating system and the computer itself behind a coding scheme, somewhat misleadingly called a programming language.

All these developments took place in a social context. Early computers were very expensive and so the organizations using them, or at least the commercial and government ones, had departments dedicated to exploiting the machinery. These were usually called data processing (DP) departments, though nowadays they are more pretentiously called information technology (IT) departments.

As DP departments became more and more important they tended also to become more and more dictatorial. Their programmers became more and more separated from the actual users, and their programs were designed more to suit the aspirations of the DP department than the needs of the actual users. As this was going on the computers became more complex and and capable, and the DP departments likewise.

However, although governmental and commercial use became dependent on DP people, the tasks and problems of engineers and scientists were much more computational. This made them harder for DP people to understand and take over. Thus engineers and scientists came to do their own programming on their own computers.

Student engineers used to be told, at least in Australia, that "an engineer is a person who can do for five bob [shillings] what any fool can do for a quid [twenty shillings]." Probably it was this attitude that led to some engineers putting together very small and cheap computers in the early '70s. These were called *minicomputers* and they became widely used in technical fields. At this stage, the larger computers came to be called *mainframe* computers, *mainframes* for short.

Inevitably, minicomputers became more commercial, that is, more complex and more expensive. The wheel turned again, and very simple and cheap machines called *microcomputers* became popular in the '80s.

Microcomputers had an advantage over minicomputers. They were very cheap indeed, so cheap that hobbyists and individual innovators could afford them. Quite a few general-purpose business applications were coded for use on microcomputers. One such application was the *spreadsheet*. Spreadsheets, large sheets of paper ruled into a rectangular grid of boxes, were once used for tabular calculations, particularly in the insurance industry, and spreadsheet programs were sometimes used on mainframe computers when typewriter terminals became popular in the '70s.

When IBM released their commercial line of microcomputers, now called the *personal computer* because it was cheap enough for many people to own personally and use individually, one of the most widely accepted programs transferred to it was the spreadsheet. At much the same time, or even earlier, Apple's version of the personal computer found wide use because of its word processing program.

The special significance of the spreadsheet and word processing programs was that these were at least as useful in the business and government worlds as they were to private individuals. Apple's great success almost wiped out the typewriter industry. The spreadsheet and word processing programs, later joined by the somewhat more business-oriented *database* programs, were widely accepted in the government and business worlds because they gave control back to the end-user, though this was only temporary.

In more recent years, the crucial spreadsheet, word processing and database programs have been continually elaborated, enormously enlarged, and precariously integrated. This has had more to do with marketing needs than user needs. What's more, personal computers are nowadays also used to run the very popular browsers, which make the Internet and its World Wide Web accessible.

Simplicity has vanished. The general-purpose machine has become harder and harder to use and control![19]

What seems to be happening is that special-purpose digital machinery is being built, particularly in the entertainment industry. In such machinery, like the increasingly popular mobile telephone, the machinery is adapted to its use by fixed programming so that the user can only do what the machine is programmed to provide and allow.

The general-purpose personal computer has become much the same, and not really general-purpose at all. The "general-purpose" programs will only do what you need if they have been programmed to allow it, and if you can find out how to get it to allow you! When you want to do something new or unusual, or even recover from an error, the barriers are many and mysterious. True, "help" facilities are provided but, notoriously, they don't.

There are implications in this, both for the computing professional and for the ordinary user. Some of these implications are examined in "Computers, Programming, and People" (essay 2.5, p. 69).

Computers and Users

As a tool, the digital computer has users of many kinds, as well as uses of many kinds. The users are either direct, writing their own programs as a community, or indirect, using programs written by others, typically in the programming community.

Early users of scientific computers wrote their own programs, coding them in Fortran or Algol, standard coding schemes developed for scientific work. The scientific and engineering community shared their program code freely, writing general and useful functions as subprograms so that they could be collected and managed in "libraries" and passed around on magnetic tapes. New algorithms were published every month in the Communications of the ACM.

Because scientific users typically used their programs to test ideas, much more computer time was spent developing programs than running their final versions. The development process was often informal and incremental, the program code being tested many times, but run once.

Early end users of commercial computers simply went on with their work. These were indirect users because the data processing department wrote the programs and ran them. The users' job was to supply data for the programs and to use the mountains of paper put out by the line printers which were essential to commercial data processing then.

Commercial computers were used in government and business mainly for repetitive work. Programs were developed formally, updated seldom if ever, and were used for decades. This discouraged firms from changing suppliers, and made the Y2K problem (p. 50) quite frightening for unprepared managers.

Program code was not shared between firms or government departments because administrative practices, if not principles, varied greatly. Enthusiatic attempts were made in the '60s to develop and sell a standard payroll program package without success.

This distinction between direct use and indirect use of the computer has persisted, though the details have changed somewhat. Much of the change follows directly from changes in the computer industry.

Perhaps the most obvious change is the growth of *embedded computing*, that is, of special purpose machines with computers and their programs built into them. Any direct user of such machinery is an indirect user of the computer within the machine. The computer is irrelevant to the user in such cases, in the sense that it merely improves prior machinery without embedded computers, machinery such as gaming machines, telephones, sewing machines and cars.

The big change for general-purpose computers is the development of the software market. Programs are now commodities.

In the scientific and engineering world, computational systems such as Mathematica, Matlab, MathCAD and Maple are popular for experimental computation. Compared to the older programming techniques, they provide a much more direct and interactive way to do ad hoc scientific programming. However, Fortran is still the most-used way to program supercomputers for very large scientific projects.

In the personal world of ad hoc computing there is little programming done by the user. Almost all use is indirect. Popular packaged programs are used for non-numerical tasks such as making enquiries of the World Wide Web and composing documents. Spreadsheet and database packages are used for ad hoc numerical tasks. Although these packages can be modified in minor ways, they effectively turn the general-purpose personal computer temporarily into a special-purpose machine.

The business and government world is doggedly conservative. Any ad hoc computing is done with personal computing packages. All other computing is done the same way throughout the organization, and with large and expensive integrated computing systems needing the support of technical specialists.

In such organizations most computer use is indirect, with the computing system driving the user along predestinate grooves. The user is a cypher, not a partner. This is unfortunate but not inevitable, as discussed in "The Usefulness of Hindsight" (essay 2.6, p. 75).

2.1   The Myth of the Computer Revolution

(1998 November)

One of the more bizarre and disquieting aspects of the Y2K Problem [see endnote] is the occasional but recurrent journalistic report that depicts a hapless Cobol programmer of 30 or so years ago lighting on the ill-fated notion of leaving the "19" off the year in order to save storage space. Where are journalists getting this idea? Surely they didn't observe it, so some person or persons in the computing industry must be promoting this misleading (if not pernicious) idea.

Indeed there are such people in our industry. Some very recent but hardly isolated evidence appeared in IEEE Computational Science and Engineering[21] [where Norris] Smith writes that in the 1960s "programmers adopted the convention of designating years through two digits rather than four." Of course this statement is not strictly erroneous. The problem is that "adopted" implies "invented at about that time."

The truth is that two-digit year encoding was adopted in the data processing industry long before Konrad Zuse built his first digital computer in the '30s. The data-processing industry didn't invent two-digit year encoding either: the practice was already widespread in the clerical industry. It's just a highly practical abbreviation that we use in everyday speech.

Iceberg of Ignorance

The misbegotten ideas about the origin of the millennium bug are only the tip of the iceberg that is computing history ignorance.

A few years ago there was a spate of stories on Australian television in celebration of the fortieth anniversary of the first commercial use of computers. According to these reports, the first computers dramatically changed the operations of those companies that were rich enough and foresighted enough to buy them. The first digital computers, so these reports said, had changed business accounting and record-keeping overnight.

The truth is that anyone associated with these innovations at the time would not have seen it that way. Early computers, in fact, were installed in well-established departments that had automated data processing decades earlier, using punched cards or paper tape. Typically, the earliest computers were installed simply to replace existing machinery, not existing processes. There was, therefore, no overnight change associated with early computing.

The first Cobol programmers did not develop new applications, they merely converted existing procedures.

Computers and Innovation

There is a related but somewhat more dangerous misconception that the computing industry seems to foster: the myth that the computer *causes* change, perhaps even revolutionary change.

The truth is quite the opposite. Computers have always been used by industry and government (the two sectors that matter the most socially) as a way to *avoid change and to reinforce the status quo*.

Many companies and departments adopted electronic computers so that they wouldn't have to innovate; so they wouldn't have to find new ways to achieve their objectives.

There is no doubt that computers did a better job than the old machines and eventually even did it cheaper. In fact they did their job too well: using computers, big organizations could exert far more control over their operations, their employees, and eventually their clients. The trend now is to use computers to replace employees altogether.

These changes have not brought innovation but consolidation. Big organizations can go on doing what they have done all along, but in far greater detail. Greater detail translates to greater control. Governments can store and administer enormously greater numbers of laws and regulations than ever before. Big business can more effectively predict and avert adverse application of those laws and regulations.

The effects of consolidation run even deeper.. As big organizations and government departments become more dependent on computing systems, they become less able to make any change but incremental change. Witness the Y2K Problem—technically trivial, organizationally immense. The Euro conversion problem is technically more difficult, and it's merely a change in a unit of measurement.

The Computer Revolution?

The Internet, in particular the World Wide Web, is usually taken to be a revolutionary innovation. Certainly its use is increasing dramatically and will go on increasing. But what looks like a revolution today will usually be seen as an evolution tomorrow. PCs seemed revolutionary in the 1980s; operating systems in the 1960s; telegraphy in the 1800s; canal transport in the 1700s; and so on and so on. PCs and the Internet may still be around some decades hence, but they will be seen as small components of technological evolution.

Things do seem to change faster and faster. Partly, at least, this is an illusion. What is new seems bright and changing, and we tend to forget that what is old was once new. Across the centuries and across the world people have seen themselves living through revolutions that in fact caused little long-term change. The old saying, "The more things change, the more they stay the same" makes just this point.

Social Revolution?

The question remains: do current social changes constitute a revolution made possible by digital technology?

In talking about the developed world, you might be tempted to answer yes. I disagree. Even in the developed world, only a minority of the population uses computers, even when PCs are factored in. Across the globe, only a very small percentage—not even one percent—of the population has ever handled a computer.

The way things are going, only a small percentage ever will. And even in developed nations, again, the most significant use of computers is by big, powerful organizations to make them even bigger and more powerful. Revolutionary social change for the general good is not their goal. Globalization is, and surely globalization is made possible by computers and networking. Unfortunately, globalization has not brought general good. If it had, we would be witnessing a reduction in the gap between rich and poor. To the contrary, the United Nations Development Program has long been reporting that the gap separating rich and poor nations is widening, as is the gap between rich and poor people in most if not all nations.[25]

This gap had begun to narrow after World War II and then began to widen when digital computers came into common use. I do not believe this is merely a coincidence. Nor is it a coincidence to me that wealth and power are stratifying more as computers and telecommunications bring globalization of business and bureaucracy.

In short, computers enable the more efficient governance of the lower class by the middle class for the benefit of the upper class. (Don't take my word for it. Read, for example, J.K. Galbraith's *The Culture of Contentment*.[6])

Rise of Neofeudalism

The current changes in social structure are all part of a natural correction that is returning us to feudalism. There is nothing unnatural about feudalism. Something like it has prevailed in most inhabited countries for most of their histories. Society seems inevitably to want to stratify into some kind of hierarchy of social power.

Liberty, equality, and fraternity: these are what's unnatural. These are the unattainable ideal. Nevertheless, those who strive for this ideal are our most noble and admirable citizens. Computer-aided feudalism—*neofeudalism*—is moving us further from it.

Neofeudalism has some new characteristics. First, it's global. Second and more worrisome, it is rapidly changing the social balance. Feudal societies have always had four main classes: upper, middle, lower, and outlaw. The outlaw class usually isn't mentioned much in the history books. It is a "non-participating" class, which means that when it gets too big it tends to destroy civilization.

This fourth class is at present evidenced in the homeless, the mentally ill, the longterm unemployed, the illiterate, the refugees, the lesser criminals. The International Labor Organization[11] puts the size of this group at more than one-third of the Earth's population and growing.

Computing contributes directly to the growth of this class in the neo-feudalistic society: digital technology displaces lower-class workers, who eventually leave the lower class and join the outlaw class. Too many outlaws and you eventually have bloody disruption.

Neofeudalism, I'm afraid, is in our future. Unless, that is, the computing profession adopts some unattainable ideals and does something concerted to move us toward those ideals rather than away from them.

Technology is neutral. It's the use of technology that can bring the good or the bad. Television, for example, could have been a wonderful aid to education; instead it has become primarily a vehicle for applied consumer psychology. The Web could be developed into a wonderful aid to education. The world's governments seem to be promoting its conversion to a vehicle for electronic commerce. The parallel with television should be obvious, and the computing profession should be strongly criticizing the more crass aspects of this development and actively working to see that the egalitarian aspects of the Internet are not drowned in the tidal wave of economic rationalism.

Perhaps what's needed is for social and technological history to be part of all education of computing professionals. This would be a basis for informed promotion of—and practical action toward—social rationalism as a counter to economic rationalism.

The Y2K Problem *mentioned at the start of this essay refers to the extraordinary and quite irrational brouhaha in the lead-up to the Year 2000, the abbreviation 2K being computer jargon for 2000, or, more strictly, 2048. It was also called the* millennium bug *although, since there was no year numbered zero, the end of the millennium was a year later than the strike date of the bug.*

The fear being promoted was the collapse of computer systems around the world because of problems associated with the customary abbreviation of the encoded year of dates to two digits. It didn't happen, which could be interpreted as a failure of the prediction or the success of the expensive precautions.

2.2   The Profession's Future Lies in its Past

(2001 October)

Teaching students fresh from secondary school about professional computing induces feelings of unreality and helplessness. The feeling of unreality comes from their belief that the profession they wish to join mainly involves using computers, and that the industry they expect to be working in is about as old as they are, if that. The feeling of helplessness comes from the extreme difficulty in getting them to believe anything else.

Unfortunately, the people most influential in their lives—parents, school teachers, career advisers, tutors, authors, and so on—all support the students' belief that a bright future lies ahead for skilled computer users in a brand-new IT industry that will pay them well.

These beliefs lack historical perspective. Ignorance of the past makes the future seem merely an enlargement of the present. It will not be. Wavelength division multiplexing should see to that. Professionals must be eager to command the future, not content to surrender to it.

The Computing Industry

We can best understand the computing industry's nature in the context of its history. Most people believe, falsely, that the industry started with the personal computer's introduction a couple of decades ago. Part of the problem here stems from the widespread misuse of the words "computing" and "computer." Computation constitutes only a minor use of computers nowadays, although quite the opposite was true, 50 years ago, of the first stored program computers. Today, the design of mass-produced processor chips specifically supports video gaming, the chips' largest market, and computers are often merely doors to the Net and its Web.

Digital technology now looms large in the consumer industry, both in various devices and in the coupling of such devices over the Internet. Computation of some kind certainly lives deep within these digital boxes, but computation is far from being the industry's main focus.

The Data Processing Industry

Fifty years ago, when most people believe the stored-program computer revolution began, "revolutionary" computers were brought into machine rooms already populated by a variety of data processing machinery used by a host of data processing workers. The stored program computer's role was to do faster and more cheaply work that people were already doing with other kinds of machinery.

When the early data-processing industry required more than addition and subtraction, it turned to hand-operated calculators or to calculators programmed by plug boards. In the world of commerce, the early stored program computers simply replaced heavier and slower calculators and tabulators.

The computing industry has a long history whose length depends on what we consider the industry to be. Viewing the industry as based merely on stored program computers supposes a discontinuity that never existed.

Even the personal computer had antecedents. The first popular computers were personal—in 1960, as a programmer of the IBM 650, the most popular computer of its time, I was allocated time slots and operated the machine myself, personally. Small, cheap computers of the time—like the LINC, IBM 610, Bendix G15, and Librascope LGP30—were often described as personal computers. A little later, in 1969, there was even a home computer, the Honeywell H316.[22]

Data Processing's History

Nowadays, when we embellish so much talk with IT—that pretentious version of the old initialism, DP—an optimist would hold that the industry seems aware that data processing is its primary concern and that our profession has thus been evolving continuously. The question is, for how long has it been evolving?

Much of the commercial machinery up to and beyond the 1950s processed data stored on punched cards. Scientific computation, when it became automated, often used data stored in punched paper tape.

Amateur historians usually trace punched cards back to Herman Hollerith's machinery, developed for use in the US national census of 1896. Around the same time, punched paper tape found use in telegraphy and music. Even earlier, Charles Babbage intended to use punched cards to program his mechanical automatic computer, an idea echoed in IBM's popular Card Programmed Calculator of the late 1940s.

Significantly, such techniques are digital in that they encode data binarily and conventionally, just as current computers and telecommunications do. The tradition lives on.

But the digital tradition goes back far more than a century. Some writings trace the use of punched cards to Joseph-Marie Jacquard (1752–1834), whose automatic drawloom greatly speeded the textile industry's evolution. But Jacquard based his loom on the work of Jacques de Vaucanson, who in turn based his work on Robert Falcon's efforts. Falcon substituted cardboard for the earlier paper tape of Basile Bouchon. Bouchon's ideas probably derived from the annotated paper strips that drawboys used as an *aide memoire* when drawing the cords for the kind of drawloom used by Claude Dangon in the late 1500s[1].

Nor was the binary tradition limited to holes in paper or card. Before the advent of player pianos, music boxes and a great variety of automatic devices ran on similar digital principles. Clockmakers often crafted these devices, the escapement clock itself being a digital device that evolved roughly a millennium ago. Computing professionals should find this clock's development especially significant. First, clocks create the discrete phenomena on which we base digital computers. No clock, no digital computer. Second, if we are to believe David Landes[15] the development of clocks made possible the mercantile and industrial development of Western Europe, which so recently culminated in the dot-com bubble.

Qualitative Data

The computational tag borne by our industry and profession is flawed because computers and the Internet process mostly qualitative data, which consists of text or other graphics rather than numbers. Printing out results has always been an important aspect of data processing, particularly in commerce and government. Indeed, the best-selling computer of the early 1960s, the IBM 1401, became popular despite its very basic computational ability because it combined the functions of a tabulating printer with those of a calculator.

Modern online printers have evolved through a variety of what might properly be called personal printers, back through the Teletype and many different typewriters. Mainframe printers have had a much richer history, back through rotary presses and the many different flatbed presses that depended on the use of movable type, a digital development distinct from that of the clock.

In the printing industry of the Western world, evolution from block printing to the use of movable type depended on developments in metallurgy and papermaking, and for a long time existed alongside and competed with the scribal industry.

The technology of written, and even spoken, language constitutes a form of digital data processing, given that we define data as "a representation of facts or ideas according to certain conventions." Taking this broad view, the data processing industry, and our global civilization with it, has evolved through three phases:

- ephemeral data in the form of spoken language,
- static data in the form of written and printed language, and
- dynamic data in the form of binary encoding and signaling.

Professions and Trades

In the very broad context of its history, what can we learn about the professional worker's role in the data processing industry?

First, useful technology sooner or later escapes from the control of the privileged few and comes into widespread use. This diffusion is happening with modern digital technology now; has already occurred with calculators, typewriters, books, and handwriting; and can be inferred to have happened with spoken language.

Second, a mature industry consists of both trades and professions, with trade workers outnumbering professionals. In the printing industry, the compositors and press operators, who actually make the books, outnumber the typographers and designers, who tailor the books to the reader. The trades and crafts focus on the product, while the professionals focus on the product's use.

These days, the computing industry's product consists of its software and the hardware that runs it. Utterly codependent, the two were never fundamentally distinct: Whatever can be done with software can be done by hardware, and usually better.

The computing industry's future depends on satisfying its products' users. Those products continue to become increasingly complex. The main producers in the industry cope with this difficulty, for the moment, by offering training in various special skills—such as network management—needed to operate their current product. Their trainees are not professionals, but trade workers.

Most people that the computing industry employs to produce its hardware and software focus on the product itself. They supervise automated manufacturing processes and code programs. They may need to be highly skilled, but they work in a trade or craft.

Most people that the computing industry's customers employ to use hardware and software work primarily in trades and in professions outside the computing industry itself. Their skills with computing machinery are, or should be, secondary to their own industry's skills.

Many of my students seem to want the glamor and unthreatening stimulation of working with computers for a living, along with the prestige and rewards of being a professional. And this is what they are being offered at present.

The computing industry has little need for true professionals because they can sell whatever they make. Marketing creates the demand they require. So industry is content, for the time being, to hire graduates versed in object–oriented computing.

Computing educators happily produce such graduates. Professional bodies create object-oriented curricula, which are delightfully straightforward for academics to teach. While the computing industry continues to grow, computing graduates will continue finding élite employment.

But history tells us that digital technology will loosen itself from the control of élites. Already, areas of professional education other than computing offer training in computer and Internet use. Already, computing industry producers offer public formal training in their products' use. Already, young adults who have used computers all their lives, at home and in school, find better jobs because of their computer skills.

Sooner or later—preferably sooner—public technical education authorities will provide intensive training in computing skills within a variety of special-ties. The trade and craft workers thus created will compete well with the uni-versities' pseudoprofessional computing graduates, and, going by experience in other trades, the good workers will be well rewarded and well respected.

The would-be controlling bodies of the computing profession would thus be well advised to assist in the development of computing trades and crafts. Further, they should broaden the definition of our profession to encompass a people-oriented focus, developed from the full context and importance of its history.

2.3   Seven Great Blunders of the Computing World

(2002 July)

Last July, for my first-anniversary column, I urged computing professionals to temper pride with humility (essay 4.2, p.156). To justify the humility, I wrote that "the computing industry's blunder rate is far higher than it should be, and we must take professional responsibility for it." No one reacted to this assertion, leaving me unsure if the silence sprang from collegial agreement or dismissive contempt.

But we must remember the blunders so we can strike a proper balance between pride and humility—assuming there have indeed been blunders. This column aims to confirm their existence by giving examples.

The seven blunders I offer here provide a mix that is ancient and modern, retrievable and irretrievable, general and particular, subtle and blatant, and arguable and undeniable. I describe some blunders only briefly because I have already given their details in previous issues of *Computer*. Further, my choice of examples reflects my background and experience. If any of you care to offer a different selection for *The Profession* next July, I would consider such a contribution both educational and entertaining.

7. Numeric Encoding

Many elementary blunders have been made during development of our system for representing numbers, such as having 10 digits instead of 12, using a minuscule symbol for the fraction point, and conflating the operation of subtraction and the property of negativity under the same symbol [more in essay 2.4, p.64].

A less obvious blunder is that we write our numbers the wrong way around. The text I am now keying goes in as it is read—from left to right— just as the digits of any number go in as they are written—most significant to least significant. Also, we say nearly all our numbers in the same digital sequence. This is a mistake, because the most recent item is easiest to recall, but we read the least significant digit last. The most significant digit, not the least significant one, should be the easiest to recall.

The blunder becomes more obvious when we do pencil–and–paper arithmetic. For example, when adding two numbers together, we write the digits of the sum from right to left. This becomes counterproductive when we try to use the computer to deliver arithmetic drill to students: the entire answer must be worked out and remembered before the student can start keying the answer in. Ridiculous—and hardly conducive to promoting numeracy.

How did we come to get this wrong? The Arabs, from whom we got our place-value notation, also put the most significant digit to the left. But to them, left is last because they write and read from right to left, so it's interesting to consider that maybe our original blunder stems from not knowing enough about Arabic. Curiously, Arabic seems to have imported the problem for numbers longer than two digits, with Arabic readers keying in their telephone numbers from left to right.

6. Text Encoding

The ASCII and EBCDIC character sets caused problems that Unicode's developers intended to put right with their text encoding system. But Unicode itself proved a bigger blunder by far. The world has many different writing systems for encoding text, and the most popular systems work with many languages. As I pointed out some time ago (essay 5.2, p. 202), Unicode's blunder was in aiming to encode every language rather than every writing system.

5. Scientific Programming

Fortran and Algol were blunders because their popular use locked scientists and engineers into lexical rather than symbolic thinking. Traditional mathematical notation, although sadly flawed in many details, supports a terse and holistic thinking style that contrasts with the verbose and sequential style of thinking that traditional program coding schemes force on us.

IBM's Ken Iverson and colleagues adapted his reformed mathematical notation, developed at Harvard, to use on computers. They called their system APL, after Iverson's original book.[12] The approach's advantages, as Iverson described in his Turing Award paper, "Notation as a Tool of Thought,"[13] were profound and clear to users. But, perhaps because of continued opposition to APL from both inside and outside IBM, or perhaps because of its symbolically rich character set, few people adopted the system, and those who did came to be regarded as fringe dwellers.

After he retired from IBM, Iverson returned to Canada where, with new colleagues, he revisited the notational approach. With the advantage of hindsight, they developed a notation and system called J, based on the ASCII character set. Added to J more recently, tacit programming arguably provides the purest form of functional programming yet to appear.

The continued neglect of APL and J by scientists, engineers, mathematicians, and actuaries delays recovery from the original blunder. Although commercially successful, the various program suites that accept the highly complex traditional mathematical notation are themselves blunders because they perpetuate the worst features of that notation, thus making it harder to teach young people mathematical skills.

4. Commercial Programming

Cobol—which certainly made it easy to write program code that could be easily understood by others—was nevertheless a blunder. Its widespread adoption, often as a matter of fashion, stopped the development of macrocoding, a more effective approach to coding based on the division of labor between system programmers and application developers.

When tackling a problem area, the system programmers would write macrodefinitions for the data fields and records, and for the basic operations on that data. The application developers used those definitions, effectively a tailor-made coding scheme, to build programs. This highly productive approach made programs easy to maintain and adapt. The assembler-based programs that macroprogramming produced were typically smaller and faster than equivalent programs written in Cobol.

Assembly coding's critics argued that it produced lengthy and cryptic source code. This argument did not apply to macrocoding, however, as the application-specific macrodefinitions could greatly reduce the lines of source code and could exploit the application area's technical terms to make the code easy to understand.

The blunder came about partly because of the rather short-sighted but enthusiastic promotion of Cobol, and partly because the macroassemblers of the mid to late 1960s were rather primitive compared to some of the earlier ones, such as the MAP for the IBM 7080. Although developers used macrodefinitions in what assembly programming there was in the later 1960s, these definitions were usually restricted to providing standard operating system interfaces. Indeed, IBM's own software development shops banned other macrodefinition uses.

This blunder has two important consequences. First, macrocoding in many ways anticipated object-oriented coding techniques by, for example, allowing data names to be protected. This approach could have provided an early basis for commercial off-the-shelf components, given that macrodefinitions essentially are components.

Second, developing the distinction between system programmers and application developers would have ensured better programs through separation of responsibilities and skills, and it would have given a natural structure to the computing profession that it sadly lacks today.

3. The Processor

Arithmetic is an essential central processor function. Computer architects blundered, however, when they persisted in keeping integer arithmetic and floating-point arithmetic separate. This decision complicated instruction sets and subprogram libraries, courting otherwise avoidable arithmetic errors and imposing on programmers the need to make a choice between arithmetics and representations.

It would have been relatively easy to compose integer and floating-point arithmetics by tagging represented numbers to signify their kind, leaving it to the hardware to convert between the kinds if and when the need arose. This approach would also have allowed including other kinds of arithmetic and numbers, such as rational, to improve results, as I noted previously.[10]

2. The Computer

The keyboard has been the main device by which users put data directly into the computer. Back when we used typewriters and similar devices as terminals, adopting the customary typewriter keyboard made sense. When terminals with display screens came into use, extra keys were needed to send nontextual signals to the computer. We blundered by adding those keys variously and variably to the outskirts of the typewriter keyboard much as leeches attach themselves to the exposed surfaces of rainforest tourists.

Although designers have given much attention to the computer keyboard's physical layout, they have given little attention to its logical design, apart from trivial aspects like the relative positioning of letters. A complete separation of text keys from control keys would allow a structured pattern of controls for navigation of the display screen and its logical components. For example, keys for the left hand could specify vertical navigation, while those for the right hand could control horizontal movements. Such a pattern would make controlling the computer much easier for neophytes to learn and for designers to extend.

The role of the mouse is important here. Ideally suited to graphical interaction, it performs logical navigation less well, as indicated by operating system designers' perceived need to provide keyboard shortcuts. But keyboard shortcuts are distinguished by their ad hockery. A separate and standard set of control keys would make it easy to establish a consistent and clear style of operation as an alternative to the mouse. Such control keys would make chording the text keyboard attractive. This option would make touch typists of us all, like it or not. After all, our hands are wonderfully suited to keying in eight-bit bytes by chording.

1. Terminology

Our profession's greatest blunder so far stems from the way it ignores its own standard definitions of data and information (essay 1.3, p.16). Briefly, the standard defines data as conventional representations of facts or ideas, and information as the meaning that people give to data.

These definitions make a clear and significant distinction between people and machines: only people can process information, while machines can only process data.

However, the computing profession, and consequently the media and the public at large, treats data and information as synonymous terms. If machines cannot easily be distinguished from people, then businessmen can blithely replace employees with machines, bureaucrats can readily use computers as scapegoats, and people can naïvely believe that computers embody genuine intelligence.

The seven blunders I've described have two important implications. First, although computing professionals have many admirable achievements to their credit, they could have done better, and they should strive to do better in the future. Second, and more specifically, some of these blunders directly affect the profession itself.

Blunders arise from an inability to see beyond the immediate problem to its full social or professional context. The adoption of Cobol has obscured and delayed the much needed structuring of the profession into professional designers and skilled programmers. The conflating of data and information has prevented making a distinction between data technology and information technology, a distinction that would beneficially separate those professionals who focus on digital machinery systems from those who focus on the use of such systems by people.

Blunders arise from a failure of imagination, from an inability to see beyond the immediate problem to its full social or professional context. If professionals acquire an education in and remain sensitive to social and ethical issues, they will commit fewer blunders and recover more swiftly from them.

There is a minor "terminological" issue that is inconsistently dealt with in this book: should the word data *be treated as singular or as plural? I have always used it as the plural of* datum, *whereas* Computer's *style is to treat it as singular. So, by and large, the singular holds in essays, the plural elsewhere.*

2.4   Truth and Clarity in Arithmetic

(2003 February)

Last year, when I argued that our sequencing of digits in numbers from the highest to the lowest significance was a great blunder (essay 2.3, p.59), I intended to show that a faulty convention could be so embedded in our everyday life that few would ever think to question it. Several e-mail messages about this blunder chided me for not mentioning that the Arabs got place-value notation from the Indians, while another respondent questioned whether the digit of greatest place value was always the one of greatest significance.

But the most gratifying e-mail supported my view and pointed out that the convention meant that reading out an integer in words could not start until the entire number had been scanned, because only then could the leading digit's place value be known. This reminded me of how I sometimes feel annoyed when using an ATM, because the amount I key in builds up in such a peculiar way: each digit causes the prior value to be multiplied by 10 by being shunted to the left before the new digit is shown. Something similar happens in most numerical machinery for personal use, particularly electronic calculators.

In a well-designed world, digits would not need to joggle around like this. However, I am realistic enough to know that pointing out this blunder will have no effect on what we so much take for granted and that most people will simply disbelieve it's a blunder at all. Only very young children struggling with the rudiments of numeracy will be conscious of this burden, though unable to explain it.

Nevertheless, in a technological world where numeracy in developed countries shows steady decline, we in the computing profession should do everything we can to remove barriers that keep people from attaining numeracy.

Cantankerous Calculators

The atrociously poor design of the ordinary pocket calculator is the greatest barrier to numeracy that the profession could do much to fix.

In 2001, I received a cute little solar-powered calculator from the IEEE Computer Society as a Christmas gift. This novel present reminded me of the last similar device I can remember owning: a slide rule. But I'd since fiddled skeptically with other people's calculators, so the first thing I did with my gift was to key in 1 ÷ 3 × 3 = upon which the device displayed 09999999 instead of the proper 1. On much closer inspection, it appeared the answer was actually 0.9999999, but your eyesight needs to be better than mine to see the difference easily.

Still, the calculator's accuracy greatly exceeds the slide rule's, so I looked for things I could do with it that I couldn't do with a slide rule. My calculator sported four buttons labeled MC, MR, M+, and M-. I assumed the designers provided these to allow use of a single-value register, but experiment suggested that they serve merely and literally as accumulators. So I haven't used the calculator since, except as a desk decoration.

My experience is not unusual. Harold Thimbleby has made a particular study of electronic calculators. In "Calculators Are Needlessly Bad," [he] summarizes his findings, although in needlessly mild language[24] Simply put, the available calculator designs are an utter disgrace to the computing profession.

Calculator Redesign

The most important calculator is the most basic one, the one used first in learning arithmetic and most in everyday life. More complex and expensive calculators should be designed to compatibly extend the basic calculator.

My solar-powered calculator is basic in most respects and typical of commodity calculators. Let's consider the flaws in its design and how that design could be improved.

Clarity

A basic calculator must first exhibit clarity. The user should be given a clear depiction of what's going on.

Clarity has many aspects. Visibility provides a static aspect, violated on my calculator by making the decimal point almost invisible. The decimal point affects the value of a number more than any individual digit, and it should be as prominent on the display as any other symbol. The conventional decimal point could be suggested by a low triangle: 12△34. In any case, it's confusing generally to have the period used as an infix in numeric values but as a suffix in alphabetic text.

Overtness provides a dynamic aspect of clarity. Consider what happens as I key 1 ÷ 3 × 3 = into my calculator. The 1 goes straight to the display, but the division symbol merely causes the display to blink. Nothing has changed on the display otherwise. The 3 goes straight to the display, replacing the 1, but keying the multiplication sign causes the value 0.3333333 to appear on the display. So, tapping the multiplication key causes a division to be carried out. The next 3 goes straight to the display, and the equal sign causes the multiplication to be carried out. This is opaque, not overt.

Two design changes beg to be made. First, before carrying out an operation, both operands should be visible, and after carrying out the operation both the operands and the result should be visible. Second, tapping an operation key should cause that operation to be carried out, and be seen to be carried out, right away. The result of a simple multiplication might be shown overtly as

```
    12
   ×34
   408
```

Obviously, we need a display of at least four lines. The operands of the most recent operation and its result usually require three lines, and we need a fourth for the next operation's second operand. The result of the previous operation will normally be the next operation's first operand.

Simplicity

Second, a basic calculator must be simple to use. The calculator's operation, particularly in its use of keys, should be as consistent and uniform as possible. Thus we require three key classes: editorial, numeric, and operational, though editorial keys are not strictly necessary.

The *editorial* keys copy and edit values from the stored list of previous operands and results. For many reasons, storing these previous values is preferable to providing only a peculiarly limited and counterintuitive accumulator.

The *numeric* keys must provide the 10 decimal digits and two signs: a prefix for the negative sign, and an infix for the decimal point. The numeric keys should all work the same way, a tap putting the symbol into the second operand at the cursor.

My calculator is defective in respect to these two signs. Although it has a decimal point key, tapping it doesn't change the display. Instead, it just frees up the permanent decimal point to move left. The calculator also lacks a negative-sign key, instead providing a toggle that switches the number in the display between positive and negative. Nor does it show negativeness with a prefixed sign in the display, using instead a suffixed subtraction symbol—all of which is highly inconsistent.

It is most unfortunate that the calculator uses the subtraction operation's symbol also as the negative sign. This fundamental ambiguity severely hampers elementary instruction in arithmetic, for example, and forces the use of the comma as a separator in parameter lists within program code. In a basic calculator, the negative sign could be distinctively shown as a high triangle such that, for example, $\triangledown100$ would represent *negative one hundred*.

The *operational* keys are the most significant because they actually cause arithmetic to be done. The other keys merely set up operands. My calculator has five black keys for *dyadic* operations: +, -, ×, ÷, and =. It also has three blue ones for *monadic* operations, labeled +/-, %, and √, of which the first is the negate operation, the second unfathomable, and the third the square root. Worse than their strange effects, these eight keys fail to provide the most important basic operations.

Presuming the numeric keys are arranged in a 3×4 block, it's simplest to provide the four most basic operations straightforwardly as a column of keys alongside the numeric keys: counting, selecting, adding, and multiplying, with key-top symbols of, say, #, ∧, +, and ×, respectively. Dyadic counting—for which x # y yields the number of xs in y—and selection are more central to basic numeracy than addition and multiplication. A count always results in an integer, and this operation is behind the long division taught in elementary education and so often confused with the remainderless division that is multiplication's inverse. The selection operation gives the higher of its two operands—another basic operation that elementary education treats inconsistently.

We need more operations than these four, and they can be provided in two different, simple ways. First, the negative sign and the decimal point—normally a prefix or an infix—can be keyed as number suffixes that will be applied as modifying prefixes to an immediately following basic operation. Second, the operation, with any modifying prefixes, can be keyed without any value being given as the second operand.

Table 1 merely suggests the richness of basic operations that could be provided with a simple keying system. The negative sign ∇ would best be used systematically to replicate the operand of a monadic operation or to commute the operands of a dyadic operation. Thus, ∇+ y would double y, while x ∇# y would be the same as y # x.

Table 1. Possible operations for an improved calculator.

Key	Monadic	Dyadic	Keys	Monadic	Dyadic
×	factor	times	∆×	reciprocal	divide
+	magnitude	plus	∆+	negate	minus
∧	increment	higher	∆∧	decrement	lower
#	floor	count	∆#	round	modulus

Truth

Only exact arithmetic makes complete truth possible without recourse to algebraic notation. All the basic calculator's arithmetic operations must yield exact results when applied to exact values, and only exact values can be keyed in. My solar-powered calculator is inexact. It lies under division, as I've shown. While many calculators show a result of 1 under the same sequence, the lie is often revealed when we subtract a real 1 from that result.

To solve this problem, we must provide a representation for nondecimal fractional values. We can do this simply, by using the ▽ key as an infix to separate the numerator of a fraction from its denominator. Although we use this negative-sign key to put the denominator point in, the display could show it as the customary virgule. Among its other virtues, this convention gives a clear notation for infinity as 1▽0 or 1/0, arising from 0#1, and for indeterminacy as 0▽0 or 0/0, arising from 0#0.

To maintain the dedication to truth, irrational and transcendental values must be approximated by rational values, but this will emphasize that they are only inexact arithmetically on more advanced calculators. For example, an approximation to π could be keyed in either popularly as 22▽7 or 3△1▽7, more accurately as 3△14159, or even more accurately still as 355▽113 or 3△16▽113.

The computing profession—indeed the engineering profession in general—has a particular responsibility to promote numeracy, both within the profession and within the community at large. The commodity calculator is an insult to that responsibility.

The IEEE should establish and promote a rigorous and detailed standard for a universal basic calculator. Professional engineers everywhere should press to have that calculator manufactured and adopted as widely as possible. Computing professionals should work with the teaching profession to have the arithmetic of the universal basic calculator taught throughout elementary schooling, perhaps using calculators with drill and practice built in.

2.5   Computers, Programming, and People

(2002 March)

In the *Technology Quarterly* that *The Economist* bundled with its 22 September 2001 issue I found an odd article called "A Lingua Franca for the Internet."[4] I found the article's pedagogical lead-in—a somewhat fanciful history of program coding—peculiar. Likewise, the contradiction between the article's title and its closing clause, "expect a whole alphabet soup of languages within the next decade," seemed odd.

More peculiar still was the contrast between the first-page highlighted claim that "the business of writing software is becoming steadily easier," and the author's observation regarding object orientation's widespread adoption that "The price to pay for objects is . . . making the language bulkier and more cumbersome to use."

An amusing appendix, "Programmer's progress," reflected this discord. Attributed to one Joe Garrick, it showed progress using different versions of the banal anthropomorphic Hello World program. The first entry, in Beginner's All-purpose Symbolic Instruction Code, read as follows:

```
10 PRINT "HELLO WORLD"
20 END
```

Garrick showed programmers' growing experience beyond this Basic sample by increasing the code's length and complexity. At the progression's high end—the Seasoned Professional and Master Programmer categories— Garrick depicted the entries as excerpts torn from complete versions too large to be shown whole.

Computer Architecture

The Economist article made a strong impression on me because recent teaching experience had brought me face-to-face with similar contradictions. Last semester, I acquired a second-semester, first-year course called "Computer Organisation and Architecture." Believing that learning can best be done by doing, I sought to build in a strong practical component.

The textbook I selected had a fairly detailed description of John von Neumann's IAS computer, complete with several diagrams and a table of operation codes. Therefore, I based two major programming assignments on direct use of simulated IAS machines, simplified to one instruction per 20-bit word. Students would write the first program in hexadecimal machine code, the second in symbolic code [see the essay's endnotes if these terms are not familiar to you].

I was completely unprepared for the difficulties many of the class experienced with this assignment, including some of the better students. For example, despite detailed online instruction and repeated demonstrations of the process in class, many students could not learn how to do bootstrapping. They seemed unable to distinguish between the commands used to operate the machine and its programs' instructions. Although some students gave thanks when I finally provided a command specifically for loading and starting programs in one step, my contribution left others yet more perplexed.

Some students shunned certain kinds of instructions, notably those with address-modifying operations—the IAS computer has no index registers—and those with immediate operands. In symbolic code, many students insisted on putting data definitions up front but still expected to start their programs at their load point.

Many students struggled to fix in their minds a clear image of the machine on which their programs would run. Discussions confirmed the impression that their prior and continuing instruction in Java programming now interfered with their understanding of the IAS machine's sequentiality. Two possibilities follow:
• there is no point to having professionals understand the nature of the machines they use and code for, or
• there is some significant general benefit to understanding these machines.
Sound arguments can be marshaled to support either view.

Computers Are Irrelevant

Now part of consumer society, and marketed globally like hamburgers and soft drinks, computers are designed to be *sold* rather than *used*.[7] Likewise, developers have designed the software that runs on them to have built-in obsolescence so that both commercial and private sales will continue to grow.

The industry's main software products are already so gigantic that supporting their continuing growth, or developing competitors for them, presents more of a management problem than a technical one. Object-oriented techniques and component technology suit such an industry ideally. Accessing the Internet—arguably computers' most popular use—involves exploiting user interaction and delivering stimulating visual experiences. Elaborate special-purpose software packages provide the perfect tools for developing such applications.

Software marketers, e-businesses, and their technicians consider having an understanding of how the underlying machinery works to be utterly irrelevant. For them, the most important skills are marketing, management, and graphical expertise.

Under this régime, computer organization and architecture should be confined to engineering schools. There, the most talented of an increasingly innumerate and illiterate public can learn to design and produce extraordinarily complex computers powered by microchips whose impressive clock speeds and astronomical transistor numbers make for such impressive ad copy.

Computers Are Relevant

Although computers now play a major role in the consumer market, their potential *noncommercial* usefulness to society and the world remains virtually untapped. Commercial computers and software could be exploited for purposes quite different than those their makers intend.

Cheap and obsolete computers, particularly when networked, could do much to help reduce poverty and inequity by supporting educators in poor and underprivileged sectors of society. They could also assist organizations that promote such poverty reduction and education, such as PCs for Kids![16]

Yet, if educators are to somehow reverse society's growing illiteracy and innumeracy, they will not do so through their use of commercial software. They must use their own knowledge and control of a variety of programs, foreseeing and prescribing the computer uses that will meet their objectives.

These potential uses can best be discovered by people who can program novel applications such as drill and practice for skills fundamental to literacy and numeracy. This trend, once started, could become self-perpetuating: any increase in numeracy or literacy would likely increase the number of people able to create innovative software.

This approach requires many people to develop uses for computers that extend beyond strictly commercial and profitmaking ones. Such applications may well be for personal or private use, but they present technical challenges rather than organizational ones. Solving these challenges will require a wider understanding of what computers can do and how they do it.

Programming And People

We put computers to novel use by programming them for such tasks. For professionals, the coding of programs has long been indirect, using coding schemes that make a virtue of their distance from the reality of the machines

on which they will run. Compare the Java Hello World applet in Figure 1—
described by its source as "minimalist"—with the Basic example I cited earlier.

```
public class HelloWorld extends javax.swing.r
  JComponent {
    public static void main (String[] args) {
      javax.swing.JFrame f = new
        javax.swing.JFrame("HelloWorld");
      f.setSize(300, 300);
      f.getContentPane().add(new HelloWorld());
      f.setVisible(true);
      }
    public void paintComponent(java.awt.Graphics g) {
      g.drawString ("Hello, World!", 125, 95);
      }
  }
```

Figure 1. Java Hello World applet.

Coding schemes like this one are unsuited to popular programming.
Quite opaque to the inexpert, they fall prey to the whims and fancies of
professional fashion because programming techniques and tools undergo
continual development and frequent reinvention.

Some coding schemes such as Basic were originally intended for popular
use, while others such as Cobol were intended for use by ordinary business
people. These languages, however, have been oriented to objects rather than
to the processes that make a sequential machine what it is. An excolleague
with very long experience in the computing industry recently described Visual
Basic to me as "truly appalling." Certainly, it's quite unsuited to popular use
given that, according to Bruce McKinney, "Visual Basic designers have chosen
to pile more and more doodads on a weak foundation, knowing that doodads,
not foundations, sell boxes."[17]

As the Java example suggests, object orientation is valuable in the development of complex programs because it brings discipline to the exploitation of
the increasingly complex services offered by operating systems and servers.
This observation implies that machine-independent coding schemes are
unsuitable for popular use—or quickly become so.

Computers And People

To exploit computers for the popular good, we must provide machine-oriented program coding in a stable and simple context. This requirement rules out using the object-oriented Java virtual machine, the hypercomplex Itanium with its 13-bit operation code, or similarly complicated approaches. Popular computing could be based instead on international standards for

• a simple, stable computer organization and architecture to be provided by simulation or emulation within commercial systems;

• a symbolic programming system supporting the coding, development, and testing of programs for that architecture;

• an operating system providing services according to the standard organization; and

• a macrocoding system to simplify interfacing with the operating system and to support exchange and reuse of code fragments.

Standards for these four components would need professional consideration and international negotiation. The following rudimentary ideas are an illustration of possibilities, not a final design.

The computer architecture should be as simple as possible to program with, but versatile. For this task, a single two-operand instruction format would be suitable, without registers but with provision for indirect addressing. Operand tagging would greatly reduce the number of operation codes. Storing instructions and operands separately might be wise as well.

The symbolic programming system should be completely straightforward, but adaptable to different writing systems. Any complexity should be subsumed by the operating system or concealable within the macrocoding system.

The operating system should be completely in the background, and it could be an existing standard such as Posix. The OS should support program testing and tracing, and it should allow other programs to invoke tested programs as though they form part of the OS. Programmers should be able to ignore the host operating system's complexities while still having access to stored files of all kinds.

The macrocoding system should make the organization of the notional computer, and the services of the notional operating system, available to the programmer in simple format. Finally, the macrosystem should let skilled programmers code macrodefinition sets to provide toolboxes for simplifying application coding in specialist areas.

Future possibilities for the computing industry and profession fall into a spectrum. At one end, the computer and its software primarily function as commercial artifacts, with users mainly filling the role of consumer. At this end, the computer is irrelevant to most computing professionals, and professional education focuses on developing and managing complex program suites for the ever more complex stimulation of, interaction with, and control of users and customers.

At the spectrum's other end, the computer serves as a household tool and the user controls its uses. Here, the profession strives to make it as easy as possible for everyone to exploit the computer on their own terms and in their own culture, and it may even champion teaching the computer's direct use in elementary schools.

As things stand, the industry seems to be going in the first direction. From any ethical and moral standpoint, the profession should be pushing to move in the opposite one.

Although this essay is rather more technical than most of the others, readers with less computing experience should be persistent with it, as the theme is non-technical. To help such readers, a few of the terms will be explained here.

Binary code is awkward for programmers to work with directly, so bits are often used in groups of four, which effectively means numbers then are based on 2^4 or 16, hence hexadecimal. *In the very early days of computing, programmers would code programs by directly representing the instructions to be used in a program by the computer. Such instructions are called* machine code. *Because writing machine code is extremely tedious, programmers now write* symbolic code, *which special programs called* assemblers *or* compilers *convert to machine code.*

Before operating systems made starting the computer automatic, programs were run one at a time. This involved using its console to put a very small program into the computer to read the real program in (load) and start it. This procedure was in many circles called bootstrapping. *The story I heard to explain this was that it referred to the looped straps which were part of rural workers' boots in some countries. These made it easy to pull the boots on, but Wild West humor insisted that, if you were strong enough, you could use these to lift yourself off the ground, which is like what you had to do to start a program. Nowadays the term is often shortened to* booting.

Computers store frequently used numbers separately from main storage in fast registers *to speed up processing with them. Numbers are often used in lists, and to speed up processing of lists,* index registers *are used to hold offsets which are automatically added to the starting address of a list.*

2.6 The Usefulness of Hindsight

(2004 November)

Recently, reading an excellent article on system engineering [by] Diane Strong and Olga Volkoff,[23] gave me an intense feeling of déjà vu. Perhaps these feelings were so strong because they took me back to the early 1960s, when I first worked for IBM Australia.

Times were quite different then than today, but early commercial data processing problems were much like those facing today's enterprise systems, to go by Strong and Volkoff's observations. Two particular points they make relate to perhaps the most important system engineering issues of all, and both relate to the development of a large corporate project.

User Issues

At one time, a well-known international car manufacturer located its Australian data processing operations and much of its manufacturing on the outskirts of a large provincial city in the State of Victoria.

The manufacturer's previous operations had been based entirely on punched cards, with their computation programmed by plugboard for a machine with a peculiar magnetic-drum main store. The data on the drum was actually stored on a single wire that had three closepacked windings for each data track, with the wire screwed to the drum at each end. When the wire broke, as it occasionally did, an impressive mess resulted. Seating the replacement wire correctly took a long time.

Implementation

A new supplier replaced this system with an IBM 1401 computer. This transistorized machine, surprisingly, didn't have any plugged panels at all. With this amazing new technology, so different from the prior art, a new role came into being. In the plugged-panel era, programming had been the responsibility of the more experienced operators, but the new transistorized machines required specialist programmers.

Further, the new equipment was expensive, which the customer planned to justify by implementing new systems for all sections of the company. Yet where were these programmers to come from? Such talent was scarce at the

time, particularly in Australia, so the customer's management people decided
to advertise internationally and offer big salaries. This dismayed both me and
my salesman partner on the project. Going by similar attempts made by other
companies and applying a modicum of common sense, we felt confident this
approach would not only be far too protracted, but would very likely fail in
the long run.

A better approach, we felt, would be to recruit team members from within
various parts of the company and teach them how to program. That way,
the essential internal company knowledge would be there from the beginning,
and we felt—and later proved—that in a week we could teach enough about
programming to the recruits to get the project off to a good and speedy start.
Luckily, we persuaded management to adopt our recommendation.

We knew that the key to this approach, the Programming Aptitude Test,
could be used to get recruits who would quickly learn to program, provided
the company accepted only those who scored well. So the personnel department undertook a companywide testing of workers with a minimum of
five years' experience in the firm. Academic qualifications were rare and not
considered relevant. We put together a team that represented all significant
parts of the company, including the warehouses, assembly line, foundry, and
the chap from personnel who ran most of the aptitude testing.

The project proved very successful, although many team members left for
jobs elsewhere when their acquired experience gave them the confidence to
venture into the rapidly growing data processing industry.

Implications

At this time, the unfortunate split between system analysts and programmers
had yet to take place, so the team both designed their programs and coded
and debugged them. The team succeeded not because they were good programmers, but because they excelled at system analysis and design. Usually,
the people working on a program knew the users and their context, what was
needed, and what would be useful. If they didn't have this information, they
knew who to go to for the best answers. In Strong and Volkoff's words, "the
best and most experienced users from the business units . . . will make an ideal
team."

This approach has some further implications for the computing profession
as a whole. Anyone with the aptitude for it can program successfully and with
relatively little training, as long as the coding system is simple.

The contrast seems to be that oldstyle programmers designed the system
to best suit the user, while enterprise-system programmers require the user
to fit the system. As Strong and Volkoff observe, "Consequently, some users
must not only learn a new system but must take on additional, sometimes
unfamiliar, tasks and responsibilities."

Consider how different the software process would be if developers designed the system to be completely adaptable by the user. In the 1960s and 1970s, mainframe computers shipped with a great variety of features and parameters, and manufacturers tailored their operating systems with macro-definitions that let a data processing department build its operating system not only to fit the computer but also to suit its users. Are enterprise systems all that different? Who are they designed to suit?

Data Issues

Another international company, famed for its tracked vehicles, went into data processing with an IBM 1440 computer. Because this represented a significant investment for the company, the general manager took a strong interest in the project and had the vendor install the computer in an open area next to his office. He liked to see the expensive machine at work when he came in from his car park in the morning.

The data processing people wrote a special program that read and punched empty cards, moved the seek arms on the disk drives, and printed noisily without moving the paper. They also scheduled an operator to come in early and start it running when no other work was ready.

Implementation

The company wasn't particularly big at that time, so it justified the computer purchase by implementing many small applications for different areas of the company. That the company had two of the relatively new 1311 disk drives—the first such relatively inexpensive drive with removable disk packs—made this strategy feasible.

The programmers bent their backs to the work and quickly and successfully implemented a variety of programs for a variety of users. Then a problem arose. With many data files sharing a disk pack, it became feasible, and certainly desirable, to share data between departments. The programmers attempted this, but had great trouble putting code together and, when they got a program going, generated results that sometimes went strangely wrong.

After much panic and bewilderment, the cause eventually became obvious. The data that one department kept often proved incompatible with data kept by another. Sometimes the data had different names, formats, or units, and so on.

When management realized this, the data processing department reluctantly stopped developing new programs and turned their programmers to documenting the different data the company used in its manual systems as well as its already automated systems. As this work proceeded and conflicts were removed, the programmers built an authoritive data dictionary that gave different data standard names for both programming and everyday use, definitions, machine and display formats, constraints, and explanations. In the final stages of this effort, the programmers revised programs already written and converted data already stored on disk.

Overall, this effort revealed a company culture that inhibited standard-ization: At the time, people across the company showed reluctance to waste their time explaining obvious things to upstart technicians. They also balked at making trivial and aggravating changes to unimportant details of their work.

However, after a while, it dawned on many of these scoffers that this data dictionary could be useful to them. By then, it was as much used by people outside the data processing department as by the programmers. Certainly, it became plain that the dictionary not only made further application develop-ment feasible, but also sped up the process.

Implications

The two most important parts of a computing system are the users and their data, in that order. Although the users' needs must be met, their most impor-tant need is that the system produce, without qualification, trustworthy data.

The actual logic in the programs and the arithmetic in the computer can give rise to errors, but thorough checking during development will rectify them. In batch programs, common practice took measures—a hash total in the case of nonnumeric data—of all data just after it was read in and just before it was written out, so that users could compare the totals at the end.

Programmers must, however, make sure the data is trustworthy in the first place. Frequent failures of this kind led to the old acronym, GIGO—garbage in, garbage out. As Strong and Volkoff note, "... data cleansing is one of the most critical technical issues for successful implementation."

This issue has two aspects: standardizing the data usage, as in the second of my two anecdotes, and blocking invalid data on its way in to programs. Good management can greatly lessen invalid data generation, but many human errors can be made while getting data into the computer.

In batch programming, common practice demanded that operators check the daylights out of all incoming data, and often supplemented this activity with independent file-checking programs. I remember reading in an old issue of *Datamation* that the US Air Force's data processing people spent 80 percent of their coding effort and space on input data checking—and considered the effort well worthwhile.

The excellent project management advice in Strong and Volkoff's article caused me to think of the two examples I've shared. However, their descrip-tion of enterprise systems, and the separation their complexity brings between the technical people and the end users, reminded me of the strengthening of data processing departments in the 1970s and the rift between the typical data processing department and its users.

Data processing departments often seemed to exert a kind of arrogant tyranny, running their systems on their own terms. The introduction of Wang minicomputers as word processors in the late 1970s started breaking down this imbalance, a process carried further when business PCs became popular.

Hindsight suggests that this cycle might soon repeat itself. What will cut the enterprise systems people down to size now? Personal database machines with hardware to ensure integrity, authority, and sharing? Could these machines enable a hierarchy of entities down to the individual, which would let users look after their own data but use a network to get a coherent view of what they need from other entities? Maybe.

Obviously, more hindsight by computing professionals and their educators could greatly lessen the extent of the problems that Strong and Volkoff so clearly document.

2.7   Notions

The notions are given here partly as a rough summary, but more particularly as topics and issues for students to study and debate. They are in the sequence of their *key word* or *phrase*. The page number to the right of each notion points to its context.

1. Although we cannot but admire modern digital technology,
   that *admiration* should not be allowed block us
   from looking closely and critically at it   41

2. The basic calculator's *arithmetic* operations
   must yield exact results when applied to exact values   68

3. Computers have always been used by industry and government
   as a way to *avoid change* and to reinforce the status quo   51

4. We must remember our blunders
   so we can strike a proper *balance* between pride and humility   59

5. In a world where numeracy in developed countries shows steady
   decline, the computing profession should do everything possible
   to remove *barriers* that keep people from attaining numeracy   64

6. Some *blunders* it is practical to fix, the older ones probably not   42

7. In the world of *commerce*, the early stored program computers
   simply replaced heavier and slower calculators and tabulators   55

8. The distinction between quantity and indication
   is quite fundamental to *computing technology*   43

9. The business and government world is doggedly *conservative*   49

10. A basic calculator must be simple to use;
    its operation should be as *consistent* and uniform as possible   66

11. Basic numeracy is essential
    for competently functioning membership of a *consumer society*   44

12. Useful technology sooner or later escapes from the *control*
    of the privileged few and comes into widespread use   57

13. The conflating of *data* and information has prevented making
    a distinction between data technology and information technology   63

14. As big organizations and government departments become
  more *dependent* on computing systems, they become
    less able to make any change but incremental change 51

15. Oldstyle programmers *designed* the system to best suit the user,
  while enterprise-system programmers make the user fit the system 76

16. Clocks create the discrete phenomena on which
  we base *digital computers*—no clock, no digital computer 56

17. To argue that binary encoding is a blunder
  would not be to invalidate today's *digital technology* 42

18. Early commercial data processing problems
  were much like those facing today's *enterprise systems* 75

19. The best and most *experienced* users from the business units
  will make an ideal system development team 76

20. Computers enable the more efficient *governance* of the lower class
  by the middle class for the benefit of the upper class 52

21. It's easy to be wise in *hindsight*, but crucial decisions
  often have to be made when no relevant hindsight is available 42

22. The *history* of digital technology is in effect
  the history of human civilization 40

23. Blunders arise from a failure of *imagination*,
  from an inability to see beyond the immediate problem
    to its full social or professional context 63

24. The computing *industry* has little need
  for true professionals because they can sell whatever they make 58

25. Revolution is the way *marketeers* would like us to see
  what is actually evolution 39

26. The development of clocks made possible
  the *mercantile* and industrial development of Western Europe 56

27. "General-purpose" programs will only do what you *need*
  if they have been programmed to allow it,
    and if you can find out how to get it to allow you 48

28. The atrociously poor design of the ordinary pocket calculator
  is the greatest barrier to popular *numeracy* 64

29. Our consumer society,
  all of commerce and finance, is based on *numerics* 44

30. Ignorance of the *past*
  makes the future seem merely an enlargement of the present 54

31. The development of printing machinery has boosted
                          the *power* of bureaucracies and priesthoods   40

32. Developing the distinction between system programmers
            and application developers would have ensured better *programs*   61

33. What looks like a *revolution* today
                          will usually be seen as an evolution tomorrow   51

34. Keyboard *shortcuts* are distinguished by their ad hockery   62

35. *Simplicity* has vanished, the general-purpose computer
                          has become harder and harder to use and control   48

36. *Society* seems inevitably to want to stratify
                          into some kind of hierarchy of social power   52

37. Whatever can be done with *software*
                          can be done by hardware, and usually better   57

38. English *spelling* is more historic than systematic   40

39. For *technological development* to keep going the institutions
            that train and educate professionals, especially teachers, need
                          to be given students with a very high level of numeracy   44

40. What is more important than the *technology*
                          is what the technology is used for   39

41. A mature industry consists of both trades and professions,
                          with *trade workers* outnumbering professionals   57

42. The users' most important need is for their system
                          to produce, without qualification, *trustworthy data*   78

43. Data processing departments exerted a kind of arrogant *tyranny,*
                          running their systems on their own terms   79

44. Technology is neutral;
            it's the *use of technology* that can bring the good or the bad   53

45. A basic calculator must give the *user*
                          a clear depiction of what's going on   65

46. Most computer use is indirect, with the computing system
                          driving the *user* along predestinate grooves   49

47. The two most important parts of a computing system
                          are the *users* and their data, in that order   78

48. The main advantage of *written language* is
                          that it is relatively and reliably permanent   40

2.8 Bibliography

The entries are in order of the first or only author's name. Where no personal author is known, as for popular news items, an indicative name is used. Where there is a page number or two in *italics* at the beginning of the annotation, they point back to where the item was cited. Where some of the annotation is given in quotes it has been taken from the item itself or from some of its publicity.

1. John Becker (1987). *Pattern and Loom: A Practical Study of the Development of Weaving Techniques in China, Western Asia and Europe.* Copenhagen: Rhodos International Publications, ISBN 87-7245-151-3, 316 pp. (*p.56*; in collaboration with Donald B. Wagner; the classical book on the topic; a second volume has 80pp., ISBN 87-7245-204-8).

2. *Committee on Science, Engineering, and Public Policy* (2006 February). *Rising Above The Gathering Storm: Energizing and Employing America for a Brighter Economic Future.* Washington, D.C.: The National Academies Press, ISBN 0-309-10045-3, xviii+524 pp. (*p.45*; under the auspices of The National Academy of Sciences, The National Academy of Engineering, and The Institute of Medicine; pre-publication version via Open Book at nap.edu/books/0309100399/html).

3. Stanislas Dehaene (1997). *The Number Sense: How the Mind Creates Mathematics.* New York: Oxford University Press, ISBN 0-19-511004-8, xii+274 pp. (*p.43*; a particularly good account of the historical and, in more detail, personal development of number sense; the beginning of Chapter 4 describes the place of manual signing).

4. *The Economist* (2001, September 22). "A lingua franca for the Internet," *Technology Quarterly,* pp. 12–16, (*p.69*; online at economist.com /displayStory.cfm?Story_ID=S%26%28%280%25QQ%2F%2A%0A for Web only or print subscription).

5. James Essinger (2004). *Jacquard's Web: How a hand-loom led to the birth of the information age.* Oxford: Oxford University Press, ISBN 0-19-2805477-0, xii+302 pp. (emphasizes the human aspect of computing history, going from Jacquard to Babbage to Hollerith to Aiken, among others; richly illustrated; reviews and more in www.jamesessinger.com/reviews.htm).

6. John Kenneth Galbraith (1992). *The Culture of Contentment.* Boston: Houghton Mifflin Co., ISBN 0-395-57228-2, ix+195 pp. (*p.52*; this book is

very readable and contentious; the author died in 2006 and an obituary is online at guardian.co.uk/print/0,,329468789-110843,.html).

7. Robert L. Glass (2001, Sept.). "Practical Programmer: Of Model Change-overs, Style, and Fatware,"*Communications of the ACM,* Vol. 44, No. 9, pp. 17–20 (*p. 70*; HTML/PDF via doi.acm.org/10.1145/383694.383698).

8. Herbert R. J. Grosch (1991). *Computer: Bit Slices From a Life.* Novato, California: Third Millennium Books, ISBN 0-88733-085-1, 260 pp. (details personal and professional in the life of a pioneer in computing who spent a lot of time with fellow pioneers; a third edition, extended to nearly 700 pages, is freely available at columbia.edu/acis/history/computer.html).

9. Brian Hayes (2001, Nov.–Dec.). "Third Base," *American Scientist,* Vol. 89, No. 6, pp. 490–494 (*p. 42*; a wide-ranging introduction to various forms and uses of ternary arithmetic; the cited link to James Allwright's balanced ternary web pages unfortunately seems dead; americanscien-tist.org/content/AMSCI/AMSCI/ArticleAltFormat/20035214317_146.pdf).

10. W. Neville Holmes (1997, March). "Composite Arithmetic: Proposal For a New Standard" *Computer,* Vol. 30, No. 3, pp. 65–73 (*p. 62*).

11. *ILO* (2006). *International Labour Organization: Home Page.* (*p. 53*; www.ilo.ch; there are many documents available, but the source for the citation couldn't be found when this entry was being put together).

12. Kenneth E. Iverson (1962). *A Programming Language.* New York: John Wiley & Sons, Inc., LCCCN: 62-15180, xxi+286 pp. (*p. 60*; describes what was sometimes called "box notation," from which the programming language APL was developed; the notation was used very effectively in the '60s and early '70s for system specification).

13. ———— (1980, Aug.). "Notation As a Tool of Thought," *Communications of the ACM,* Vol. 23, No. 8, pp. 444–465 (*p. 60*; his very thoughtful Turing Award Lecture; PDF at elliscave.com/APL%5FJ).

14. Michitaka Kameyama (1990, May). *Toward the Age of Beyond-Binary Elec-tronics and Systems.* Charlotte, North Carolina: Proceedings of the 20th International Symposium on Multiple-Valued Logic, ISBN 0-8186-2046-3, pp. 162–166 (*p. 42*; the arguments for ternary and other bases are briefly reported in csdl.computer.org/dl/mags/co/1990/08/r8112.pdf).

15. David S. Landes (1983). *Revolution in Time: Clocks and the Making of the Modern World.* Boston: Harvard University Press, ISBN 0-674-76802-7, xx+480 pp. (*p. 56*; plus 8 pp. color plates, 32 pp. figures and an appendix on escapements; the very interesting argument is that clocks made the modern mercantile world possible).

16. Megan McAuliffe (2001, July 20). "Microsoft charity dispute draws attention," *CNET Networks* (*p. 71*; "An Australia charity said it had re-

ceived applause from around the world after standing up to Microsoft in a dispute over software licences."; news.com.com/2100-1001-270306).

17. Bruce McKinney (2006). *Hardcore Visual Basic: A Hardcore Declaration of Independence.* (*p.72*; this interesting item has moved around a bit, and now is at vb.mvps.org/hardweb/mckinney1.htm).

18. Karl Menninger (1969). *Number Words and Number Symbols: A Cultural History of Numbers.* Cambridge, Massachusetts: The M.I.T. Press, SBN 262 13 0400, xiv+480 pp. (*p.43*; translated by Paul Broneer from the revised German edition, *Zahlwort und Ziffer*, of 1958; compendious and richly illustrated).

19. Donald A. Norman (1998). *The Invisible Computer: Why Good Products Can Fail, the Personal Computer Is So Complex, and Information Appliances Are the Solution.* Cambridge, Mass.: The MIT Press, 1999, ISBN 0-262-64041-4 (paperback), xiv+302 pp. (*p.48*; very readable and extremely perceptive).

20. Denise Schmandt-Besserat (2003, December). *Accounting With Tokens in the Ancient Middle East.* University of Texas at Austin, Linguistics Research Center, Numerals Project (*p.43*; an intriguing story with both technological and social significance; the Numerals Project site holds much more of interest; utexas.edu/cola/depts/lrc/numerals/dsb/dsb.html).

21. Norris Parker Smith (1998, April–June). "The Millennium Is Close At Hand: Stock Up on Zeroes," *IEEE Computational Science and Engineering*, Vol. 5, No. 2, pp. 104–C3 (*p.50*; on the Y2K Problem).

22. Dag Spicer (2001, August 12). "If You Can't Stand the Coding, Stay Out of the Kitchen: Three Chapters in the History of Computing," *Dr. Dobb's Journal* (*p.55*; early home computers; now available online at ddj.com/184404040 though the URL keeps changing).

23. Diane M. Strong and Olga Volkoff (2004, June). "A Roadmap for Enterprise System Implementation," *Computer*, Vol. 37, No. 6, pp. 22–29 (*p.75*; "Drawing on five years of enterprise system implementation observations, the authors developed an informal roadmap that can help managers achieve . . . technical and organizational objectives . . . "; doi.ieeecomputersociety.org/10.1109/MC.2004.3).

24. Harold W. Thimbleby (2000, June). "Calculators are needlessly bad," *International Journal of Human-Computer Studies*, Vol. 52, No. 6, pp. 1031–1069 (*p.65*; damning of a particular calculator in detail, more briefly of others; PDF at www.uclic.ucl.ac.uk/harold/srf/hucalc.pdf).

25. *UNDP* (2006). *United Nations Development Programme: Home Page* (*p.52*; undp.org, and the various Human Development Reports are at hdr.undp.org).

Chapter 3

Computers and Education

The word *educate* comes from the Latin *ēducāre*, meaning *to rear* or *to bring up*. The closely related *ēdūcēre* means *to lead forth*. Thus education aims to bring the child out of infancy and into full membership of society, able to take part in and contribute to a full range of community activities. A good education system will aim to do this for all children and to the full extent of their abilities.

Both for the child, and for society, nothing could be more important than education. The better their education, the more adults can benefit from the community, and the community from its adult members. Education depends on communication.

Our human society is based on digital technology. From prehistoric times, spoken language has been used primarily for personal communication, in the day-to-day life of the family, and of the tribe or village. From historic times, written language has been used to communicate within the larger community, across both time and space.

The use of written language is responsible for the complexity and richness of our modern society—its culture and learning, its commerce and technology, its governance and principles. The development of electromagnetic digital technology with its ability to collect, manipulate, store, and transmit data of very many kinds in vast quantities has made accelerated development of our society possible.

Modern development is dismayingly and thoroughly lopsided. The dream was that technology would bring improvement throughout society, would make everyone healthier, wealthier, and wiser. Instead, life has been improved for a very few, worsened for most.

Ill-health, inequity, illiteracy and innumeracy are all increasing, tragically even in "developed" nations, as the United Nations Development Program's data clearly show.

The basic problem is poor education. People are being rejected by society instead of being led into it. And digital technology, instead of being used to better education, is rapidly worsening it.

This conclusion is one I reached many years ago. It was strengthened by my involvement in school systems at various levels over many years, both as a parent and as a computing professional. One result was my formal article, "The Myth of the Educational Computer" (essay 3.1, p. 99), published a little before I was offered the editorship of *The Profession*.

Developments since then have confirmed my concerns, not confounded them. The pity of it is that digital technology has such enormous potential benefit in the field of education, especially and crucially in the Third World, yet so little of that potential is being realized.

The article examines the nature of education, and suggests in broad terms how a school system might be better structured for present day needs. Two important uses of digital computers in schooling—drill and practice (p. 109), and academic gaming (p. 111)—are briefly described in appendices.

In the article a three-stage structure for a school system was suggested in passing (see p. 106). What was not provided in the article were details of how digital technology might best be used within that structure. In the following, the three stages are described in detail primarily to allow the different uses of digital technology to be shown in a clear context, *not* to dictate what is properly the concern of professional educators and sociologists.

A Structure for Schools

Education must go through stages. Computers are important in different ways in the different stages. One way to stage the process is the following:

• Primary social education for basic skills, intrapersonal ones like reading and arithmetic, and interpersonal ones like conversation and cooperation.

• Secondary liberal and progressive education for acquiring, organizing and evaluating knowledge.

• Tertiary vocational education for applying skills and using knowledge in particular broad areas.

Such a structure would need to be adapted to different conditions, and adaptable to changing conditions. Also, this structure does not include a place for university education, which is discussed separately below (p. 94). But whatever the structure, the clear and urgent need is for more social investment in teacher training and in school facilities.

Primary Social Education

The crucial need, at the very least in today's developed countries where single parent families and families with both parents working have become much more common, is for earlier schooling. There are disturbing reports of more and more children beginning school inoralate, that is, unable to converse. Many do not know how to use cutlery, and some don't even know to use the washroom or toilet. Besides, developmental psychologists tell us that the very earliest years are the best for learning, especially for learning how to learn.

This need for an earlier and better formal start to schooling is beginning to be recognized. In the Australian state of Victoria, policies are being drawn up for bringing the many informal preschools or kindergartens within the main school system. Special training is being given to inoralate school beginners in some parts of Britain.

Primary schooling is where basic skills must be learnt and reinforced. The earlier they are learnt the better they are learnt.

While teachers are necessary for training in social skills, basic skills in the use of the digital technologies of spoken, written and arithmetic language can be superbly developed by using modern digital machinery. Drill and practice can be designed to adapt to the individual user with inhuman patience and accuracy when it is delivered by computer.

Reading skills are in the news at present. *Whole word* methods were adopted in most classrooms some years ago, at least in Britain and Australia. But now *phonics*, a method that focuses on the correspondence between letter patterns and sounds, has become officially favoured.

These methods are more faddish than systematic, and the switch seems to be more a hasty reaction to the symptom of rapidly growing illiteracy than a considered decision based on a cultural change in society.

The two methods can't be isolated from each other. English spelling is not consistent in its patterns. The way common words like *reject* and *row* are pronounced can depend on nearby words. Compare *to reject* and *the reject,* and the two *rows* in *a row about who is to row.* Even *the* is pronounced differently in *the dog* and *the otter* in many varieties of spoken English. Anyway, however reading of English is learnt, skilled reading is done in words and phrases.

Simple digital machinery could deliver drill combining both methods, with the balance changed to suit the talents of the learner. It could even be that dyslexia could be detected automatically and countered by special drill.

With digital speech technology, the learner being taught the word *dog,* for example, could be shown a picture of a dog with the word *dog* as caption and with the word *dog* spoken in the learner's own voice. This technique could be adapted to teach reading, spelling, pronunciation, singing, music, writing, keying, vocabulary, grammar, observation, counting, arithmetic. It could even be adapted to help teach the art of conversation to the inoralate.

What is the role of the teacher in all this? Two roles stand out, and all primary school teachers would need to be thoroughly trained in those roles.

The first and most important role is that of the social catalyst, ensuring that the basic skills are being employed properly and fully in the society of the classroom by all its members. Great skill and close observation would be needed to maintain a reasonable balance and harmony in the class.

The second role is that of monitor and mentor of the individual students, particularly in their learning by drill.

The drill device could be made personal, like a mobile phone but simpler and cheaper. It would connect wirelessly to the primary school network so that all the details of the student's drill could be copied and analysed by computer to identify students in need of extra help. Teachers could review the work and progress of any student at any time, and adjust their drill parameters if necessary, or load special drill at need. Specialist help could be seamlessly enlisted in special cases.

This outline merely suggests some clear possibilities for digital technology in primary education.

The drill and practice techniques used in early primary school for basic skills could be adapted in later primary schooling to specialist knowledge in areas such as botany and geography, breeds of dogs, and kinds of foods, and to the use of foreign languages. Drill would not only be diversified through the years of primary schooling, but also continued, though less centrally, in later schooling.

The important issue to stress, however, is that by using modern digital technology to administer intensive drill for developing reflexive skills, both physical and mental, and by training teachers to have those skills put to use in social settings, even the poorer students of the future could be brought to superb levels of oralcy, literacy and numeracy.

The important danger to be continually aware of is that this same modern digital technology can equally be used to develop skills and attitudes that are antisocial. This danger is described in the essay "Digital Technology, Age, and Gaming" (essay 3.2, p. 112).

The skills built up in primary education should empower and encourage students to think purposefully and independently. These skills are necessary for secondary education to succeed.

Secondary Liberal Education

Primary education builds up basic skills, learnt in youth and among youth. Socially, the learner learns within and from immediate groups, both inside and outside school.

Secondary education builds up knowledge and understanding of the larger world, the world outside the school and the family. The learner observes and analyses sociality itself from within the school and local community.

Sociality exists at various levels, from the family to the world as a whole. Students need to understand how these levels work internally, and how they work together. As to whether and to what degree levels don't work internally, or don't work together, students need to learn to observe, analyse and judge for themselves.

The most basic social interaction level is between people as individuals. While the family and the primary school build skills in social interaction within the family and the classroom, secondary school will be able to use voice and video over the Internet to widen personal social interaction far beyond the physical classroom. In effect, classrooms in different areas, for example city and country, could be joined for shared lessons and activities.

By interacting directly with students and classes in different circumstances, social skills will be enlarged and understanding of other communities will be swiftly gathered. Provided the teachers are trained to make best use of such opportunities, learning of foreign languages tackled in primary school could be swiftly reinforced and extended, say by joining classrooms internationally.

At the next level of social interaction students need to understand how national societies work in general terms, and how their own national society works in more detail. Here digital technology has two very important roles.

The World Wide Web can provide excellent material for group discussion, especially through its daily newspapers and weekly magazines, increasingly published on line, and websites of public broadcasters. The Web also holds an enormously rich archive of social material, which can be used to study areas such as history, art, literature, law, commerce, and much much more.

However, social studies exploiting the Web are relatively passive. They need to be backed up by active learning provided by academic gaming (see p. 111) in which the operation of social and government entities can be learnt. Provided teachers are well trained in managing their use, these games can also teach skills useful in daily life, skills in areas such as project planning, risk assessment, financial management, negotiation and reporting.

At the top level of social interaction, the supranational level, the student needs to understand the activities that permeate all nations and communities in much the same way. Areas for study include industry, commerce, law and government, science, nature, agriculture, technology, and communication.

Learning about what people do in these areas is basically a contemplative activity in secondary schooling, and less amenable to group learning. Though some academic gaming would be useful, the most important uses of digital technology are likely to be in simulation and in interactive tuition.

A simulation takes a model of a system of some kind and shows how the system behaves over time. The model has parameters that affect its behavior during a simulation. The student learns by changing the parameters' values, observing the effect and trying to find values that achieve a particular result. A simulation might run a simple model over and over again, with the student setting all the parameter values at the start. A dynamic simulation would allow parameters to be changed during the simulation.

Interactive tuition is needed to enhance simulation. Such tuition would explain the model to the student, instruct in the use of the simulation, assist in analysing the results, test the student's understanding of the model, and describe the wider context, in particular its social implications.

Secondary education is about understanding and evaluating what happens in society at various levels and in various areas. This is an essential grounding both for tertiary education and for success in life beyond school.

Secondary education must not be cloistered. Although digital technology is invaluable for bringing experiences into the school, the danger is that the student becomes merely an unthinking spectator. Here the teacher is of central importance in ensuring that students analyse and evaluate the significance of their experiences both for themselves and for other people.

The social significance of the digital technology used in their education is especially important for students to understand. Some aspects of this are outlined in "Rationality and Digital Technology" (essay 3.3, p. 117).

Tertiary Vocational Education

Tertiary education (as explained on page 88, this is not university education, which is discussed starting page 94) aims to take students with the skills and knowledge given by primary and secondary education, and turn them into useful and satisfied members of society. This is done by providing the students with opportunities to apply their skills practically, and to extend those skills in ways that will increase their sense of identity and feeling of worth in the community.

The process is one of phasing the student into society. At the start of tertiary education students will spend most of their time at school. At the end they will be spending most of their time out in the community. In the meantime they will be deciding in what areas of work and recreation they will be spending their life beyond school.

Different students will graduate into society at different rates and along different paths. However, the learning experiences need to be of a systematic variety so that students can understand the possible ways they can fit into the community, make an informed choice, and start to focus their learning of topics relevant to that choice.

The variety needs to be quite systematic so that students can consciously examine and develop their feelings and talents in pursuit of a role in society that will give satisfaction to themselves and benefit to the community. This involves an analysis of what people can do with their lives, of the dimensions of their activities.

One possible analysis makes out four distinct dimensions: the personal, the objective, the subjective, and the methodical.

The *personal* dimension is about the context of the activities. It ranges from private and domestic activities, through school and community participation, to professional and occupational activities. Different skills are needed to cope successfully with life through all waking hours, and even sleeping.

The *objective* dimension relates to what the activities deal with, ranging from people, through animals, plants, materials, constructions, to machines of various kinds. Again, different skills are needed to understand and interact successfully with the various objects around us.

The *subjective* dimension relates to the mentality of activities, how the mind affects the activity, and how the activity affects the mind. Two subdimensions are relevant, one the traditional introvert to extrovert spectrum, the other the contemplative to sensual spectrum. In other words, activities may require us to be aware both of what we ourselves and those we are with are thinking and feeling. We must also be able to combine thinking, the use of the mind itself, with sensing, the use of our perception, with emotions linking the two.

The *methodical* dimension relates to how the activity is planned and carried out, and so to the nature of the activity itself. Activities are usually directed to achieving objectives, and so can be thought of as problem solving. In society at large, problems are usually complex and continuing. Teamwork is needed to deal with them. Some team members are needed, therefore, to be strategic, and some tactical. This dimension is explored in a computing context by the essay "Why Johnny Can't Program" (essay 3.4, p. 122).

This dimensional analysis is, of course, merely speculative. However it does bring out two important issues at the tertiary vocational stage.

Firstly, the task of leading the student to full and active membership of society is a social one involving the identification of fruitful areas of activity for the student based on the student's interests and skills. But the teacher's role here is more that of a prompter than that of a mentor. The role of mentor shifts to people in the world outside the tertiary school who are involved in helping the student.

Secondly, opportunities for the student to learn, while taking place more out in the community in the later stages, lean more to practical work, with the teacher in the role of practical supervisor. This implies that tertiary schools should be more a collection of workshops of different kinds, with membership of learning groups more a matter of the nature of the activities than of the age of the student. Indeed the students in a group are likely to learn more from each other than from the instructor.

It should be noted here that to call tertiary schooling *vocational* is going a little beyond the usual meaning of vocation. One's vocation is, going by the second edition of *The Oxford English Dictionary*, "One's ordinary occupation, business or profession." Given that these all primarily concern the application of skills, and that ordinary adult life is nowadays likewise concerned, taking *vocation* to mean generally "applying skills" is surely justified.

The need for a great variety of workshop experience means that tertiary schools will need to be either large or specialized, so that different kinds and levels of workshops and laboratories can be afforded.

Also, the emphasis on workshop work means that there is an emphasis on equipment. This is where digital technology comes to the fore, because both domestic and vocational equipment is more and more driven by embedded computers.

While students have, at the primary and secondary levels, used computers primarily for learning, at the tertiary level they will be more and more learning how to use computers as tools or within tools of various vocations.

Further Education

The three-layered education system described above will never come about just like that. Social and political systems are too complex to allow such reform to take place. In any case it's most unwise to undertake any significant reform except as a gradual process. Abrupt change often triggers chaos.

However, painting such a picture can provide a context for bringing out possible benefits and opportunities of using digital technology in schooling in particular ways. It can also suggest new approaches to meeting educational needs.

Universities and vocational education

The purposes of the three layers are, in brief and in sequence:
- building personal and social skills,
- acquiring knowledge and understanding, and
- learning to apply the skills, knowledge and understanding.

The last layer is importantly vocational (with meaning as discussed on p.93), helping the learner to select and fit into various roles in society. But how much time a student spends in vocational learning will vary with the selected vocations and with how much learning the student needs and how much the vocation needs. Moreover, many people will need to come back from time to time either to change vocation or to improve their skills.

This has implications for the way the vocational education is carried out, and for the teachers.

Firstly, classes or learning groups will be focused on a particular category of applied skills and so will not be of any standard duration. Indeed the duration may well be made to depend on what the students want as they go along. Furthermore, with a wide range of ages and experience among the students, teaching may be shared between staff and students.

Secondly, teachers will be focused on their own special areas of expertise, and will be guiding their groups' learning rather than persistently instructing.

Thirdly, a large and continuing investment in equipment and materials will be needed.

In many countries there is already a network of vocational or technical training institutions, but these are, at least in Australia, focused on job training for adults.

The suggestion of the three-layer model is that vocational education build up life skills as well as job skills, and do this for older children as well as for adults. Proper use of digital technology in the first two layers can accelerate the building of basic skills and the acquiring of basic knowledge so that what used to be done in say twelve years can be done, and done better, in two or three years less. This would allow all students to be concentratedly trained in the third layer to apply their skills and knowledge both to their personal life and to their work life.

What has not been discussed here so far is education for the professions. The essays "Why Johnny Can't Program" (essay 3.4, p. 122) and "Jobs, Trades, Skills, and the Profession" (essay 3.5, p. 128) explore the distinction between professions and trades in the context of the computing profession. However the same distinction holds for other professions, at least to some extent.

The essays make the significant point that while tradespeople apply skills, professionals design and supervise what tradespeople do. Professionals have traditionally been educated in universities by researchers. Researchers are people who design and evaluate what other professionals do.

Universities nowadays are facing severe difficulties, at least in Australia and apparently elsewhere. Because governments see a need for more students to get more education, many more students are going to university. With levels of literacy and numeracy falling, universities are finding it hard to produce graduates with a satisfactory level of professionalism. This has led industry to prefer graduates with combined and higher degrees, and the better students to prefer to study such degrees.

With a vocational tertiary school system, universities could resume their traditional role. The need to simply provide bulk education beyond ordinary schooling would disappear because ordinary schooling would last longer and do very much more. University entrants would do the vocational training relevant to their intended profession at tertiary school.

Teaching about digital technology

Because use of computers and the Internet is becoming more and more part of professional life, computer laboratories are found in most university faculties and departments. Most undergraduate courses have some teaching about the basic use of digital technology.

A tertiary school system would take over this teaching of basics, allowing universities to assume competence in this area for all their entrants.

A more intriguing consideration, though, is the possible effect of general competence in the use of computers on university courses with names like

Computer Science and *Information Systems*. Even if these disciplines fade away, as they might very well do, there will remain a real need for professionals who will work with people in other professions to ensure that digital technology is used to best effect. This profession would properly be called the computing profession, and the role and education of computing professionals is examined in "Jobs, Trades, Skills, and the Profession" (again, essay 3.5, p. 128).

Educational Support

School students need both to learn about, and learn to use, digital technology. Therefore digital technology's importance in the school system is second only to that of the educators and teachers.

Educators and teachers are responsible for the education of their students. The digital computers and networks they use are merely equipment.

The responsibility means that school staff deserve the very best training and education themselves, and an appropriately high level of remuneration. The importance of digital technology in the school system means that the teachers should be given the best possible support by their equipment.

Teachers' roles

School education might well be done by teams comprised of teachers working tactically and educators working strategically. Each kind would see digital technology in their own light and exploit it with their own distinct skills and experience. The teachers would focus on the students and their use of digital technology, the educators would focus on the educational outcomes and on the use of digital technology to achieve them.

Another matter that the three-layer model of the school system brings to the fore is that the education at each level is different, though of course the transition between layers would need to be made easy for the students.

Primary school staff would need to be expert in handling young children and their building up of basic mental, physical, and social skills.

Secondary school staff would need to be expert in supporting social groups and social learning, as well as in fostering the acquisition of knowledge and understanding of the outside world.

Tertiary school staff would need to be expert in supervising the building up of vocational skills in various areas, both in the personal and the public context.

Staff at all levels would also need to encourage and support activities that promote cultural and physical capabilities and fitness. Staff at all levels would also use computers and other digital machinery both to support their own work, and as technology that their students need to learn how to use in an enabling way.

However, the most significant potential benefit of computers in education is probably to free the teachers from the stigma of marking, the inappropriate responsibility of aligning students by numbers that spring so artificially and temporally from tests and examinations. This practice is no more valid than that of IQ testing (essay 1.4, p.21), and forces an adversarial role on classroom teachers.

If digital machinery is given the task of drilling basic skills and embedding basic knowledge, then the machinery *ipso facto* is measuring the learning and telling each learner how they are getting on, and in great and helpful detail as needed. Moreover the machine can quite naturally and impersonally tell the learners of their rate of progress in any area at any time, rather than giving a single climactic mark of approval or disparagement in a classroom context.

This allows the teacher to be, and be seen to be, primarily an advisor and mentor, even colleague and friend, for each student. Data collected for each student during the drill would help the teacher in this role.

Teaching support

Networked computers can be used in schools to support both students and staff in various ways, for the students to learn both from and about, and for the staff to administer and monitor the learning.

Throughout schooling, particularly early schooling, students will each need their own special-purpose computer for drill and practice. In later schooling, particularly vocational schooling, schools will need a variety of computer-based equipment for students to learn to use.

All this teaching and learning will be greatly supported and enhanced by networking of the computers.

On the one hand, the network will collect data about what students are doing, and how well they are doing it. This will enable materials, such as drill lessons and subject matter coaching, to be selected to suit the individual student and loaded into their personal computer.

On the other hand, the network, being connected to the world outside the school, will not only allow classes to be joined as suggested above (p.91), but also to allow teaching and learning materials to be widely shared and their effectiveness measured. Perhaps more importantly, students will be able to use the World Wide Web for learning on their own initiative, which their teachers would encourage.

The World Wide Web has enormous potential as a promoter of learning, but there are problems with it, as discussed in "The Internet, the Web, and the Chaos" (essay 3.6, p.133).

Utopia and Dystopia

My description above of possibilities for digital technology in schools is quite utopian. Such a school system will never come about. Political and economic interests will see to that.

Nonetheless, two facts are becoming increasingly evident. Firstly, the school systems in many of the more economically prosperous countries are becoming increasingly less effective. Secondly, the absence of school systems in less prosperous countries goes a long way to explaining why they are less prosperous.

The actualities of education world-wide are decidedly dystopian, and the dystopia feeds on itself. Worsening education worsens society itself, which in turn worsens education further.

The tragedy of this is that, as I have suggested above, digital technology could be used to make education much more effective than it has ever been, except for a very few students. My description of a model for a school system aimed at exploiting modern digital machinery for the betterment of learning can only point out directions in which improvements can gradually be made.

If my descriptions of this introduction, and of this chapter generally, seem prolix and declamatory, this must be put down to my belief, firstly, that there is no more important aspect of a society than the education of its young people, and secondly, that modern digital technology has the potential to help make this education more socially effective than we can yet dream of.

3.1 The Myth of the Educational Computer

(1999 September)

Some time ago I was at a forum attended by many teachers who were concerned about the shamefully high level of youth unemployment in Tasmania. There had just been an election, and the new State government had announced that it would slow down a project that was putting large numbers of PCs into schools. Attendees at the forum were unanimously dismayed. Not a single one doubted that putting lots of computers in the schools would automatically bring benefits.

This unquestioning trust in the good to be brought by computers reminded me of the Melanesian cargo cults. In the first half of this century, ignorant of technology, natives of Papua New Guinea and nearby islands fervently believed that ships and planes would bring them cargo from their ancestors, and no one could tell them otherwise. The Myth of the Educational Computer has been so widely accepted that there was about as much point in disagreeing with the forum attendees as there would have been in trying to argue with the natives.

The current computer-as-educator delusion is extremely harmful and yet seems to go largely unquestioned, even by computing professionals. I don't mean to say that computing professionals aren't doing very good work technically in developing courseware and so on. What seems to be missing, though, is a full appreciation of the relationship between technology and education. The literature suggests that much of the work done by computing professionals is isolated from what goes on in schools generally. Our profession's focus seems to be on how to find smart ways to use computers in the classroom, not on how to solve the really important problems deplored in the educational literature.

If, on the other hand, we were doing all our educational computing work in close partnership with professional educators, more of us computing professionals would be pressing for the reforms needed to exploit digital technology properly. The lack of such reforms and the rise of this delusion—that the computer by itself can educate—have already led to a sad waste of resources and enthusiasm![11]

Exploding the Myth

High hopes and modest fears about the use of computers in the classroom were voiced more than 30 years ago[8] The hopes have proved much too high, and the fears much too low. Although in many instances computers are very well used in education, the vast potential benefits of computers in schools are not being realized. Nor can they be in the present political climate and under the prevailing social conditions.

I have three general arguments about computers and education:

• *Computers alone cannot educate anyone.* Training and support of professional educators must both precede, and take priority over, placing computers in schools. This training and support must extend teachers' capabilities, not merely reorient them. If properly done, it will cost much more than the computers themselves.

• *Computing professionals must become active in support of reforms that aid the teaching profession.* Only then can digital technology become of general benefit to our children and young people, and thus to our society.

• *There are grave, worldwide social problems, arguably caused in part by the misuse of digital technology.* We must solve these before we can improve the generally failing educational processes.

To understand these problems and to evaluate the prospects for computers in education, it helps to put the issues in the context of just what education is expected to achieve.

The second edition of *The Oxford English Dictionary* gives two relevant meanings of education: "To bring up (young persons) from childhood, so as to form (their) habits, manners, intellectual and physical aptitudes" and "To train (any person) so as to develop the intellectual and moral powers generally." What these definitions lack is any statement of just what habits, manners, aptitudes, and powers education should aim to develop in the pupil, and why it should choose to develop those particular qualities. This is what education theories attempt to answer.

Education in Theory

Writers with Western European or North American backgrounds typically describe three theories of education: social, liberal, and progressive. Can computers help realize any of these idealistic theories?

Social education

Before there were schools, education was oral and the responsibility of the family and the community. Carried out as ritual and role play during daily life, its purpose was to sustain the community.

School systems are political entities that are larger than the oral communities. Setting up a school system is always at least partly a political act, intended to support and perpetuate the social entity that provides the system. In stable, affluent societies, children are educated in formal schools, where they are intended to be made literate.

In a typical school system, the rituals and activities within the school are patterned after those the conforming adult is expected to submit to. Teachers are primarily social workers, who aim to fit their pupils into society.

Role of computers. Can computers be used to help inculcate social norms? Those who look to computers to contribute in this way have a dual problem: Not only is the idea of a society poorly defined,[40] but also the nature of society is rapidly changing.

In any case, it is difficult for teachers to build socialization when their pupils lack even the rudimentary inter– and intrapersonal skills necessary for a traditional classroom to function. Committed parents used to provide this preschool socialization, but they are disappearing as are the skills themselves.[18] It is also pointless to model progression through public life when the gap between rich and poor is widening at an accelerating rate, and many long-standing social institutions and values are fading. These social problems have been repeatedly documented by the UN Development Programme, which makes its annual reports available.[38] Nevertheless, if it is essential to foster basic social skills—and I believe it is—computing technology can effectively support teachers in planning and controlling social interaction by inducing the very basic skills underlying the use of language and numbers (see "Drill and Practice," p. 109).

Liberal education

Liberal education, usually traced back to Plato's *The Republic*, aims to deliver a curriculum of elevating subject matter presented in a logical sequence to make it easy to learn.

Liberal education is élitist in principle. In many English-speaking countries, the traditional higher school subjects are English and French, history and geography, mathematics and science—choices clearly not based on social utility. Although few would master these subjects and few would really need them in later life, they were deemed to be "good for the mind"—and the mind was liberal education's target. Teachers are primarily subject matter experts, who seek to impart knowledge and understanding to their pupils.

Role of computers. The liberal educators have been at the same time the most involved, the most optimistic, and the most threatened of all educators since computers have been adopted for school use. There can be no doubt that modern digital technology could deliver, and in many cases does already deliver, liberal and vocational instruction satisfactorily (that is, reliably and cheaply).

Liberal education is likely to be well served by digital technology, whether in the form of electronic page turning or of highly interactive and realistic simulations, providing it remains under the control and direction of liberal educators. The very real threat is that political influence or commercial greed will force out the liberal educator, leaving the education system to crystallize and allowing machines to regiment our youth.

Progressive education

Progressive theories of education seek to help the pupil develop into a complete person in a "natural" way. These theories are often traced back to Rousseau, whose ideas were extended in America by John Dewey and in Europe by Jean Piaget. The aim is to provide each pupil with experiences and opportunities that change as the pupil develops. Ideally, the experiences and opportunities depend on how the pupil develops, so each pupil's individual potential is fully realized. In progressive education, teachers are primarily mentors and facilitators, who aim to promote individual learning and development.

Role of computers.   Preventing regimentation in education should be the role of progressive educators, who focus on developing the individual. Their position in relation to computers is precarious. One of the strong themes of the liberal educators who extol computer-administered lessons is individualized instruction. The very inhumanity of programs administering instruction allows the programs, with the appearance of infinite patience, to adapt what they do in response to any pattern of input a pupil might present. But this is still regimentation, with the difference that the students can be regimented at the most effective pace for each one.

When it is suggested that computer-administered instruction might regiment rather than educate, the usual response is that artificial intelligence will sooner or later surmount all such difficulties. The reprise of the progressive educator would be this: there is a machine on one side of the interaction and a human on the other. The more the program adapts to its student user, the more effective its brainwashing, and the more subtly the student is steered to the required responses.

Progressive educators seek to help individual students develop themselves by providing them with an appropriate sequence and variety of experiences. They could well give priority to interpersonal interaction, using technology as a support and tool, but not relinquishing control to it. One appropriate technique is academic gaming, which goes way beyond simulation (see "Academic Gaming," p. 111).

Education in Practice

Education in practice, perhaps better described as schooling, is not the same as education in theory. When we refer to a person's "education," we really mean their schooling, and level of education is commonly equated to level of schooling attained. Schooling is determined more by political forces than by educational ideals. In some cases, the effect of political influence is to modify the application of educational theory; more often it is to ignore if not negate educational theory. Three major styles of institutional education are evident: *custodial* schooling, which goes through the motions scholastically but is primarily protective; *vocational* schooling, which aims to equip pupils for the workforce; and *economical* schooling, which seeks to spend as little as possible on education (in the poverty-stricken majority of the world, this boils down to no schooling at all).

Custodial schooling

Government school systems are often very sensitive to community pressures—parents usually vote. This leads to educational distortions, most notably when the bureaucrats see it as more important that the students come to no harm than that they come to any good. Another motivation for this custodial emphasis is the fear of litigation.

Custodial schooling therefore tends to promote pupils through the classes automatically, either by stipulating that test results be ignored or that students never explicitly be failed. Custodial schooling is an institutional approach to achieving passivity in the schools and to reducing problems for administrators. In custodial schooling, teachers are primarily guardians and supervisors, and the aim is to avoid problems and responsibility.

Role of computers. One of the hopes that seem to lurk behind the political push for computers on every school desk is that they will engross the pupil and thus fulfill the custodial aim. The student surfing the Web or otherwise being driven by a computer can come to no harm and will be too absorbed to bring harm to others.

Unfortunately, computers can bring harm to their users. Teachers in schools with computers have long been familiar with the occasional student who becomes obsessed with using computers to the exclusion of other important activities. The Internet has made this kind of addiction more accessible, and not just for school children, as a virtual visit to the Center for Online and Internet Addiction[41] will quickly show. Absorption in the Internet could also lead to harmful behavior—there are reports of school computer use reducing socialization[23] The point is that custodial responsibility cannot and should not be shunted off to machines.

Vocational schooling

While social education seeks to deliver to society recruits that will better the community, vocational education seeks to deliver to industry workers that will better the workforce. In this kind of schooling, teachers are primarily agents of industrial and commercial organizations, and indeed governments nowadays actively promote the support of education by industry. Even universities, once bastions of liberal education, are becoming vocational.

Role of computers. The hope that computers can contribute to vocational education is more overt than the custodial hope: Students should be given experience with computers, the chorus goes, because they will need the skill to use such machines in their jobs. I call this a doubly blind conclusion.

First, many young people won't get jobs, whether they use a computer or not. In Australia in September, 1997, 17 percent of young adults (aged 20 to 24 years) were either formally unemployed or employed part-time but not in school. Another 9 percent were neither employed nor in school.[13] The number of youthful unemployed and underemployed has been increasing in many countries over the past decade, and the trend is likely to continue, even with economic growth. Moreover, unemployment statistics are misleadingly optimistic. Nowadays, only those who are actively seeking work are usually counted as unemployed, not those who have given up seeking work, voluntarily or otherwise.

Second, the jobs the young can get aren't what they used to be. Many jobs are being "deskilled" by computers so that workers in fact require fewer skills, not more. Grocery store checkout clerks, for example, need no computing skills, not even keyboarding. Their jobs are threatened not by their lack of skill but by self-service technology and by Internet supermarket shops. This deskilling trend is expected to continue, and not just for intermittent and part-time jobs, but even for professional jobs.[1]

So if more and more people are to be without jobs, vocational education becomes less and less relevant. And if more and more of the jobs that are available are unskilled, acquiring skills with computers is not the kind of vocational training that is needed.

Economical schooling

As part of the political imperative of reducing public spending, governments in many countries are also reducing spending on schools. This, and pressure from the International Monetary Fund on Third World countries, is why economical education is widespread. In this kind of schooling, teachers are lowly paid and insecure, while their administrators are highly paid and may be paid more the less they manage to spend on schools.

Role of computers. To the politician and bureaucrat, probably the most compelling argument for putting networked computers into the education system is the prospect that they will cut costs. Experience so far gives little support to this. Earlier technologies like movies, overhead projectors, and television have each gone through a "cycle of ecstasy, disappointment, and blame."[11] And the Web today is what television was yesterday: the great hope of the educational world—and of the commercial world.

Computers seem cost-efficient because it is easy to overlook the associated costs. Many grand plans do not provide funds for equipment installation, housing, maintenance, and obsolescence; nor for the employment of skilled support staff; nor for the training of teachers; nor for adapting timetables, curriculum, and examinations. Worse, because the need to cut costs is usually seen as urgent, computers are installed in a hurry. Schools and their staff have no time to adapt their ideas and techniques to the new methods.

The cost-cutting imperative is at its bleakest when employed at the highest levels of education. The virtual university has been described as a university "reduced to an underprivileged provider of information, with no greater identity than an icon on a Web page, and the academics reduced to employed authors of directories of information peddled by an electronic kiosk, serviced by technicians and an occasional graphic artist."[26]

Relatively few virtual universities will be needed, so the competition will be fierce. A recent *Scientific American* article reports a view from Oxford University that five universities will survive worldwide.[17] If the virtual university can be made to "work," virtual schools will not be far behind.

Recommendations

Thus, if we are to realize the enormous potential benefits of digital technology not only in education but throughout society, our society must be dominated by the wisdom and compassion that comes from good education. And good education comes from good teachers, not from machines.

Indeed, I believe that digital technology will eventually be used to make all the world's education systems more beneficial, beyond our present dreams. But benefits have so far come at a snail's pace. If this is to change, the computing profession and its members must be active in making it happen.

The following recommendations [addressed to computing professionals]— both for general and particular support—put forward activities that will likely lead to the greatest benefit from digital technology for teachers and pupils.

General support

These recommendations, which relate to the social context of education, must be tackled primarily by professional computing societies working with other community bodies. In short, our educational problems are *political* and as such can be overcome only by *political activity*. Computing people should urge their professional societies to be active politically and should personally support such activity.

Show and tell.   Computing professionals should realize—and help others to realize—that machinery is not the solution; rather, its misuse is a large part of the problem. Our professional societies are best positioned to point out the opportunities and dangers of digital technology and to influence and support our community leaders in moving communities away from increasing inequity, oppression, and social alienation, and toward a balance of equality, liberty, and community.

Lobby for more funds. Our profession should press for much more to be spent on schooling. We should persistently declare that in the long run good education is a precondition for good use of technology, not the other way around. An important focus is to improve the lot of children everywhere. In 1995, 84 percent of the world's spending on education was by the developed countries, which have only 21 percent of the world's population. Among the rich Western countries that make up the Organization for Economic Cooperation and Development, an average of $4,636 is spent per pupil on primary and secondary education. In the developing world it is $165. One in four adults in the developing world is unable to read or write, and the number is growing.[15]

Be active in reforming the school system. Today's school systems are plainly failing in their educational aims. The typical developed-country school system has a century-old structure quite unsuited to modern educational needs. In their early days, such systems provided elementary education for all, a high school education for an élite few, and a university education for even fewer. With expanding educational ambitions resulting from increasing average material wealth, a high school education appropriate to an élite few has gradually become inappropriately universal, and a traditionally academic university education has become completely subverted.

To reform the system, computing people—as designers of systems—should heed the appeal of educational reformers to start compulsory schooling much earlier.[18] Compulsory schooling should also continue longer, and do so outside the traditional university system. Perhaps a good way to do all this would be to move to a structure with three layers of at least five years: a primary school social education, a secondary school progressive education, and a tertiary school vocational education, where the vocational component should engender skills for self-employment as much as for being employed.

Politicians will of course publicly proclaim such ambitions as hopelessly expensive, and privately bewail them as dangerous. A concerted political effort from outside the political party system will be needed to bring in these reforms, and professional societies everywhere should join with the relatively few societies that are conspicuous in promoting public good worldwide. The very strong IEEE Computer Society would do well to support their allied but much weaker IEEE Society on Social Implications of Technology, which has shown that it is at least alert to some of the dangers of technology.[35]

Particular support

These recommendations, which relate to schooling itself, can be taken up by computing professionals individually or in groups.

Teach and learn from educators. Educators are the key professionals in improving the education of our children. Computing professionals should never try to solve educational problems by themselves. A computer is not the solution to any problem, it is a tool for solving problems. If educators seem unable to exploit technology properly, we should take the time to train them and also take their advice about relevant educational objectives and techniques. Many of us do this already, but we need much more help.

Look for varied uses of technology. As systems analysts, computing professionals should look for uses of digital technology beyond the Internet and its World Wide Web, which at present seems to be an educational obsession. Digital technology should be used wherever good uses can be found, not just in fashionable ways. Educational techniques such as drill and practice and academic gaming promise at least as much educational benefit when supported by digital technology as does the Web.

Provide equipment and services. Systems analysts should strive to protect educators from the vicissitudes of computing practice and provide them with the hardware and software they need. Educators need simple, reliable machines and standard, adaptable programs and operating systems. They do not need complex, transiently fashionable, and inherently obsolescent computers.

Programmers should provide software that educators can adjust to their needs, as well as the training they need to best exploit the programs. We should discourage the use of programs that simply drive students unless they are intended to develop basic reflexive skills.

Computer engineers should work to provide schools with equipment that is inexpensive and easy to use, especially for less-developed countries. General-purpose computers should be simple and robust, physically and logically. Special-purpose computers should also be widely usable across different cultures, ages, and skill levels.

Perhaps the best indicator of the health of a civilized society is the way it treats its children and youth. Modern society depends on high quality education. Digital technology has enormous potential, yet it is completely neutral. It can be used to create a utopia or a dystopia. Which one we are moving toward at any time depends on those who use the technology, not on the technology itself. By emphasizing dystopia here, I am opposing the popular cargo-cultist view of the computer and its Web as a cornucopia full of blessings available to those who believe. The dangers are but rarely mentioned.

The primary responsibility for what happens in schools must remain with the professional educators. But educators need the support of the computing profession to ensure that they are fully and properly trained and supported in their use of computers. Any suggestion of replacing teachers with teaching machines ought to be promptly and loudly condemned by the computing profession.

Appendix: Drill and Practice

The primary school classroom of a half-century ago was dominated by drill and training. The marks in my 1939 Grade 1 report were for reading, spelling, writing and transcription, written arithmetic, practical arithmetic, mental arithmetic, art, and handwork—all of which suggest drill or training. In my memory, this was no bad thing.

Nowadays, training is considered authoritarian and therefore harmful. It is also associated with very narrow forms of vocational preparation. But fluent reading, writing, and arithmetic can only be built on training in basic skills, which is precisely where automatic machinery excels. Skills must be speedy and automatic, noncontemplative and unquestioning, otherwise true literacy and numeracy are unattainable.

Machine-administered drill should not be confused with computer-assisted instruction (CAI). Instruction is much broader than training. A general-purpose computer is of course a powerful instructional medium, but not only would it be wasted on mere drill, it would be less effective than a machine designed specifically for that purpose.

The ideal machine

An ideal drill machine would be exact and exacting, adaptive and consistent, impersonal and unthreatening. Such a machine would give swift and clear presentation and immediate and reliable feedback. It would be simple and cheap, rugged and small. Because the skills it seeks to induce are general and uniform, such a machine could be made in millions and sold for a few dollars, so that all children could have one when starting primary school.

For basic numeric and arithmetic skills, one drill machine design might be usable in most of the world. For basic language skills, one machine design might do for each writing system, though it would need to be adaptable for different languages.

Such drill machines would not be internally simple—their cheapness would spring from the huge quantity needed. They would also need to be very carefully designed, though they could be steadily improved. As vehicles for attaining basic skills, they would draw on the experiences and techniques of interactive gaming to make the training interesting and absorbing, and they would aim to provide feedback and competition for the user to improve speed and accuracy.

Although a drill machine for number skills would double as a calculator, it would be a great mistake to base its design on that of present-day calculators. For one thing, their ergonomic design is wretched, and their arithmetic is badly flawed [essay 2.4, p. 64]. For another, they just don't have enough of the functions needed for elementary numeracy, such as functions to return the higher or lower of two numbers.

A drill machine for basic language skills should be able to combine training in reading, writing (and perhaps even keying), spelling, vocabulary, and grammar. Combined training, made practical with such machinery, should be much more effective than separate training in each skill. With the advance of technology, such machines might even be able to recognize and produce speech. They could provide very powerful feedback in early education. Imagine letting preschoolers see words immediately after they speak them.

Drill machines need not be confined to training for basic number and language skills. Equally simple drill machines could be imagined for musical and spatial skills, and somewhat more expensive drill machines already exist for some basic kinesthetic skills.

Warning

Literacy is not merely skill with words, just as numeracy is not merely skill with numbers, though in each case the former is completely dependent on the latter. This was well realized even 150 years ago, when a correspondent wrote in the *Launceston Examiner*: "The notion that education for the general people is comprised in the faculty of tumbling over words letter by letter, and syllable by syllable, . . . has surely had its day by this time, and a long day too."[4] Possibly it is the fear of making this mistake that has deterred use of computers for drill and practice.

Literacy is a hierarchy of reading skills that successively takes in coding, semantic, pragmatic, and critical competencies.[27] Drill and practice is ideally suited to attaining the first competency, and of great help in attaining the second, but the third and fourth correspond roughly to intrapersonal and interpersonal skills which come from practice in social interaction, not from interaction with machines.

Appendix: Academic Gaming

Computer-mediated instruction and computer-delivered simulation can free the teacher to give more attention to students who need more attention. Also, in computer laboratory work, students give great value to peer interaction. Academic gaming goes beyond simulation to provide for systematic peer interaction, in which the role of the teacher is switched from that of authoritative expert to that of facilitator, or even collaborator.

The most familiar example of academic gaming is a business management game in which participants form teams that interact through some kind of business model. Each team makes periodic business decisions, which are fed into a simulation program, and then acts on the results of the simulation to make the next cycle of decisions. With skilled supervision, participants can not only learn about running a business, but can also acquire skills in teamwork and decision making.

Academic games use simulation *as the basis for cooperation and competition*. They therefore have much more educational potential than simple simulations. And an academic game can, with some exercise of imagination, be based on almost any model, not just a business market model, and so can be used to foster a great variety of learning, including interpersonal and intrapersonal skills. Belief in the educational value of such techniques led in 1970 to the formation of SAGSET, the Society for the Advancement of Games and Simulations in Education and Training[34] and later to ISAGA, the International Simulation And Gaming Association.

Academic gaming is a very powerful tool, but its competitive aspects can cause great damage if it is not carefully developed and if teachers who use it are not sufficiently trained. This makes it expensive. On the other hand, a large amount of highly educational activity can be based on intermittent use of a single computer.

Academic gaming does not have to be strictly competitive. I remember many years ago reading about a very impressive game based on the fishing industry. It was a fairly conventional game, but the model was of an ocean of fish with a realistically limited capacity to reproduce. While the teams might start by briskly competing, the benefits of cooperation become apparent in later stages.

3.2   Digital Technology, Age, and Gaming

(2005 November)

The Economist of August 6–12, 2005 featured a special report on video gaming[14] that revealed how marketing people view the field. I felt that computing professionals would see it somewhat differently, but that it wasn't worth arguing about. Then I stumbled on an interview[36] in *The Guardian* of September 19, 2005 where Edward Castronova, an economist, alarmingly claimed that "Computer gaming is so powerful a tool we could use it to meet our emotional needs and even spread democracy." Though, like Alfred Nobel, I have always been very skeptical about economics as a science, the few economists I know seem to be quite reasonable people. But this apparently unreasonable economist has crossed over into our field and written a book on computer gaming.

Then the September *Computer* issue arrived with Michael Zyda's "From Visual Simulation to Virtual Reality to Games."[43] This splendid article, both interesting and informative, left me with the feeling that a severe generation gap separates Zyda and me, and that in our differences lie several issues of particular importance to the computing profession.

The report in *The Economist* stated early on that "three important factors are generally overlooked: that attitudes to gaming are marked by a generational divide; that there is no convincing evidence that games make people violent; and that games have great potential in education." At least two of these factors seemed to me to be anything but overlooked, and two of them are misconstrued. Before looking at these factors in turn, though, it is helpful to define what kinds of gaming there are.

Gaming and Play

The terms *gaming* and *play* largely overlap nowadays, but gaming used to mean gambling, that is, an activity in which a bettor stakes money. Gambling has been greatly extended by digital technology, through geographical dispersion by telecommunication as in lotteries or keno and financial markets, by machinery running the gambling as in poker machines, and by credit card systems providing players with easy finance. The converse of gambling is sport, in the sense of active participation, though games can have an element of both.

Video games and computer games seem to differ only in the physical equipment used to play them. Zyda contrasts *video games* as "played for amusement, recreation, or winning a stake" and *serious games* as based on video gaming but using "entertainment to further government or corporate training, education, health, public policy, and strategic communication objectives."

Mindset constitutes another dimension of gaming, one that highlights the contrast between contemplation and sensuality. Card and board games, and puzzles like sudoku and crosswords, focus on contemplative analysis. Games like tennis and football focus on perception and reaction. Analytical gamers try to get correct answers, or at least better ones than their opponents, while physical gamers try to apply physical skill or strength, often where speed is an advantage. Computer games like *Minesweeper* are contemplative, whereas games like *Tetris* are predominantly sensual.

Solitary games involve one player only, while social games involve more than one. Traditionally, most computer-free games have been social, most computer games solitary. Although this might seem a binary classification, the Internet has bred two hybrids:

- normally social games such as bridge played by isolated players, and
- video games played by many players.

Neither of these is truly social: online bridge takes place outside a social context, while the multiplayer video game offers a social context that is artificial in both its nature and its participants.

Subject matter provides video games' remaining aspect. For example, in *Secrets of the PlayStation 2* Michele Davis classifies video games along two dimensions[12]:

- *Ratings*. These range from early childhood through all ages, teen, mature, and adults only.
- *Theme*. These break down into the following game genres: action, adventure or horror, arcade, classic and puzzle, driving and vehicular combat, fighting, role-playing, simulation, sports, and strategy.

The Generational Divide

The *Economist* report states that "Games are, in fact, played mainly by young adults. Only a third of gamers are under 18." In the same article, Marc Prensky of Games2train claims that not-so-young adults, never having played them, don't understand "that these are complex games, which take 30, 40, or 100 hours to complete." What Prensky and many others don't understand is that to many adults, particularly old ones like me, having to spend anything like that amount of time in total surrender to someone else's imagination is a thorough turnoff.

But to describe this gap in appreciation as generational is misleading. It is cultural, not necessarily correlated with age, and somewhat related to gaming's mindset dimension.

Old people like myself grew up before television, when recreation in the home occurred socially through playing board and table games and participating in mealtime conversations, or personally through reading. This contemplative culture emphasized learning how to play and discuss well and how to understand people in other societies and circumstances.

Today's youth culture emphasizes the sensual. Watching and listening to television, or immersion in video games, dominates recreation. These activities commandeer perception and channel thought.

When you read a book, you construct mental images of people and places, follow and interpret sequences of actions and events, and develop feelings about the personalities and behaviors. When you watch a movie or television show, you are presented with the images of people and places, you mostly just observe the actions and events because there isn't time to think much about them, and the feelings you develop are strongly influenced by your direct observation of the actors' behavior—or by canned laughter.

Although people like me prefer the contemplative culture, many others seem to prefer the sensual. This is a matter of upbringing, not simply of age, and not a matter of one culture being right and the other wrong. So it's my culture that makes me strongly prefer *Minesweeper* to *Grand Theft Auto*, not my lack of video game expertise.

The Tendency to Violence

The report in *The Economist* builds a case for refuting the idea that video gaming induces violent behavior and includes a graph that shows violent crime in the US declining steadily over the past decade. It also outlines an experiment in which the group that had to play a violent video game for two hours daily for a month showed a frequency of aggressive behavior similar to the control group. I didn't find this refutation convincing because it's possible to explain the results in other ways.

Everyday experience does suggest an increase in violence and aggression. While I was writing this essay, a local man in my small provincial city was sent to jail for driving his car onto the sidewalk to knock down a pedestrian whom he then drove over to ensure his death. The pedestrian was unknown to the driver, who did it, he said, because "it seemed funny at the time."

About the same time, the media reported the failure of an appeal against the conviction of a man for murdering a motorcyclist in a fit of road rage. On that same day, researchers released the results of a study that showed that 44 percent of Australia's drivers had experienced road rage, up from 22 percent in 1996, and that 82 percent of them believed their rage to be justified.

But concentrating on the symptom of violence ignores its cause, which is arguably the shift to a sensual culture. A sensual culture encourages uncontemplative reaction to stimulus. Road rage is simply one kind of uncontemplative reaction.

Commercial television's whole point is to promote the uncontemplative buying reaction a consumer society depends on for economic growth. Marketing people now see the Internet and video games as extending and perhaps supplanting commercial television. Thus, advertisements increasingly add their clutter to Web browsing, along with brand placement in video games.

The Potential For Education

The unpleasant consequences of this dominance of the sensual raise the need for a rational balancing of the contemplative and sensual cultures—a task that could take generations of systematic and intense education to achieve.

Zyda commendably supports the adaptation of video gaming to training and education by having a human-performance-engineering team interact with game developers. Given that Zyda's aim for these serious games is to "engage the game player's mind via sensory stimulation and providing methods for increasing the sense of presence which contribute to building a feeling of immersion," his approach clearly lies deeply in the sensual culture, and it is an excellent one for the inculcation of high-level reflex skills. But it will be at least as effective in forcing the uncontemplative absorption of dogmata, which can be socially dangerous.

This is not a theoretical danger. As *The Economist* points out, in *Sim City*, a video game widely recommended for school use, "the player assumes the role of a city mayor, [and learns that] no amount of spending on healthcare is ever enough to satisfy patients, and the fastest route to prosperity is to cut taxes." Dogma indeed!

Educators adopted an older approach, *academic gaming*, for traditional business games in which a market is modeled for teams of players forming the companies active in that market. Each team makes decisions quarterly. The simulation is fed the decisions quarter by quarter and produces documents that describe the results.

Two kinds of skills are learnt in these business games: the understanding and use of accounts and balance sheets and the social negotiation needed to make joint decisions within a team.

Academic gaming can be extended beyond business to many fields and skills at many levels. It provides the social and contemplative counterpart of sensual video gaming. It also has the potential to be extremely valuable in schools, as I outlined in "The Myth of the Educational Computer" (essay 3.1, p.99). Academic gaming has not taken off in schools, possibly because teachers need special training to exploit the technique and this has not yet been accepted by those who teach teachers.

About 30 years ago, I attended a conference of the Society for the Advancement of Gaming and Simulation in Education and Training[34] in Loughborough, U.K., where highly competent people expressed great enthusiasm for the potential role of academic games in schools. They surely deserved success more than their near oblivion.

For some time there has been an international federation of similar societies, the International Simulation and Gaming Association. These societies lack prominence, however, and at least one seems to be defunct. Nonetheless, they deserve the strong support of the computing profession.

Academic games suffer from the problem of relying on their players having basic knowledge and skills, but students nowadays do not develop these attributes sufficiently. Basic knowledge or vocabulary and basic skills such as reading, spelling, and arithmetic are ideally suited to being imparted by drill and practice using simple video gaming techniques. This kind of instruction doesn't require immersion. Schooling would be tremendously helped by the development of simple machines to deliver drill and practice, provided teachers could be trained in their use.

Drill and practice also have value outside early schooling. I can't help feeling that, given the nature of the conflict in Iraq, the soldiers there would have been better off if video gaming had been used to drill them in reading and speaking Arabic. With modern voice-processing technology such drill could be made very effective.

The development of basic skills has particular significance for the computing profession, and indeed for engineering and science generally. Fewer young people study mathematics and science at school, and universities are closing down some important technical areas.

The number of engineering graduates in many advanced countries declines steadily, forcing industry to rely increasingly on importing professional skills from countries where contemplative culture still dominates. This situation can only be countered by emphasizing the development of basic skills in early schooling. This could be achieved far more effectively with gaming technology than with the classroom chanting used when I attended primary school.

3.3 Rationality and Digital Technology

(2004 September)

With the increasing pervasiveness of digital technology, the computing profession faces new circumstances. Not so long ago, digital technology and computing were just different names for the same thing. Now that digital networking has taken over the communications world, and digital recording looms large in the entertainment world, computation as a numerical activity has been relegated to a quite minor use of computers.

This change forces computing professionals to deal with a much greater variety of digital technologies. While there will still be a need for communications, software, and digital hardware engineers, they will be specialists and will need training focused on their specialty. The more numerous generalists will need much broader training and education, along the lines of the pioneering course at Guelph-Humber University.[37]

But computing professionals must be alert and responsive to the wider social implications of digital technology's ever-growing adoption. Further, they must base this alertness and responsiveness on an understanding of digital technology and its role in social change, which is much wider than commonly acknowledged during the education of computing professionals.

Basic Issues

I found the struggle to succinctly present an encompassing picture of the relationship between society and its digital technology in this column extremely difficult. Desperate, I decided to take my mind off the problem by reading *The Inside of the Cup* written by an almost forgotten American novelist named Winston Churchill.[10] But rather than distracting, I found the book remarkably relevant. It describes the social effects of the technology in use a century ago. Ultimately, the main character, a clergyman, came to much the same conclusions I reached.

The social effects of technology reflect the contention between rationality and irrationality, and they result from the contrast between personality and authority in affecting the contention. By personality, Churchill meant the taking of personal responsibility for values and actions, which is very much the essence of professionality as far as learned professions of any kind are concerned.

The contention

Rationality is not a straightforward idea. It is often equated to logicality, the idea that—given the facts of a situation or problem—a single correct evaluation or solution will follow by the application of reason.

But we may properly doubt even the "facts" that come into our consciousness from our perceptions and memories. It might be that my perceptions are of a virtual world, fed into my virtual consciousness by some kind of program being run by an unimaginable creature in a real world. I cannot prove logically that this is not so, and the deep philosophical arguments I have tried to read that claim to prove it have not convinced me. Thus, I fall back on a reasonably illogical belief that my perceptions are of a real world.

Similarly, that world, and I and my memories in that world, might have been created by some other unimaginably superior creature last Saturday evening at 7:30 p.m., Australian Eastern Standard Time. Again, even though I cannot prove logically that this is not so, I can reasonably assume that my memories were in fact built up from my perceptions over the past 70 years or so.

All rationality is based on beliefs or assumptions about our perceptions. On the other hand, irrationality springs from impulse and emotion. In human society, rational behavior is overwhelmed by the irrational. A glance at the newspapers confirms this.

The intellectual tradition that praises rationality and decries irrationality is invalid in daily life. In the extreme, an entirely rational society would consist of automata alone. Joy and sorrow, friendship and enmity are, and always have been, essentially human, and they give society its zest and vigor as well as its tragedy and misery.

The contention between rationality and irrationality determines the quality of society. Professionals must apply rationality in irrational contexts to improve that quality.

The contrast

Technology's tools and techniques develop through the often ardent application of rationality, based on the accumulation of beliefs gained through experiment and computation. A select few people determine the facts of technology, which many others then trust to be correct. My knowing that the speed of light is about one billion kilometers an hour is not knowledge in any absolute sense, but merely a belief. I back this belief by reading about the use of that fact by reputable professionals and by the absence of any persuasive refutation.

On the other hand, technologists do not rationally determine the uses for technology. Instead, the people who control the commercial and bureaucratic processes that exploit technology determine these uses, deciding in an impulsive and personal way just what goods and services technology shall be used to produce.

This is not to say that the technology's exploiters are irrational. The contrast lies rather between the beliefs on which technology is based—scientific beliefs accumulated formally and stringently—and the beliefs on which the exploitation of technology is based—social beliefs made possible by and affecting society's very structure.

To a large degree, because the exploiter is an authority employing the professional developer, the responsibility for any social effects of this exploitation might be thought to rest with that authority. Nevertheless, society accepts as a matter of principle that individual professionals must consider the social effects of their technology and personally strive to make these effects socially beneficial. In this perception lies Churchill's contrast between personality and authority.

Digital Technology

Considerations of rationality and irrationality, of personality and authority, acquire much greater strength in the present context of complex and widespread digital technology. Because digital technology is the basis of human society, its social implications can only be properly understood by looking at the way it has developed and how it has affected society.

The success of digital technology derives from the notion that facts and ideas can be most effectively represented by composition from a set of distinct components and, in present-day technology, from two components, called *zero* and *one*. This simplification means that data can be stored in a tiny space and transmitted in huge quantities, yet it can be reliably recovered in the face of severe deterioration.

Digitality's origins

Spoken language is a digital technology that requires its users to restrict themselves to a limited number of components to communicate facts and ideas. Because it requires perceptions to be classified by vocabulary and can be used to predict and inform, orality facilitates using rationality to improve human interaction. However, oral societies seem almost always to be hierarchical, with a minority using oral lore, often as mythology or superstition, to maintain authority. Personality is controlled or ejected.

Written language, developed in many different ways from simple depiction, adds a permanence to spoken language. On the one hand, this means that facts and ideas can be accumulated and developed more effectively and suppressed with more difficulty, thus extending the role of rationality in human society. On the other hand, by restricting the use of literacy, a minority can use scripture as laws and regulations to inculcate beliefs in the majority that establish the minority's authority. In a society with literate administrators and illiterate administratees, developing an independent personality complete with rational beliefs and values becomes difficult.

Arithmetic, the representation and combination of quantitative data, is the third digital technology. Although number words are part of spoken language—and some cultures extend these words gesturally—the technology became much more important when written language made it possible to use them in commercial interactions?

The gradual development of techniques and tools made all these digital technologies possible. Spoken language depends on having a particular kind of respiratory passage and on developing the neural equipment to drive its various parts. Written language depends on having equipment to write with and a medium to write on. Likewise, tokens, tally sticks, quipus, counting tables, and abaci helped arithmetic develop beyond merely speaking and writing.

Digital machinery

More complex digital equipment has only recently been developed. Printing machinery has a relatively long history, and calculating machinery has also undergone fairly steady development. The mass production of books and newspapers beginning more than a century ago has made general literacy possible in some countries, but the cost of other digital machinery has meant that it is still mainly used by government and business.

Science and technology provide a notable exception. Scientists and engineers have long been trained in the use of measuring and calculating equipment. This has led to the rational accumulation of an immense amount of carefully checked data, which eventually led to the development of present-day digital machinery and techniques. Indeed, the development of science and technology has been made possible by the rational cooperation of many kinds of professional workers in a social subsystem that requires findings and reasoning to be rigorously checked.

Scientific and technical development depends increasingly on digital data gathering and computation. In this field, digital technology can be considered an amplifier of rationality. The use of digital technology outside the professional community is quite another matter. Mobile telephones, the Net and Web, and a host of other digital products and services help administer and preserve large commercial and other social hierarchies while creating and satisfying individual and community needs. In this respect, digital technology can be considered an amplifier of irrationality.

Digital technology has been wonderfully effective in amplifying human rationality and irrationality and will continue to serve in this role. The profession has a responsibility to monitor—and, if necessary, influence—how the technology is used.

It may be that the technology is being ill used. When it first came in, radio broadcasting was hailed as a boon for education and culture. Instead, it became a boon for marketing. The same thing happened when television arrived. Will the Net and its Web see the third iteration of this cycle? Professionals must consider questions such as this and act on the answers if necessary. Yet, without a broad enough education, they won't be able to do so. Education, and not just professional education, must cover not only technology and its uses, but also its history and social effects.

Human society must blend rationality and irrationality, for the role of digital technology should be to promote whatever is deemed to be the best blend. Who will determine this blend? Authority will naturally press for the blend that would bring the greatest benefit to those in authority, typically expressed as benefits in property. Professionals, on the other hand, must press for the blend that brings the greatest general benefit, typically benefits in personality.

3.4   Why Johnny Can't Program

(2000 December)

This essay includes examples of program code. Those readers without a background in computing should not try to figure out just what these examples mean as program code is highly conventional, and mysterious to the uninitiated. Those with an interest in understanding them, however, may find helpful the explanation starting on page 275 in the Appendix. The term Object *used below, and signalled in the* OO *initialism, refers to a style of programming and design called "Object Oriented Programming," which is described briefly at the top of the next page, but not in the appendix.*

Although written nearly a year ago, this column quite neatly follows last month's, in which I charged that misguided attitudes to programming restrict the layout of program code too much [see p. 285]. This month, I claim that programmers are not educated well enough to code really good programs.

Johnny's problems were highlighted for me by Bertrand Meyer's "A Really Good Idea,"[29] which I read for two reasons. First, I've long been bemused by the prevalence of Objects. Never having had much to do with them, I've found that what I read about Objects either passed over my head or resembled a strictly applied version of what I knew long ago as modular programming.

Second, I wanted to know why Meyer, an authority on the topic, thought Objects such a good idea. Although Meyer explained why in his column, most entertainingly and eloquently, I still felt confused about the nature of the really good idea.

One really good idea seemed to be about software construction in the large: "... when it comes to building complex, evolutionary, mission-critical systems, OO solutions are our best bet. Nothing else has come to challenge them." This passage bespeaks an emphasis on technical management. Indeed, there's nothing like the thorough and controlled application of a clearly specified and well-tested technology to ensure a complex technical project's prosperity. So, as a basis for good technical management, Object Technology (or is it Component Technology?) should be a really good idea.

The other really good idea seemed to be about what developers once called systems analysis, the arena of the promoted programmers who specified the programs and modules to be coded by their less-experienced or less-talented workmates. Meyer gave as examples two general principles, although objectives might be a better word:

- "the OO view [is] that we are building little machines, each with its official control panel . . . serving as the obligatory path to the internals," and
- "to keep modules independent from each other's implementation decisions and hence from variations in each other's implementations."

Had these examples of objectives appeared early in the column, I probably would have dismissed the piece as another case of modular programming revisited. But by the time I got to them, I had slogged through two rather disturbing programming exhibits. True, Meyer offered these exhibits as examples of bad programming. My only quarrel with him is that he didn't show how really bad they are.

His failure to do so caused me to conclude that OO technology focuses on technical management and systems analysis, and away from program coding. Methodology has drowned the craft. Johnny may be a software engineer now, but he can't program anymore—at least not properly.

Why can't Johnny program? Meyer's two programming exhibits suggest several reasons.

Johnny Is Innumerate

Evidence for asserting that Johnny is innumerate lies in the pivot "solution" to the main Y2K problem, referred to in Meyer's column as the "windowing Y2K technique." He properly lambastes it, then later asserts that the solution lies in the use of information hiding.

That might be so at the systems level, or even at the coding level, but Meyer's criticism overlooks that the pivot technique is simply an innumerate corruption of a perfectly good programming technique that uses what school mathematics curricula call "clock arithmetic."

To keep the explanation simple, let's forget about minutes and suppose that in a program we must deal with a 24-hour clock precise to the nearest hour; thus our code must deal with integers in the range of 0 to 23. Such clocks mainly allow us to compute periods of time. In this example, our starting time and our finishing time will be integers in the range of 0 to 23.

The program computes the elapsed time by subtracting the starting time from the finishing time. What happens if the computed elapsed time turns out to be negative? Such a result indicates that the period of time included midnight. No problem in clock arithmetic—you just add a modulus of 24, with no pivot necessary.

The 24-hour clock compares directly to double-digit calendar-year encoding, but with a modulus of 100. Clock arithmetic, as taught in elementary school and as known and used by skilled programmers for at least 40 years, easily and correctly deals with such encoding. Therefore, innumerate Johnny encoded all programs with this particular Y2K bug. Johnny also wrote the pivot patches.

```
//function to eliminate blanks from a string
  void eatspaces (char * str) {
     int i=1; /* copy to offset within string */
     int j=1; /* copy from offset within string */
     while ((*(str + i) = *(str + j++)) !='\0')
       if (*(str + i) != ' ') i++;
     return;
  }
```

Figure 1. Coding example with illiterate comments.

Johnny Is Illiterate

Meyer's second programming example—drawn "from one of the most frequently used C++ introductory textbooks" and shown in Figure 1—supports the claim that Johnny is illiterate.

Meyer says of this example that it "can't have anything to do with object technology" and proceeds to spell out why. What disturbs me about the example is not the points Meyer makes against the algorithm, which I heartily agree with, but the point he *doesn't* make about the coding, at least not directly: that the code is so bad that he must explain it in bitter detail speaks volumes. Good code is self-explanatory, at least to anyone familiar with the coding system used.

Why is the example's code so bad? The comments provide one clue. Comments—as opposed to *remarks*, which address aspects external to the code—explain the code itself. To quote a saying that once circulated among programmers: "A comment is a confession of failure."

The most significant aspect of a program is the names given to its data—a good programmer will put great effort into choosing names that explain the data. This practice makes expressions that use the names much more meaningful, and should make comments unnecessary. Let's try it—Figure 2 shows the results.

If anything needs to be explained now, it's the details specific to the C++ coding system; we no longer need the original comments. This matter is not trivial. Good programming practice focuses on functional coding, not on decoration with comments. Developers should design code, at least public code, so that it can be understood.

```
//function to eliminate blanks from a string
  void eatspaces (char * string) {
    int to = 1;
    int from = 1;
      while ((*(string + to) =
              *(string + from++)) != '\0')
            if (*(string + to) != ' ') to++;
      return;
  }
```

Figure 2. The code of Figure 1 with explanatory data names added.

Johnny shows himself to be illiterate in more than his choice of names. Problems crop up in smaller details, too. Compare the code of Figure 2 with that of Figure 3.

```
//function to eliminate blanks from a string
  void eatspaces (char * string) {
    int to = 1;
    int from = 1;
    while ('\0' != (*(string + to) =
                    *(string + from++)))
            if (' ' != *(string + to)) to++;
      return;
  }
```

Figure 3. The code of Figure 2 with reversed comparisons.

There's only a small difference—the conditions of the `while` and the `if` have been rearranged internally. We read this kind of code from left to right, putting together the meaning as we go. The meaning of both the `while` and the `if` hinge on the comparison `!=`. These meanings become more obvious in the rearranged example, first because the comparisons come up early, where you see them before your attention starts to wander, and second because you don't need to store a complex comparand in your working memory while waiting for the comparison to appear.

This code needs further literate improvements. Most conspicuously, the blank and end-of-string characters should be declared and everywhere used as named constants.

These may seem minute details, but, as Meyer says, "The in-the-large aspects of programming rely on the lower-level parts, and you can't get them right unless you get the small things right too."

Listing Johnny's inadequacies does not, however, reveal why Johnny got that way. It's too simple merely to accept that the community as a whole is getting more illiterate and more innumerate. Presumably, Johnny received training. So why didn't it make him numerate and literate?

Johnny Is Overwhelmed

I believe that Johnny, trained as a software engineer and employed to develop software systems, has bitten off more than he can comfortably chew. Meyer borrows a metaphor from Isaiah Berlin to tell us that object technology has "a little of the fox and a little of the hedgehog." Object technology, Meyer insists, requires that Johnny be competent both in the small, like the fox, and in the large, like the hedgehog.

But consider this point: in other branches of engineering, the professional engineers deal with the in-the-large tasks while the tradespeople deal with the in-the-small ones. Each group has its particular training, skills, and duties. With so much to learn and know and do in an endeavor such as building a highway or a ship, a single profession or calling cannot skillfully perform all the work. Yet we blithely insist that software engineers must be both foxes and hedgehogs.

The best way to build Meyer's "complex, evolutionary, mission-critical systems" involves creating a team that consists of both foxes and hedgehogs, rather than a single group that vainly strives to acquire the traits of both. Such a team will consist of

- system engineers with in-the-large skills like, but not limited to, those Meyer describes, and
- programmers with in-the-small skills that include and lie behind those he describes.

I deliberately use "system engineer" rather than "software engineer." The professional programmer must know and understand clock arithmetic, but the system engineer must be responsible for determining whether a mere 24-hour clock provides a safe system solution. I don't think that "software engineer" describes this role well.

In real life, engineers should be designing and validating the system, not the software. If you forget the system you're building, the software will often be useless.

Computing professionals must know vastly more now than they needed to know 40 years ago, but even then the field often distinguished between programmers and systems analysts. Meanwhile, Johnny must know too much to be at the same time a skilled programmer and a skilled system engineer. That's why he's overwhelmed.

But Johnny's problem goes deeper: If he wants to be a professional programmer, he must learn on the job. Programmers have few trade courses to select from, many fewer than those available to carpenters, plumbers, and electricians. Further, very few professional courses will assist Johnny if he wants to become a straightforward, generalist, humanist, system engineer. Specialists such as computer system engineers and software engineers appear to dominate the field.

No wonder Johnny has a problem. Let's move to give him the proper training to become whichever he wants to be—programmer or system engineer.

3.5   Jobs, Trades, Skills, and the Profession

(2002 September)

Recently, I got an e-mail message from someone who assumed I wrote the June column, "Using Computers in Our Daily Life."[3] This person took issue with the statement that those who "remain tied to the past and refuse to adopt digital technology ... can expect nothing but poverty." That Ana Asuaga, the June column's author, lives in Uruguay, a Third World country, gave a particular edge to that assertion.

This e-mail came from the US, where its author benefits from a First World environment and skills: he writes his own software, maintains Web pages, exposes security holes on the Internet, and rescues computers from dumpsters so that he can refurbish them. Yet he cannot get a job in the computing field, complaining bitterly that "just because you have a ton of computers and can program them doesn't mean jack squat."

IT Skills Shortage

Such a plaint might, in the absence of further information, suggest that some aspect other than talent and experience makes this person unemployable. However, shortly after receiving this message, I chanced on a column by the highly respected Australian technology journalist Graeme Philipson, who sees the IT skills shortage as nothing less than a political scam.[32]

So do many of his readers, who contributed to a response he describes as by far the greatest he has experienced in 20 years of writing about IT[33] All but one of his more than 250 respondents agreed with Philipson—those he quoted echoed the sentiments of my own irate reader.

Nor is this solely an Australian phenomenon.   Certainly, Norman Matloff's testimony to the US House Judiciary Committee's Subcommittee on Immigration indicates that the situation is much the same in the US[28] Further, the main government measure to counteract the supposed shortage— encouraging people with IT skills to emigrate from less-developed countries— is common to both Australia and the US, and it also seems to be popular in Western Europe.

Who is behind this myth?   In his June column, Philipson suggested that "many in the IT industry are manufacturing fears of an IT shortage to get handouts from government and to be able to hire cheaper immigrant labour." And in the US, an H-1B Hall of Shame lays blame similarly.[42]

Blaming the IT industry or a servile government for this deceit is unfair. The main fault lies with the computing profession.

IT and the Profession

Information technology concerns itself with processing data, particularly digital data. The computing profession takes this activity to be its special bailiwick.

But what kind of a profession are we? We can lay some claim to being a branch of engineering. The various engineering branches exist to exploit technically physical materials and other resources. Civil engineering exploits materials in static structures, mechanical engineering exploits kinetic energy, and electrical engineering exploits electrical energy. The computing profession exploits data: conventional representations of facts or ideas.

The computing profession and traditional engineering branches differ in two respects: their professionals' responsibilities and the nature of the resources they exploit.

Professional responsibility

In traditional branches of engineering, professionals lead and take responsibility for the work of those skilled in particular trades:
- civil engineers oversee machine drivers and concrete workers,
- mechanical engineers oversee machinists and other metalworkers, and
- electrical engineers oversee riggers and electricians.

In traditional engineering, professional work is clearly and formally distinct from construction work and from the work the constructed products' users do. Not so in the computing profession. Where segregation of this kind exists, it is local and informal. The computing profession seems instead to want to separate into branches, each of which engineers a specific type of system: information, computer, software, knowledge, and so on.

Industry generally sees the computing profession as a variegated and vacillating collection of leaderless skills. That's why industrial leaders can rant about IT skills with little fear of contradiction—they see no clear structure because the profession itself sees none.

Engineers and tradespeople have distinct and essential roles. Engineers lead by bringing their education and experience to bear when applying general principles to new problems. Tradespeople carry out assigned tasks using a variety of tools and techniques coupled with skills acquired through training and experience.

General principles are stable and only slowly extended, and engineers apply those principles continually to develop new tools and techniques for using them. Thus, training and continual retraining are much more important for the tradespeople who use those new tools and techniques than for the engineers who develop them. In many countries, specialist schools for technical or vocational education supply this training. If they were better supported in specialist areas of computing by the profession, and if computing professionals were prepared to lead computing tradespeople, any real shortage of particular IT skills would be short-lived.

If the computing profession recognized and encouraged the development of computing trades, we would have little need for separating the profession into branches, and the education of computing professionals could be redeveloped along generalist lines, perhaps even as a unified data engineering discipline. Let's face it, programming is a craft and trade, not a profession.

The secondary profession

A data engineering generalist would seek to exploit data. As a resource, data and the machines that process data differ in kind from the resources and machines that other engineering branches exploit. Engineering's traditional branches exploit resources and phenomena derived from them, such as structural materials and kinetic and electrical energy.

Data, on the other hand, subsists in immaterial representations imposed on material derived from natural resources. Data is thus a secondary, indirect, and limitless resource that all professions and occupations use. Indeed, humanity has based its civilization on the formal use of data.

Although we once could imagine a profession distinguished from others by its exclusive use of digital computers, this notion is now ludicrous. Yet computing professionals continue to talk loosely of the *computer profession*, a phrase echoed in the "Innovative Technology for Computer Professionals" tagline that, unfortunately, appears on [*Computer*]'s front cover.

All professions—and those who educate their practitioners—will increasingly depend on machines based on digital technology. Therefore, educators should teach future computing professionals more than data engineering. They should educate students to accept and promote their profession as secondary: one that aids and abets other professions. The students' education should include project work carried out in cooperation with students from other professions. To survive and flourish, the computing profession must abandon the idea of living in splendid and oracular isolation.

We do need a branch of engineering devoted solely to the design and manufacture of digital computers, which might well be called computer engineering. But computer manufacturing's oligarchic nature means that the field will need relatively few such computer engineers, so their professional education and affiliation would be better regarded as a specialization within electronic engineering.

Beyond Professions

Digital machinery is rapidly coming to dominate upper- and middle-class domestic life in developed countries, most significantly in entertainment applications. In such an environment, children receive a significant amount of computer and Web training during their daily activities. Many occupations will rely increasingly on using computers and computer-based machinery, and training in the vocational use of computers and such machines—training distinct from that of computing tradespeople—should be demanded by the relevant trade organizations.

Using appliances based on digital computers lies beyond the computing profession's proper concerns. Using computers to compute does not. The profession has a responsibility to promote and support the effective and knowledgeable vocational and domestic use of computation. It should thus give attention to how marketing objectives dominate such computation.

Ordinary users and their teachers feel flummoxed by the ever-growing complexity of the personal computers, operating systems, and software suites they must upgrade continually. If the automotive industry behaved as the computer industry does, it would sell in place of the private car an articulated 18-wheeler containing a bathroom and private theater, with an automatic transmission supplemented by a 233-speed manual gearbox necessary for curves and hills.

We desperately need a program suite that combines *basic and stable* spreadsheet, database, document, and graphic processing under a *basic and stable* operating system on a *basic and stable* personal computer. With such a foundation, *all* children and apprentices might effectively learn persistently useful skills. The digital divide might then start narrowing rather than continuing to widen. Further, if we could make available *basic* RPG, Cobol, and Fortran in the simple style of the 1960s, many more young people might learn to do their own programming.

All this talk of IT skills masks a deception: The phrase itself suggests that such skills form some kind of esoteric capability distinct from all others. The computing profession should assert most vigorously that everyone should possess the skills to deal with data effectively. Basic education should have this aim. After all, we expect schools to inculcate literacy and numeracy in their students—skills essential to IT. In this age and in the developed world, the essential aspects of literacy and numeracy should include acquiring basic competency in document and spreadsheet manipulation.

Vocational education should also aim to impart skills in the literate and numerate use of computation within every trade. Schools should avoid vocational training in IT skills per se. Rather, the aim should be to produce workers in specialist fields, such as computer security and programming, who can work with professionals in various fields, but particularly with computing professionals.

If we accept computing as a secondary profession, and if we view all professions and vocations as benefiting from skillful data use, people seeking *professional* jobs will see that having computers and being able to program them matters "jack squat" compared to being able to help other people use them and benefit from that use. With luck, employers and government will come to see this, too.

3.6   The Internet, the Web, and the Chaos

(2005 September)

The public and, I suspect, many computing professionals discern at best only a vague distinction between the Internet and the World Wide Web. In many popular writings, authors use the simple phrases "the net" and "the web" interchangeably, which is understandable as these terms are synonymous in ordinary speech. Admirably, the *International Herald Tribune* uses an initial capital in *the Net* and *the Web*, but professionals should go further and always refer to *the Internet*.

As an observer, I can dissect the digital networking world into usefully distinct major components, although the boundaries between them may be blurred. If we do not make such dissections, this world will seem hopelessly chaotic both to the profession and the public. The profession at large will not understand what we do, and the public at large will not properly appreciate it. The chaos will continue.

The Internet

Today, the communicating world moves most of its digital data around via the Internet. Its creators designed the Internet, once simply a network connecting digital computers, to be resistant to disruption by all manner of disasters— including, for example, nuclear warfare.

The Internet has two major layers: the physical, in which the signals travel, and the logical, in which the data travels. In turn, each layer has two aspects: the nodes and the links between the nodes.

The physical layer

The physical Internet has many different kinds of links. Signals are transmitted electronically over wires, an increasingly unpopular medium, and photonically through fibers, cables, and space. Electronic mail in transit, or in storage, is not usually electronic, but rather photonic in transmission and magnetic in storage. Engineers use many different technologies and standards for signaling, and these technologies and standards come and go.

The physical Internet also has many different kinds of nodes. The mainframe computers that were nodes of the original Internet are now relatively few. Routers perform the buffering and forwarding of signals at intermediate nodes, while digital computers of various kinds dispatch and receive signals at terminal nodes.

Servers—straightforward digital computers—personal computers, hand-held computers, and personal digital assistants now can all be Internet nodes. So also can the bewildering variety of mobile phones or cell phones. Further, we face the very real prospect that a huge assortment of automatic data-gathering equipment will be connected to the Internet to, for example, handle security surveillance and the identification and location of prospective customers.

Such a variety of technologies, standards, and equipment can seem chaotic. But professional engineers in the field will try to subdue this chaos and to make the Internet and its terminal nodes simple and reliable. Yet, one in every seven mobile phones sold in the UK last year was faulty,[6] which shows that this objective is not always met.

The logical layer

Signals carry message data along Internet links in complex packages. The messages have a sequence of wrappings that carry transmission-management data for use at the nodes. One of these wrappings contains a numerical value that specifies the package's terminal node destination—its Internet Protocol address.

The Internet functions as a single entity because all data traveling across the network must be packaged with an IP address, and these addresses define the Internet's logical structure. The logical Internet is chaotic in two ways: addressing and packaging.

The size of the IP address puts a natural limit on the number of nodes that can be in the Internet at any time. Under the current IP version 4, that size is too small. The accepted version 6 would solve this problem, but its use is being smothered largely by commercial interests for short-term financial benefit, and by lack of international support. The result is that IP addresses are no longer fixed in their identification because of the tricks that must be employed to let everybody who wants to use the Internet do so. This in turn causes many further problems.

Developers intended the use of data packaging to make the Internet robust, and they succeeded. However, the Internet's success has led to a burgeoning of both the amount of data and the kinds of traffic on it.

In general, an increase in the amount of traffic can be handled simply by investment in the network's equipment. However, for the transmission of video data of one kind or another, it's not just a question of the transmission equipment's raw capacity, it's also a question of transmitting the huge amounts of data quickly and smoothly. There is reason to doubt whether the Internet can handle video data satisfactorily in packages.

The Web

The Internet, in the simplified way I have described it, is to the World Wide Web what an engine and transmission are to a car: the Internet makes the Web possible. It plays host to many different systems, such as e-mail and instant messaging, but these appear to be on their way to being subsumed within the Web.[24]

The original Web, which forms the foundation for the current Web, functioned as a logical network of links joining files. The files, stored at Internet nodes, held text encoded with the HyperText Markup Language to specify the text's structure and nature. Uniform Resource Locators provided the links, which pointed to specific HTML files or to points within them.

The reasoning behind such links, as devised by Vannevar Bush—although his links had the advantage of being bidirectional—focused on finding details of specific ideas in a document if needed simply by following a chain of links, a generalization of formal documents' citations and bibliographies.

A URL has up to three parts that contain addresses: one for the Internet node at which the file is stored, one for the file's location within the node, and one for the HTML-labeled spot within the file where the specific details can be found.

The node address within the URL is not the IP address but a symbolic address that special Domain Name System servers scattered around the Internet can translate into an IP address. This node address consists of a sequence of names, vaguely and unsatisfactorily related to trademarks, which are used in marketing commercial products and warfare. URLs, often with just a node address, are now used as pointers to many different entities beyond mere text files.

Browsers

To access the Web, users need a browser, first to fetch and display a text file and any files associated with it, and second to follow a link within the current file to another file. The Web is useless without a browser, and only the success of various browsers has let it achieve its current popularity. But the browsers have brought chaos with them.

The Web no longer seems to be a worldwide collection of linked text files because browsers have gone far beyond merely wandering the Web. The browser provides an interface to most of the Internet's services and also has become an interface to the computer running the browser. Vendors, hackers, phishers, and anyone else who can persuade or trick a browser user into interfacing with a computer can run their programs on that user's machine.

There would be less chaos if browsers could only load passive files and if another kind of program, a *seller* let's call it, could interface with files that provide active and potentially dangerous services. The seller program's developers could focus on security and, since most of these services are commercial, on identification and payment. There could well be a market for simple handheld devices specialized to run sellers.

Search engines

The Web's success has meant that a huge variety and stupendous number of text files have become available on it. To make these files more accessible amid the chaos, many users turn to *search engines*.

The search engine has two components. The *crawler program* continually extracts text files from the Web and constructs an inverted file from their content and URLs. The *responder* uses textual queries to select entries from the inverted file and constructs a list of URLs that match the query, then sends the list with some relevant context to the browser that sent the query.

Search engines have been remarkably successful programs because they hide the chaos. Even so, they only provide access to a small fraction of the Web's content and use somewhat arbitrary methods to select and rank what they process—making their activities more of a raid than a search.

Clearly we need some way to formally separate the Web's wheat from its chaff, something like a reviewing procedure to qualify Web files for inclusion in inverted files for searching. The people responsible for the reviewing in any area could also be responsible for making sure all the qualified files are stably and permanently stored.

Addressing the Web

Web addresses, or URLs, are themselves textual and based on the Latin alphabet. This raises important issues for those who use other writing systems—a population that is rapidly increasing its Web usage.

The Latin alphabet's predominance is unlikely to continue, particularly when the Chinese realize that their wonderful writing system needs encoding by radical rather than by character to save it from chaos. Segregation of Web content by writing system, if not by language, seems inevitable and will be much easier to implement if anticipated.

A primary requirement will be meeting the need to separate DNS server complexes for each writing system. This challenge seems closer to hand given that the US government has opted to retain its overall control of the present DNS complex.[5]

After all, the vast majority of Internet messages, whether selling or searching, use only one writing system. Most machinery and applications are specific to a particular writing system, and trying to mix systems usually proves difficult and unsuccessful. Everyday keyboards in English-speaking countries can't even properly handle other languages that use the same alphabet.

The Populace

Another global network runs alongside the Internet and the Web: the social network. Introducing new technology to so-called backward societies can bring chaos,[25] but it can also disrupt developed societies. At one time, shopping provided a rich social activity populated by real personalities like grocers, greengrocers, butchers, bakers, chemists, newsagents, and clothiers. The social component of today's supermarkets is minuscule, and seller programs will remove it altogether.

Functions like management drift further and further from personal contact to digital mediation, using e-mail, spreadsheets, and PowerPoint via BlackBerries and their like. I have heard modern management called a parallel world, and I suspect that middle management may soon move to outsourcing on its way to becoming completely automated.

The biggest threat I see is that entertainment and marketing will take over the Web as they have taken over television and radio, media that at first seemed to offer great potential benefit to personal society in areas such as education and information.

Perhaps the best way to get a truly social benefit from the Web will be to support and extend efforts like Wikipedia[39] and Project Gutenberg,[20] and move toward a stable and organized Accessible Authoritive Archive (AAA), as the British Broadcasting Corporation has tried to do against determined opposition.[9]

Chaos might seem too strong a word to describe the modern Internet and its Web, but even if it's only an awful mess, the computing profession must take some responsibility for that mess. To clean it up, we must start by cleaning up the terminology, then proceed by imposing a clear structure on the Web.

A good first step might be for our IEEE Computer Society to press, perhaps through the International Federation for Information Processing,[22] for professional computing societies to pool their publicly accessible publications in a common AAA complete with inverted file. Open documents from the computing industry could also be brought in, such as those at [IBM[21]].

Since writing this essay I have become aware of an interesting system for countering URL volatility, the DOI System.[31]

3.7   Notions

The notions are given here partly as a rough summary, but more particularly as topics and issues for students to study and debate. They are in the sequence of their *key word* or *phrase*. The page number to the right of each notion points to its context.   Sadly, many of the maxims below express hopes rather than reality.

1. The *absence* of school systems in less prosperous countries
goes a long way to explaining why they are less prosperous   98

2. Social studies exploiting the Web are relatively passive and need
to be backed up by *active learning* provided by academic gaming   91

3. Education *aims* to bring the child out of infancy and into
full membership of society, able to take part in
and contribute to a full range of community activities   87

4. An entirely rational society would consist of *automata* alone   118

5. *Basic skills* must be speedy and automatic,
noncontemplative and unquestioning, otherwise
true literacy and numeracy are unattainable   109

6. The vast potential *benefits* of computers in schools
are not being realized   100

7. The more the program adapts to its student user,
the more effective its *brainwashing*, and the more subtly
the student is steered to the required responses   102

8. Educational distortions come when the *bureaucrats*
see it as more important that the students come to no harm
than that they come to any good   103

9. Abrupt change often triggers *chaos*   94

10. The best indicator of the health of a *civilized* society
is the way it treats its children and youth   107

11. In programming, a *comment* is a confession of failure   124

12. The people who control the *commercial* and bureaucratic
processes that exploit technology determine its uses   118

13. Education depends on *communication*   87

14. *Computers* alone cannot educate anyone   100

34. Digital technology amplifies *irrationality*
                                        outside science and technology   120

35. *Liberal educators* have been at the same time the most involved,
        the most optimistic, and the most threatened of all educators
                            since computers have been adopted for school use   101

36. *Literacy* is a hierarchy of reading skills that successively
            takes in coding, semantic, pragmatic, and critical competencies   110

37. The most significant potential benefit of computers in education
                    is to free the teachers from the stigma of *marking*   97

38. There are grave, worldwide social problems
                        caused in part by the *misuse* of digital technology   100

39. Not only is the idea of a society poorly defined,
                    but also the *nature of society* is rapidly changing   101

40. Another global *network* runs alongside
                        the Internet and the Web: the social network   137

41. As digital networking and recording loom large in the world,
            computation as a *numerical* activity has been relegated
                            to a quite minor use of computers   117

42. To survive and flourish, the computing profession must abandon
                the idea of living in splendid and *oracular isolation*   130

43. Committed *parents* used to provide preschool socialization,
                but they are disappearing as are the skills to provide it   101

44. Custodial schooling is an institutional approach to achieving
            passivity in schools and reducing problems for administrators   103

45. Schooling is determined more by *political* forces
                                        than by educational ideals   103

46. Digital technology has enormous *potential* benefit
        in the field of education, yet little of that potential is being realized   88

47. Society accepts as a matter of principle that
            professionals must consider the social effects of their technology   119

48. The in-the-large aspects of *programming* rely
                on the lower-level parts, and you can't get them right
                            unless you get the small things right too   125

49. There's nothing like the thorough and controlled application
                of a clearly specified and well-tested technology
                        to ensure a complex technical *project*'s prosperity   122

50. The school systems in many of the more economically
            prosperous countries are becoming increasingly less effective   98

3.8   Bibliography

The entries are in order of the first or only author's name. Where no personal author is known, as for popular news items, an indicative name is used. Where there is a page number or two in *italics* at the beginning of the annotation, they point back to where the item was cited. Where some of the annotation is given in quotes it has been taken from the item itself or from some of its publicity.

1. Stanley Aronowitz and William DiFazio (1994). *The Jobless Future: SciTech and the Dogma of Work.* Minneapolis: University of Minnesota Press, ISBN 0-8166-2194-2, 408 pp. (*p. 104*; "challenges beliefs in the utopian promise of a knowledge-based, high-technology economy").

2. Marcia Ascher (1991).   *Ethnomathematics: A Multicultural View of Mathematical Ideas.* Pacific Grove, California: Brooks/Cole Publishing Company, ISBN 0-534-14880-8, xii+203 pp. (*p. 120*; a very interesting and rich book, not directly relevant where it is cited, but with many curious insights on the different uses of numbers in different cultures).

3. Ana Asuaga (2002, June). "The Profession: Using Computers in Our Daily Life," *Computer*, Vol. 35, No. 8, pp. 104, 103 (*p. 128*; "more than just business tools and toys, computers can become vital agents of socially beneficial change").

4. Albert Gordon Austin and Richard Joseph W. Selleck (1975). *The Australian Government School 1830-1914: Selected Documents with Commentary.* Melbourne: Pitman Publishing Pty. Ltd., ISBN 0 85896 3132, xvi+356 pp. (*p. 110*; the cited quote is anonymously given on page 12).

5. BBC (2005, July 1). "US holds onto key Internet role" (*p. 136*; news.bbc.co.uk/1/hi/technology/4640441.stm).

6. ———— (2005, August 4). "One in seven new mobiles 'faulty'," (*p. 134*; news.bbc.co.uk/1/hi/technology/4745205.stm).

7. Stephen Paul Benson (1998, January). "Village People? The Net Generation," *IEEE Communications Magazine*, Vol. 36, No. 1, pp. 32–35 (*p. 108*; "the changes to lifestyle, culture, society, and architecture emerging ... as a direct result of developments in communications technology").

8. Don D. Bushnell and Dwight W. Allen (edd. 1967). *The Computer in American Education.* New York: John Wiley and Sons, Inc., SBN 67-22407, xxx+300 pp. (*p. 100*; 19 essays, 393 item annotated bibliography; a very influential book, now mainly of historical interest).

9. Edward Castronova (2005). *Synthetic Worlds: The Business and Culture of Online Games.* The University of Chicago Press, ISBN 0-226-09626-2, 344 pp. (*p. 145*; "offers the first comprehensive look at the online game industry, exploring its implications for business and culture alike").

10. Winston Churchill (1913). *The Inside of the Cup.* New York: Grosset & Dunlap, 513 pp. (*p. 117*; a very enjoyable novel on a surprisingly modern theme).

11. Larry Cuban (1993, Winter). "Computers Meet Classroom: Classroom Wins," *Teachers College Record,* Vol. 95, No. 2, pp. 185–210 (*pp. 99, 105*; "Examines why computers are used less often in classrooms than in other organizations"; tcrecord.org/Content.asp?ContentId=82).

12. Michele E. Davis (2000). *Secrets of the PlayStation 2: An Unauthorized Guide to the Hottest Entertainment Machine.* New York: ibooks, inc., ISBN 0-74-34130-4, 160 pp. (*p. 113*; revealing of attitudes; mixed reviews on Amazon).

13. *The Dusseldorp Skills Forum* (1999). *Australia's Young Adults: The Deepening Divide.* Sydney, Australia (*p. 104*; dsf.org.au/features/ol/yr99; a 1998 report is at /yr98).

14. *The Economist* (2005, August 6–12). "Video gaming: Chasing the dream" (*p. 112*; economist.com/printedition/displayStory.cfm?story_id=4246109).

15. Larry Elliott (1999, Mar. 28). "A Lesson the Whole World Must Learn," *Guardian Weekly,* Vol. 160, No. 13, p. 21 (*p. 106*; a review of *Education Now: Break the Cycle of Poverty,* Oxfam International, a report now gone from oxfam.org/educationnow).

16. Howard Earl Gardner (1985). *Frames of Mind: The Theory of Multiple Intelligences.* BasicBooks, ISBN 0-465-02509-9, xx+440 pp. (a very persuasive argument for the complexity of intelligence).

17. Wendy M. Grossman (1999, July). "Cyber View: On-Line U.," *Scientific American,* Vol. 281, No. 1, p. 25 (*p. 105*).

18. A. H. Halsey and Michael Young (1997). "The Family and Social Justice," pp. 784–798 of *Education: Culture, Economy, and Society,* A.H. Halsey et al., edd., Oxford: Oxford University Press, ISBN 0-19-878187-3, 842 pp. (*pp. 101, 106*; the last of 49 interesting essays).

19. Ben Hammersley (2005, July 7). "A moral imperative," *The Guardian,* (*p. 137*; about the problems encountered by the BBC's Creative Archive; technology.guardian.co.uk/online/story/0,3605,1522351,00.html).

20. Michael Hart (fndr. 1971). *Project Gutenberg: Home Page,* Project Gutenberg Literary Archive Foundation (*p. 137*; "the first and largest single collection of free electronic books"; gutenberg.org).

21. *IBM Journal of Research and Development.* (*p.137*; complete and open archives at www.research.ibm.com/journal/rd).

22. *IFIP* (2006). *International Federation for Information Processing: Home Page* (*p.137*; under UNESCO auspices, a "non-governmental, non-profit organization for national societies working in the field of information processing."; www.ifip.or.at).

23. Robert Kraut et al. (1998, Sept.). "Internet Paradox: A Social Technology that Reduces Social Involvement and Psychological Well-Being," *American Psychologist*, Vol. 53, No. 9, pp. 1,017–1,031 (*p.103*; asks "whether the Internet is improving or harming participation in community life and social relationships").

24. Neal Leavitt (2005, July). "Instant Messaging: A New Target for Hackers," *Computer*, Vol. 38, No. 7, pp. 20–23 (*p.135*).

25. David Leser (2000, May 27). "Global Warning," *Good Weekend* (*p.137*; an interview with Helena Norbert-Hodge that touches on the problems of the Ladakh people; unitedearth.com.au/HNHinterview.html).

26. Lorraine Ling and Peter Ling (1998, May). "The Virtual University: To Be and Not to Be," *Melbourne Studies in Education*, Vol. 39, No. 1, pp. 27–42 (*p.105*).

27. Allan Luke (1995). "When Basic Skills and Information Processing Just Aren't Enough: Rethinking Reading in New Times," *Teachers College Record*, Vol. 97, No. 1, pp. 95–115 (*p.110*; "argues that reading is a malleable social practice with identifiable moral and ideological consequences"; tcrecord.org/Content.asp?ContentId=1411).

28. Norman Matloff (1998, April 21). "Debunking the Myth of a Desperate Software Labor Shortage: Testimony to the U.S. House Judiciary Committee's Subcommittee on Immigration," *University of California at Davis* (*p.128*; last updated 2002, Dec. 9; this highly detailed and well documented report can be found at heather.cs.ucdavis.edu/itaa.html).

29. Bertrand Meyer (1999, Dec.). "Component and Object Technology: A Really Good Idea," *Computer*, Vol. 32, No. 12, pp. 144–147 (*p.122*; the final essay of this column, reviewing past essays).

30. Seymour Papert (1992). *The Children's Machine: Rethinking School in the Age of the Computer*, New York: BasicBooks, ISBN 0-465-01830-0, xiv+241 pp. (in "a truly modern School the computer will be as much part of all learning as the pencil and the book have been in the past"; for more recent Papert see papert.org).

31. Norman Paskin (fndr. 1998). *Digital Object Identifier System*, Oxford: International DOI Foundation (*p.137*; managed by "an open membership consortium including both commercial and non-commercial partners, and has recently been accepted for standardisation within ISO."; doi.org).

32. Graeme Philipson (2002, June 18). "IT skills: a shortage or a scam?," *The Age*, (*p. 128*; "many people in government and the IT industry would have us think [there is a shortage], but only because it suits them"; theage.com.au/articles/2002/06/15/1023864366686.html).

33. ———— (——, July 16). "Testimonials put the lie to the myth of IT skills shortage," *The Age*, (*p. 128*; a follow up to the preceding item; theage.com.au/articles/2002/07/15/1026185154255.html).

34. *SAGSET* (2006). *Society for the Advancement of Games and Simulations in Education and Training: Home Page* (*pp. 111, 116*; "a voluntary professional society dedicated to improving the effectiveness and quality of learning through the use of interactive learning, role play, simulation and gaming."; simulations.co.uk/sagset, affiliated with ISAGA, www.isaga.info).

35. *SSIT* (2006). *Society on Social Implications of Technology: Home Page*, Institute of Electrical and Electronic Engineers, Inc., (*p. 107*; ieeessit.org).

36. John Sutherland (2005, Sept. 19). "The ideas interview," *The Guardian*, (*p. 112*; an interview with Edward Castronova of *Synthetic Worlds*[9] fame; guardian.co.uk/g2/story/0,,1573071,00.html).

37. David A. Swayne, Qusay H. Mahmoud and Wlodek Dobosiewicz (2004, Aug.). "The Profession: An 'Offshore-Resistant' Degree Program," *Computer*, Vol. 37, No. 8, pp. 104, 102–103 (*p. 117*; "will proficiency in both computer science and communications give students a global edge?").

38. *UNDP* (2006). *United Nations Development Programme: Home Page* (*p. 101*; undp.org, and the various Human Development Reports are at hdr.undp.org).

39. *Wikipedia* (2001). *Wikipedia: Home Page*, Wikimedia Foundation (*p. 137*; "the free encyclopedia that anyone can edit."; wikipedia.org with English description at en.wikipedia.org/wikipedia/Wikipedia:About).

40. John Wilson (1997, Sept.). "Education Versus Society," *Oxford Review of Education*, Vol. 23, No. 3, pp. 333–343 (*p. 101*).

41. Kimberly Young (Fndr. 1995). *Center for Online and Internet Addiction*, subsidiary of ebehavior, LLC (*p. 103*; ". . . dedicated to helping those who suffer from out of control online behavior."; netaddiction.com).

42. *ZaZona.com* (2006, March 24). "Get the Facts on Nonimmigrant Work Visas" (*p. 128*; was "The H-1B Hall of Shame"; zazona.com/ShameH1B; populist and political).

43. Michael Zyda (2005, September). "From Visual Simulation to Virtual Reality to Games," *Computer*, Vol. 38, No. 9, pp. 25–32 (*p. 112*; "leveraging technology from the visual simulation and virtual reality communities, serious games provide a delivery system for organizational video game instruction and training").

Chapter 4

Computing and Professions

Many of the essays included in the chapters above have mentioned, often stressed, issues about the computing profession. This is because most of them were written for a column called *The Profession* in the IEEE Computer Society's monthly house journal, *Computer*.

With a theme insinuated so often already, why would I believe it necessary to devote an entire chapter to it and risk boring, if not annoying, the reader who has got this far?

Perhaps I should first make clear that, although the readers of *Computer* are all particularly interested in the computing industry, if not employed in it, the points I am continually making to them about the computing profession are not in their principles specific to the computing profession.

In any case, my reasons for having this chapter are many, and are based on my conviction that professionalism is not widely understood, by professionals themselves, in the trades they depend on, or by the public at large.

It is also my observation that professions are losing the respect and trust they need to fill the social role in which their activity is so important. There are quite a few symptoms of this malaise.

Litigation alleging professional malpractice or negligence is increasing, and there are reports of professionals refusing to take responsibility in dangerous situations because of their fear of its consequences. Fear also plays a part in the failure of professionals to blow the whistle on unprofessional or illegal activities on the part of their employers.

Membership of many professional organizations is going down, even in those fields, such as computing and telecommunications, where commercial activity is booming. Governments in some developed countries are taking an interest in supervising and regulating the activities of professionals under the pretext of encouraging competition and enforcing responsibility.

The dependence of countries like the US, UK and Australia on immigrant professionals such as doctors, nurses, dentists, engineers and scientists implies that there are grave deficiencies in the education systems and culture of those countries. This is one reason why I felt it necessary to use Chapter 3 to describe how digital technology could be used to improve education greatly. What is worse, many of such immigrant professionals come from countries where the need for their services is much greater.

Although the essays later in this chapter deal mainly with the computing profession, the points being made are relevant to other professions, and very important to everyone. As our global society becomes more complex and more threatened (see Chapter 6) more and more professional people are needed, both because already we don't have enough and because even more will be needed as the big problems wax.

The Nature of a Profession

A profession is not the same thing as a trade or a craft, nor is a trade the same thing as a craft. The differences lie not primarily in what is done but mainly in the context in which it is done.

A professional has traditionally held a privileged position in society. The rights that society gives to a professional carry certain duties. The main duty of a professional is to put the needs of a client, and of society at large, above those of an employer or of a government.

The essay in which this is most straightforwardly discussed is "Fashioning a Foundation for the Computing Profession" (essay 4.1; p. 152), which was the first in *The Profession* series.

This essay also looked briefly at the nature of the computing profession. However, it did not make the important point about it being a secondary profession, which is spelled out particularly in "Jobs, Trades, Skills, and the Profession" (essay 3.5, p. 128), and elsewhere in this book.

As well as being distinguished by an overriding concern for people and society, professions are also social activities in themselves. They have long directed and regulated the professional activities of their members through professional societies, though there is now a trend for governments to take over this responsibility.

The considered regulation of a profession is best done by its members working through their professional society. Unfortunately, personal attitudes and interests of members interfere with this, which may be one reason for the decline in membership of such organizations, and for the regulatory attention of governments.

Membership of a professional organization has been seen, especially by its members, to confer prestige. This often tempts members to see themselves as somehow above and beyond ordinary people, and can make the profession distrusted by the community at large.

These issues are discussed in the context of the computing profession in "Vanity and Guilt, Humility and Pride" (essay 4.2, p.156), published on the first anniversary of *The Profession*.

Professions and Society

The status of a profession in society depends on its reputation. Having a good reputation in society depends on the profession doing what society sees as "the right thing" and on it turning out to indeed be the right thing.

Many professionals, and especially computing professionals, interact more with their employers and their clients than with the public at large. If for any reason their employers or their clients see them as having been incompetent, or can blame their professional employees for a failed project, then this tends to worsen the reputation of their profession with the public.

Although these issues are discussed in "To See Ourselves As Others See Us" (essay 4.3, p.160) as they apply to the computing profession, the conclusions apply to all professions. And because digital technology is used by more and more professions, and because their reputations depend to some degree on how well they use that technology, the issues affecting the reputation of the computing profession are most relevant.

Doing the right thing merely to maintain a reputation is too passive and reactionary, however.

Professionals have special training and experience in applying observation and reason to problems they encounter in their professional career. They are particularly fitted to do this because their training and education are intended to inculcate such skills and understanding. In the past, professional training and education have been subsidized by the government in the interests of the community.

The interests of the community are not served if professionals keep aloof from developments in the community about which they can make professional judgements, and if they refrain from making those judgements public in their professional personæ. Indeed, many professional societies have codes of ethics and behavior which require their members to act in the public interest in such cases.

There are dangers in this because professionals speaking out in the public interest will often be decried as speaking out politically in their own interests. A distinction must be made between political activity on a community's behalf and political activity on a profession's behalf. That is why some professionals may belong to one or both of two organizations—one strictly professional and the other looking after the interests of the professionals in areas like working conditions and remuneration.

Professional engineers in Australia, for example, may join the Institution of Engineers, Australia[13] as their formal professional body, while they may join the Association of Professional Engineers, Scientists and Managers, Australia[1] as their industrial body.

These issues are illustrated by considering the computing profession in "Should a Professional be Political?" (p. 166), which was also an anniversary essay.

Professionals and Their Field

An important factor in how professionals are viewed in the community, and within other professions especially, is how they tackle the professional work they do. Of course there is a lot of variation within a profession, but it averages out into a general perception of that profession.

Here medical people, both doctors and nurses, have a splendid advantage. They plainly—most of them, anyway—are trying to improve things for other people. Other professions are viewed with less admiration, often with plain scepticism.

Sadly, the computing profession, although certainly not the profession least admired by the public, seems to go out of its way to generate suspicion and engender dislike. All too often the most visible motivation for the broader use of digital technology in government and business is to lower costs by replacing people by machinery or by workers in other countries. And indeed it's digital technology that makes it practical to use workers in far countries.

Too many computing professionals are openly supporting these aims and developments. The irony is that, thirty or forty years ago, the new world of computers was touted by computing professionals as being about to bring higher wages and shorter working hours for all as automation would greatly increase economic growth.

It's all too easy to see the computing profession as spoilers who are more concerned with "improving" their technology than with its consequences. This public scepticism about computers and their minders, sometimes even going as far as fear and loathing, is supported by such things as unreliability of software, planned and frequent obsolescence of personal computers and their software, prevalence and apparent invincibility of spammers and hackers, and conspicuous and frequent failure of gigantic digital technology projects[8]

But a more subtly ominous face much too often presented to the public by computing professionals is the equating of people and computers, or, far worse, the trumpeting of the tremendous superiority of computers over people and of the imminent and inevitable increase in that superiority.

The falsity of such attitudes, and their dangers, are discussed in "Artificial Intelligence: Arrogance or Ignorance?" (essay 4.5, p.171). "The Myth of the Intelligent Computer" (essay 1.4, p.21) provides a shorter introduction to some of the points.

While the computing profession may well be leaders in looking inwards at their technology rather than outwards at its users and their clients, many other professions have similar symptoms.

There are two major tasks that professionals need to undertake. The first is making sure that their technology is used to the greatest general benefit. The second is making sure that the solutions they design for solving problems in their field are understood and accepted.

Getting benefit from technology is a task that professionals must undertake in partnership with their technicians. That's why professional education needs to include technical training, as well as some management training, so that this partnership is effective.

Getting technical solutions accepted is a task that professionals must take sole responsibility for. This is a marketing problem. That's why professional institutions will often require all candidates to have had industrial experience under the supervision of a fully qualified member of the profession before they are accepted as full members of the institution.

Professional education needs to give some training in marketing, though students are often not able to appreciate and practise simple marketing while they are being given a technical education. Frankly, they are almost never able to see the point of it. But at the very least they should be given some training in matters like teamwork, project management, meeting procedures, contract law, and presentation skills.

Probably getting students to give presentations is the most effective way to start them off thinking about marketing. Some advice and a strong warning are given in "In Defence of PowerPoint" (essay 4.6, p.176).

4.1   Fashioning a Foundation
for the Computing Profession

(2000 July)

To paraphrase the opening sentence of Jane Austen's *Pride and Prejudice*, it is a truth universally acknowledged that a new column must be the better for a solid foundation. If that column is called *The Profession*, the foundation must provide a clear appreciation of what a profession is and is not. A profession must in turn be distinguished from a craft and from a trade. All three of these collective nouns—profession, craft, and trade—denote a college of practitioners who share a body of skills and knowledge. But each differs in the responsibilities it places on its members.

Crafts and Trades

A craft's members are primarily responsible to their fellow practitioners. A craft will survive only if its products attract continued custom, and those who are not sufficiently skilled in a particular craft will not be acknowledged as members of it by those who are.

Members of a trade, on the other hand, are as responsible to their clients as to each other. Further, a lack of skill or knowledge in trade workers, such as electricians or auto mechanics, can endanger their—or their employers'—clients. Thus, government regulations typically control a trade's conduct, while official certification controls its membership.

A trade's members have traditionally supported each other by joining together in guilds or unions. These organizations can negotiate with employers and governments to ensure that their members are well paid and well provided for in the workplace.

A craft's members are not usually regulated in what they can charge for their work, nor do they have any power to prevent outsiders from practicing their craft. Members of a trade are regulated, and outsiders usually cannot practice the trade in public.

Because it is unregulated, a craft—such as acting or athletics—will have a few successful members who are extremely well rewarded. Most of its members, however, receive no compensation beyond their own satisfaction. On the other hand, even modestly successful tradespeople can expect a remuneration generous by ordinary standards, and assured for them by regulation. Unless they establish a large business of their own, however, tradespeople cannot expect to be paid even a small fraction of what the entertainment and sports industries pay their star performers.

Professions

Like trades and crafts, professions are distinguished by a shared body of knowledge and skill. Professions typically publish magazines, journals, and books that confirm and promote their particular body of knowledge.

In a craft, such as woodcarving or ice hockey, knowledge is focused on the materials or performances being crafted, while skill is focused on applying techniques—and possibly tools—to the work at hand. In a trade, such as plumbing or auto mechanics, knowledge is focused on the trade's tools, while skill is focused on the procedures in which the tools are exploited to achieve a standard result using standard materials. In a profession, such as doctoring or engineering, knowledge is focused on improving the material health or welfare of the community, while skill is typically focused on the process of guiding others in their trades, businesses, or private lives.

It follows that a profession, in contrast to a craft or trade, has a direct effect on the community and its members. Thus a profession has a primary responsibility to the community that the profession's effect upon it be a benevolent one. A profession that seeks to have digital equipment—computers, or machinery driven by them—used beneficially within the community, and which seeks to guide others in the use of such equipment, is therefore truly a profession, providing it is based on a distinctive body of knowledge and skill.

The Computing Profession

The body of knowledge and skill that defines the profession to which the IEEE Computer Society's members belong is suggested by the technical articles that appear in the Society's publications. The computing profession is relatively new, still forming, and as yet uncertain of its identity. It is in danger of losing the respect of its wider community, which associates the profession with apparent fiascoes like the Y2K affair, or feared fiascoes like the Internet stock bubble.

The future health of the computing profession depends on its members taking an interest in issues outside its body of knowledge and skills. These issues fall into three classes, those that relate to

• the profession itself: its identity, territories, the trades it should encompass (if any), how it distinguishes itself from other professions and chooses to cooperate with them, how it seeks to influence those who educate its would-be members, what that influence should be, and so on;

• the constraints that might or should be imposed on the profession by the external community: constraints of law and professional conduct, the effect of national and international government policies, how business practices relate to the profession's management and careers, and so on; and

• the profession's effect on the external community: its effect on education, personal behavior and health, business behavior and ethics, community welfare and equity, and so on.

In this column, we will emphasize the professional importance of issues such as these, provide a basis and stimulus for members to consider them, and offer an outlet for members' opinions. Some issues overlap the classes, and all involve problems more appropriately resolved through discussions than computations. Nevertheless, the social status of the computing profession and its members doesn't ultimately depend on resolving these issues. Rather, our status depends on our members' being aware of, well informed about, and able to express reasonable opinions on these issues when challenged by people outside our profession.

Figure 1. The nine dots puzzle.

In the early days of computing, many thought that a competent system analyst must be able to "see outside the nine dots." This expression sprang from the puzzle, in which you are required to draw four end-connected straight lines through the nine dots.

The Nine Dots

Back in the early days of computing, when it was more a trade than a profession, those who belonged to it consisted largely of programmers and systems analysts. To be considered competent, common wisdom decreed, a system analyst must be able to "see outside the nine dots." This expression sprang from the popular puzzle, shown in Figure 1, that required the victim to draw four end-connected straight lines through nine dots arranged in a three-by-three dot grid.

Figure 2 shows that the nine dots puzzle can only be solved by realizing that its rules allow a corner—where one line starts and the next begins—to lie outside the square that the dots define. The puzzle challenges the analyst to consider the entire circumstances of a problem when designing its solution.

Now, when the computing profession encompasses so much more than systems analysis and coding, when the affluent throughout the world use personal computers, and when the digital network connecting the world's computers has become at least as significant as the computers themselves, it has become essential for those who would be members of a true computing profession to look beyond the problems they are paid to solve, taking note of how their profession and the world at large affect each other.

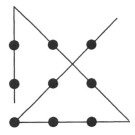

Figure 2. The solution.

To solve the puzzle with only four lines, you must extend the lines beyond the square defined by the nine dots.

Oddly, few "nine dots" solvers ever look outside the sheet of paper on which the nine dots are drawn. Thus they fail to realize that all nine dots can be lined up on a single straight line. The procedure is best done in three steps:
1. Draw a straight line through each row of three dots so that you have three parallel lines.
2. Make a simple cylinder out of the sheet of paper so that the three original lines make three circles.
3. Move the two adjacent edges along each other—angling one upward and the other downward—until the ends of two of the lines on one edge line up with two of the lines on the other edge, leaving one line end free both above and below the two joined lines.

It will be easiest if you draw the three original lines along the length of the paper because, when curved, the sheet makes a broad cylinder that adjusts more easily to movement of its edges. The resulting spiral connects all nine dots with an unbroken line.

Granted, this second solution to the nine dots puzzle is far from obvious. Custom has it that you need four lines to solve the puzzle, just as custom imposes on us certain attitudes toward our trade or profession. In this column, we shall strive to provide content that helps us remove those blinders so that we might better see beyond the bounds of our daily professional lives.

4.2   Vanity and Guilt, Humility and Pride

(2001 July)

This anniversary essay relates thoughts about some of the e-mail messages stimulated by the seven essays I have contributed since this column first appeared a year ago. Of snail mail there has been none—a reflection of the times, no doubt.

The e-mail responses fall roughly into four categories, defined by the axes of brief-to-lengthy and positive-to-negative. Each month, *Computer's* editors choose some of the more substantial responses for the Letters to the Editor column, usually publishing readers' responses to an essay a couple of months after its publication. Some of these messages—and many of the longer unpublished ones—cause me to wonder about my success in provoking thought and discussion about truly professional issues.

Merely Secondary Details

Typically, the author of a disquieting e-mail starts by congratulating me on the essay, either enthusiastically or perfunctorily. That person then goes on to dispute my reminiscences and observations, although in most cases they are merely secondary details intended to give an air of nostalgic conviviality to an otherwise dry and unrelenting narrative.

My first essay was meant to provoke discussion about what constitutes a profession and how a profession differs from a trade or craft. As secondary enlightenment, I used the well-known nine-dots problem to observe that, while a technician should be able to find a four-line solution by seeing outside the box formed by the dots, a professional should be able to see outside the piece of paper that the nine dots are drawn on to find a *one-line* solution.

Much of the e-mail this essay generated found fault with my one-line solution on various grounds, but none denied that it worked. The typical objection was that rolling the paper into a tube is, for various reasons, such as going into a third dimension, invalid. I suspect that many such objections arose from a perceived threat to the popular cliché, "outside the box."

Although I enjoy such exchanges, the persistent focus on secondary topics causes me to worry that some readers are not getting past the details to the major issues.

Vanity

Even the secondary e-mails can incite thoughts about professional issues, however. At the moment, I am involved in an e-mail exchange with the American Dialect Society over my speculation about the origin of the term *floppy disk* (essay 1.3, p.16). This exchange has involved no less a celebrity than Eric S. Raymond, the widely renowned author of *The New Hacker's Dictionary*,[24] who described my recollections as "a thin, unsupported, and very implausible tissue of conjectures . . . ."

I found Raymond's condemnation especially stinging because I had received an e-mail a couple of weeks earlier, provoked by the February column, "US Electoral Reform,"[18] that baldly told me I am "a complete idiot." Such accusations raise an issue more general than the quality of my memory or intellect: they raise a professional issue. If our profession, however it might eventually evolve or be defined, is to gain the community's respect—a necessity for our profession's members to be fully effective—those members must first respect one another.

Apart from any question of politeness, professional disagreement must be handled in a professional manner, even through e-mail. If an author makes a factual error, the reader should simply point out the error and cite the appropriate authority. A reader who questions an author's recollections should describe any disparity with enough background to show that the contrary recollection has more weight than the original, or at least enough to require reconsidering the original assertion.

In matters of opinion, however, professional respect is paramount. The opinions and judgments developed by a profession's members distinguish that profession from a trade. To cite the Charles McCabe quote that once adorned *Computer*'s Open Channel column, "Any clod can have the facts, but having opinions is an art."

When debating opinions and recollections, we must acknowledge their subjective nature; bear in mind that other professionals can be as convinced of their judgments' value as we are of ours; and be prepared to change our opinions in the light of professionally delivered alternatives.

Professional respect should extend even to intemperate comment from other professionals, a principle whose validity became plain to me when I checked what I had actually written about the origin of the term "floppy disk." I certainly recall that marketers of the time had rendered "flexible" meaningless, and thus made "flexy" descriptively useless. But to my dismay, I discovered that I had gone overboard and asserted that the marketers had coined "floppy." I have no recollection of any particular group of people—other than the general body of users—being blamed or credited with this coinage. Therefore, Raymond was correct even if he wasn't right. This mistake exposes another professional principle: always double or triple check what you actually write when you record a recollection or opinion.

But honest mistakes, even careless ones, should not be bluntly scolded in public. In a very real sense, the fault behind vituperation is vanity, insofar as vanity lies in putting self-regard above respect for others.

Guilt and Humility

Self-regard of a slightly different kind manifests itself as guilt. A reader commenting on the first several installments of *The Profession* accused me of "building up [readers'] guilt," presumably because he felt guilty.[17] This accusation puzzled me quite a bit at the time.

Guilt is an extremely personal and unconstructive feeling. If we make specific *personal* mistakes, such as the recollection error I just confessed, we may well experience some feeling of personal discomfort and even guilt. But feeling guilty about professional issues—in this case, about "paradigm shifts"—seems to imply a very personal and complete identification with the profession, an attachment that runs very close to vanity.

A larger problem with allowing self-regard to dominate our attitude toward the computing profession involves how this behavior appears to the public and other professions. The closing two paragraphs in Robert Whelchel's "The Digerati," written as his swan song when he retired as editor in chief of *IEEE Technology and Society Magazine* bite particularly deep[29]:

> As a teacher of electrical engineering I use technical software daily. I am more in awe of its educational benefits than most of my students. ... I have nothing against computers and nothing against properly functioning software. What I do oppose is the digerati attitude spawned by excessive pride and arrogance, which promotes disregard and disrespect for the rest of us. It is time for the digerati to learn humility.
>
> There undoubtedly is a paradigm shift in learning due to ubiquitous computing power. ... Trying to figure out how to live with and control this and similar paradigm shifts requires serious effort. Those of us involved in such tasks could benefit greatly from digerati input if they would abandon their used-car salesman attitude that everything they do is the greatest thing in the world.

Although we must take remarks such as these seriously, we should not react by feeling guilty, as doing so will not promote our profession.

Whelchel urges that we "digerati"—his encompassing and somewhat disparaging term for computing professionals—learn humility. We should indeed do so. We should also realize that the computing industry's blunder rate is far higher than it should be and that we must take professional responsibility for it. In acknowledging and working to reduce this blunder rate, we will show that we are indeed learning humility.

Pride

Whelchel accuses us of "excessive pride and arrogance." Any arrogance is bad, but excessive pride deserves special condemnation—for it springs from vanity, from an excess of self-regard. We must base proper pride in our profession on respect for our fellow practitioners, and confidence in the value of the profession to clients, and, more importantly, to the community.

Our pride in the computing profession should impel us to make our products, services, and general behavior more professional. As professionals, we must work to improve the computing industry's record, and we must humbly and respectfully strive to support people like Whelchel, who seek to apply digital technology for the benefit of the greater community.

In some areas, such as the field of education, we are in grave danger of continuing to achieve far less than we should have. But we can take genuine pride in the computing profession's achievements so far, and the possibilities for the future are almost unimaginably rich.

The new millennium seems an appropriate time for the computing profession to become more concerned about professionalism. Significantly, *Communications of the ACM* started its *The IT Professional* column this year under the leadership of Peter Denning. Although its tone differs somewhat from this column, readers with an interest in the computing profession should find Denning's column interesting.

The e-mail *The Profession* column has provoked thus far strongly suggests that computing professionals have a real interest in professional issues. Anyone who contributes an essay to the column is, I believe, assured of a wide and interested readership.

IEEE Computer Society members might also consider joining the *IEEE Society on Social Implications of Technology* so that they can receive its quarterly publication, *IEEE Technology and Society Magazine*. Many of the articles in that publication relate directly to digital technology, and all of them would be of interest to computing professionals.

4.3   To See Ourselves As Others See Us

(2002 January)

By tradition, each year *Computer*'s January issue describes the wonders that computing professionals and their industry anticipate most keenly. Doubtless our professional duty lies in designing and implementing these wonders. However, we have an equally important duty to consider the effect of these innovations on the world at large and to be aware of how our dreams and our efforts to realize them will shape others' opinions of us.

To maintain an awareness of the world outside our profession, we can choose any of several methods. For example, I subscribe to and diligently scan *The Economist* for a rational, economocratic view of the world. For a more democratic view, I read the *Guardian Weekly*, which includes sections from *Le Monde* and the *Washington Post*.

Last year, a column by editor and journalist Simon Caulkin appeared in the *Guardian Weekly*.[6] The article gave a succinct and very critical evaluation of the role computers play in the business world.

Digital Binges

Caulkin opened by observing of economic growth that "the great Internet binge has given us levels of improvement that haven't been seen since, er, the 1930s." According to him, the notorious dot-com bubble is not, alas, a singular phenomenon.

Caulkin reported that Paul Strassmann, at one time the Pentagon's information chief, has observed eight "build-and-scrap" cycles in computing investment since 1946, with each cycle greatly surpassing the previous one both in absolute value and percentage of overall business investment. Strassmann projects the next binge to be two and one-half times more expensive than the last, and suggests somewhat optimistically that we won't have enough money to pay for it.

Caulkin saw these binges as "sustained by some kind of arms race in that, short of any profitability justification, companies invest simply to keep up with rivals." It's easy to blame these binges on management and absolve our profession from any responsibility. On the other hand, company managers usually employ computing professionals to advise them on technical matters, which strongly implies that professionals have supplied bad advice—or none at all.

The PC binge

I remember best the personal computer binge, which I presume qualifies as one of Strassmann's cycles. The professional failing there was twofold. First, professionals didn't cater to their end users. Second, they succumbed to the PC hyperbole.

By the time the PC binge began, computing people in the business and government worlds were organized into politically powerful data processing departments notorious for their large budgets and disdain for end users. They saw themselves as answerable only to upper management's needs. These professionals cherished their status as big-project people. When cheap personal computers with useful full-screen generic applications like spreadsheets became available, the DP departments ignored them. However, end user departments bought lots of PCs so that their workers could run these applications. The low cost of a single PC allowed DP departments to avoid prohibitions on large equipment purchases, and gave individual workers what they really needed.

The typical DP department then made the mistake of trying to suppress these initiatives, rather than moving to provide a comparable level of personal service with their existing equipment. When suppression proved impossible, and the benefits of desktop PCs became obvious as they quickly spread, the tradition-bound DP departments strove to bring the proliferating PCs under their control—with two quite natural consequences.

First, PC hardware and software, having evolved from hobbyist origins, proved much harder to use and maintain than professional mainframe software driving dumb terminals would have been. Thus, the already expensive DP departments adopted the only rarely successful Help Desk approach in a vain attempt to retain centralized computing control.

Second, as more and more end users in business and government organizations did increasing amounts of work on growing numbers of PCs, they needed to exchange and share data more frequently. This led to the widespread adoption of local area networks, with file and print servers attached, to link the PCs.

An alternative

The time had clearly arrived for computers that provided services *directly* to end users. The PC binge could have been turned into a more gentle evolution if DP departments, or their mainframe or minicomputer suppliers, had developed generic end-user applications to run on full-screen dumb terminals. Today, thin-client computing revisits this approach—one that the profession still fails to take seriously enough.

Computing professionals must bear responsibility for missing this obvious solution. Or, if they did see it, they must bear responsibility for failing to convince their management or their suppliers that existing systems could provide the needed end-user services in an evolutionary way.

The difficulty here is that computing professionals tend to see themselves only as system engineers responsible for analyzing their client's needs and designing and implementing a system that satisfies those needs. But a professional also has a responsibility to management. All too often, the computing professional's manager remains relatively uninformed about trends in digital technology, but, being higher on the pecking order, hesitates to ask for or take advice. Professionals have an important responsibility to inform management when potential technical problems or opportunities arise, even if their counsel might fall on deaf ears.

Too few computing professionals combine both technical and management skills. This problem can be tackled by making computing professionals knowledgeable about management science, sensitive to their responsibility to management, and interested in assuming management responsibilities themselves. Computing courses should include instruction in professional ethics and basic management. Computing students with an interest in management should be allowed to minor in the discipline, or could be advised to study management after finishing their first degree.

Frankenstein Systems

Caulkin also observes that highly complex computer-based systems become ends in themselves, just as Frankenstein's monster assumed a life of its own. Computing professionals could think of many examples, but Caulkin gives special attention to airline reservation systems and call-center systems.

Voracious child

A consortium of airline companies developed Sabre, the "granddaddy" of airline reservation systems. This system proved highly profitable because, rather than pricing seats according to their cost, it allowed them to be priced according to the fluctuating demand.

Sabre's success, and that of similar systems, led to spin-offs as independent businesses. According to Caulkin, Sabre now levies what is "effectively an impost of $10–$12 on every ticket its former parents sell." Such overhead makes the larger airlines vulnerable to low-cost flat-fare competitors, a vulnerability that I imagine the September 11 tragedy has only magnified.

"Not surprisingly, the [major] carriers are squirming uncomfortably, trying to remove themselves from a hook of their own creation," Caulkin writes.

Problematic "solution"

Call-center systems offer another example of complex systems developed "as a 'solution' to service cost or quality issues." They sprang from the idea that a sufficiently complex computer-based system would let low-cost, low-skilled outsourced workers respond to customers from a variety of businesses. These workers could also sell raffle tickets to the general public during slack time— the high-tech version of door-to-door salesmen.

As Caulkin sees it, "Requiring IT–scripted call-centre staff to sort out service problems often just increases the number of irate calls, leading to apparent demand for yet another information factory." My own experience with call centers makes me think they're not all bad, at least for simple inquiries. However, the financial systems that the larger banks and credit card companies use demonstrate a more blatant example of complexity's cost. These institutions' rapidly increasing charges and persistently high interest rates are attracting much criticism.

Monstrous complexity

I view Frankenstein systems as a professional failure that has resulted from complexity worship. It's a long-standing and widespread failure. Two of the finest articles ever published in *Computer*—"A Plea for Lean Software"[30] by Niklaus Wirth and "Why Software Jewels Are Rare"[23] by David Lorge Parnas— eloquently argue the case for simplicity in software, but seem to have gone unheeded.

Often complexity seems unavoidable, even desirable. Management demands an all-encompassing system to reduce labor costs. Marketing demands continual accretion of advertisable capabilities. Clients want a system that does more than their last system, and more than their competitors' systems. Professionals seek the safety of shared responsibility within a large team, and complexity justifies large teams.

Simplicity does not come merely from doing everything on the computer. Computing professionals should seek simplicity in all aspects of a system. Often, the software can be made simpler by designing independent machine capabilities that the user integrates into adaptable work patterns. Typically, users will be more effective if their work can be designed to give them a feeling of achievement, and if they can develop skills. Education of computing professionals would ideally include the study of human psychology and even of cognitive science generally.

Information Factories

Binges and complexities can arise from the isolation of computing professionals in a kind of organizational priesthood. Caulkin repeatedly depicts "information factories"—a phrase he attributes to Thomas Johnson—as detrimental to business. Information factories extend computing isolation by bringing specialist computer users into what is really a new kind of DP department.

Overpaid underproducers

In manufacturing, Caulkin observes, digital technology "has greatly increased the productivity of direct labor. But these gains are generously offset by an invisible IT overhead." He also comments that information-factory workers often outnumber and earn much higher salaries than "real ones."

Caulkin's use of the term "real" conveys the view that computing professionals aren't *really* workers, that they don't produce real value. He emphasizes that "Much computerization is what environmentalists call 'end-of-pipe'—it is applied to an existing process to make it manageable. But this is a solution only in the sense that liposuction is a solution to obesity."

An alternative

Caulkin proceeds to cite Toyota as a success story showing that industry functions better and more profitably without an information factory. At Toyota, he writes, the "work-flow is designed so that the manufacturing processes themselves carry all the information that those operating it need to know." Caulkin thus implies that Toyota's computing professionals work with the "real" workers, as part of the team on the factory floor. The traditional DP department and the modern information factory, which not only separate professionals and their clients but also the management of both groups, discourage such close cooperation.

To be most effective, computing professionals should work as closely as possible with the workers they support. Were computing professionals to be integrated into their client departments and teams, as at Toyota, they would be better able to design and support the needed systems, and to adapt them to new requirements.

Our service profession

In some ways the computing profession can be seen as a secondary profession, providing services to other professions and occupations. Thus, the wider IEEE's general publications often have articles that might well have been published in *Computer*. For example, last September's *Proceedings* focused on soft computing, and *Spectrum* carried pieces on IBM versus Intel, computer-controlled cars, Lego Mindstorms, and Apple OS X.

Organizational dispersion of computing professionals should have benefits beyond improved systems. Skills in computer use could be built up more effectively throughout a company, making technical advice and support more easily available. Fellow workers would more naturally share credit and responsibility for successes, and would be more concerned with ensuring that success and preventing failure.

A mature profession, like a mature person, values and seeks to attain a good reputation. A reputation ultimately lies not only in evaluating our own actions, but also in observing and taking seriously how other people see and value what we do. As Robert Burns once wrote, this would "frae mony a blunder free us, and foolish notion."

When critics like Caulkin find fault with the use of computers, we must look for the cause in our professional work. When Caulkin observes that the New Economy was "sustainable only as long as the illusion lasted that computers did anything genuinely new," we as professionals should not scoff, but should look instead for truth in his opinion. Truth is there to be found, and a mature profession will find and be guided by it.

We cannot earn respect unless we are prepared to give it—to users as much as to critics. When the public believes that the "New Economy was a gigantic computer-aided pyramid scheme," then the reputation of our profession suffers as much as the speculators' pockets.

The education of professionals, in the classroom or on the job, must stress that computers are only justified if they help the people who use them and the people whose lives are affected by them. It is our professional responsibility to ensure that computers are used to actually help people.

4.4   Should Professionals Be Political?

(2003 July)

Three years ago, in my first *The Profession* essay (essay 4.1, p.152) I laid out what I considered this column's proper concerns. Recently, some readers have questioned the propriety of some essays I have written, finding particular fault with my treatment of political issues. Several readers questioned whether political issues should be treated at all in an IEEE Computer Society publication.

This controversy has prompted me to revisit the topic of what it means to be a computing professional, what such a professional should be concerned with, and what *The Profession* should be about.

What Is a Professional?

The problem with the term *professional* is that it has two main contrasting meanings. First, we have those professionals who do for money that which others might do for pleasure or personal improvement: musicians, athletes, or photographers, for example.

The other kind of professional belongs to a learned profession such as medicine, law, or engineering. Their particular education and experience—and often their membership in a professional institution—empowers them to practice their profession.

When discussing professionals, we must distinguish them from technicians. Typically, professionals provide advice and guidance. Technicians exploit technology for others—often professionals. Opinions and judgments are professionals' stock in trade, while technicians rely on skills and techniques. The two roles complement each other, but exhibit important differences:

• Technicians focus on making something work properly. They directly apply their skills and knowledge to machines and processes to make them run and keep them running.

• Professionals focus on predicting the outcome of decisions under new or varying circumstances so that the more beneficial alternatives can be selected or so that better machines and processes can be developed. Professionals arrive at their opinions and judgments by applying their education and experience to rational analysis and argument.

Therefore, those who participate in activities such as writing articles or essays for professional publications or commenting on such articles or essays should display rational analysis or argument. In the essays I write for *The Profession* I try to be as rational and factual as possible, and I feel other contributors do the same.

Unhappily, not all readers display this professionalism when commenting on essays in *The Profession*. This is particularly the case when the topic is one close to people's daily lives. Thus, I still receive e-mail messages prompted by my essay on terrorism (see essay 6.3, p. 255) that accuse me of antisemitism.

The trigger for this accusation appears to be that I cited a list of US actions in the Middle East, compiled by a Middle East expert, that aid "Those who wish to make trouble ... to depict the US as the villain." Among the seven items I paraphrased was "ongoing military and financial support for Israel." Nowhere else did I mention Israel, Judaism, or Jewry, although I did argue that "Religion, like technology, is inherently neutral."

In a quite recent e-mail message about this essay, another reader told me that "I can't imagine what moved you to write such a stupid, ignorant article or why you think a professional magazine should be an outlet for your political and social fantasies." Yet he failed to mention any specific error I had made. Indeed, a rereading of my essay suggests to me that subsequent events have supported rather than refuted my analysis.

Clearly, such readers are not using rational analysis and argument when reacting to what they read in *The Profession*.

What Does Political Mean?

A more sober comment from a reader reacting to my "The Profession and the World" column (see essay 6.1, p. 245) raised a matter of principle. This reader wrote quite dispassionately that "*Computer* is not the correct forum for what, in my opinion, are political or ideological views having no preferential connection to the engineering profession."

By way of contrast, responding to a clarification[11] of that same essay in which I gave a specific example of how greed could reduce the value of money, another reader simply dismissed the example as "spouting discredited ideas from Marx or Mao."

First, a secondary point. In my view, the computing profession is preferentially connected to any activity in which digital technology plays a prominent role, and the widespread adoption of that technology means that this preferential connection is widespread.

But my primary point is that the word *political* is ambiguous.

On the one hand, *politics* refers to the highly human social behavior reflected in phrases such as "office politics" and "marital politics" at one end of a behavioral spectrum and by "party politics" at the other. Such activities are more ethology than politics proper. They mainly concern computing professionals through their effect on any system design and implementation—that is, as context rather than as subject matter.

On the other hand, *The Oxford English Dictionary* strictly defines politics as "the science dealing with the form, organization, and administration of a state or part of one, and the regulation of its relations with other states." This is a different matter altogether, a matter relating to one of the major components—arguably the most important one—of our civil lives. But why should computing professionals concern themselves with such matters? Why should they be political?

Why Be Political ?

In my first *The Profession* essay [essay 4.1, p.152], I argued that "a profession has a primary responsibility to the community that the profession's effect on it be a benevolent one," and gave reasons that no reader disputed at the time: the community gives learned professions rights and privileges and thus they owe the community certain duties and responsibilities.

Being a benefit to the community is a responsibility generally accepted by professional institutions everywhere. This primary responsibility requires us to look beyond the technical results to consider the longer-term, wider-scope social and political effects of what we do when we apply our professional knowledge and experience. If we can plausibly apply our technology in ways that would better the community, we should argue loudly for doing so. We run into difficulties, however, when we try to evaluate exactly what would constitute "better."

Suppose that, as a systems engineer, I study the system of corporations, these entities being the most significant feature of successful modern economies. Suppose I determine that the corporate system's downside stems from its technologically enabled complexity, the intricacies of cross-ownership that lets money be laundered, laws and taxation avoided, and assets hidden—this is all supposition, remember. It occurs to me that the structure could be simplified by forbidding any corporation from owning part of any corporation that owns part of any another corporation—or, more succinctly, by limiting corporate ownership to two levels.

If I then publish details of this scheme, explaining and comparing both the benefits and drawbacks of the two systems, that would be quite professional. It would also be political, in the strict sense. If another systems engineer rationally disputed my analysis, that, too, would be quite professional.

A salient issue here is the basis on which I compare the two systems' benefits and drawbacks, as I need some comparison to justify talking about the alternative system at all. There must be at least some subjective component to such a comparison, most benefits being unquantifiable, but it would be professional to make that component as small as possible.

Also, it remains open for someone to claim, for example, that to let governments apply regulation of this kind—limiting the powers of corporations—is improper. Such a claim moves us into the realm of ideology and party politics, and it would not be professional for me to argue for or against it as a systems engineer. Further, it would be questionable for me to dispute it as a citizen once I have opened the topic in a professional role.

I have chosen this fairly abstruse example to illustrate the professional issues. My actual experience in *The Profession* is a little more involved.

On one hand, I have twice written on electoral processes[18] (and essay 5.5, p.218) and no reader complained that either essay should not have been published. On the other hand, the essays on terrorism (essay 6.3, p.255) and global inequality (essay 6.1, p.245) have drawn allegations of professional impropriety. Why the different reactions?

The protest-free essays examine bureaucratic process, topics that make it difficult to infer any ideological bias on my part. The other two address topics ordinarily steeped in ideology. Yet I believe computing professionals must consider all such topics equally important, and I have tried to treat them as professionally, rationally, and dispassionately as I know how. If I have failed in this, then readers should point out such failings rationally, by detailing errors of fact or reason rather than by denunciation.

What Is Rational?

My advocacy of rational argument does not make me blind to its inherent weakness. For, while rational argument must always be consistent with the facts, it can never be based on facts alone. Behind every argument somewhere sits an axiom, a dogma.

In politics, for example, US President George W. Bush laid down dogma in September 2002, citing "a moral principle," in *The National Security Strategy of the United States of America*[4]: "If you can make something that others value, you should be able to sell it to them. If others make something that you value, you should be able to buy it. This is real freedom, the freedom for a person—or a nation—to make a living."

Nobody, except perhaps an ethicist or philosopher or grammarian, can argue with this assertion professionally. A US citizen has a right to argue with it as a US citizen, but not as a computing professional. A computing professional might analyze how well it is being applied, or suggest how it might be better applied, but those two roles must be kept separate.

Does this mean we members of the IEEE Computer Society can have no dogma? It does not. Professional institutions are based on dogmata that they require their members to adopt and that they spell out in, for example, codes of ethics or conduct. These codes typically require separating professional acts from civil political acts.

More importantly, behind these codes—as one reader spelled out in an email message—lie for us the IEEE Vision and the IEEE Mission[20] The Vision urges us "to advance global prosperity by fostering technological innovation, enabling members' careers and promoting community worldwide." The Mission asserts that "The IEEE promotes the engineering process of creating, developing, integrating, sharing, and applying knowledge about electro and information technologies for the benefit of mankind and the profession."

Promoting community and technology for the benefit of mankind is political activity. Thus, as professionals we are required to be political.

4.5 Artificial Intelligence: Arrogance or Ignorance ?

(2003 November)

Wojciech Cellary's remarks on decision making and intelligence in *Computer*'s September 2003 issue[7] brought to mind Bob Colwell's "Engineering Decisions" column[9] and my disappointment with Adrian Hopgood's article, "Artificial Intelligence: Hype or Reality?"[19] Shortly afterward, under the Artificial Intelligence heading in the book review section of the May 2003 issue of *American Scientist*, I found descriptions of two books on the chess-playing computer, Deep Blue,[26] as well as a book on the "sociable" robot, Kismet.[12] When the September 2003 special issue of *Scientific American* titled "Better Brains: How Neuroscience Will Enhance You"[25] arrived the same day, I felt pressed to move in a predestinate groove. Although I previously had resolved not to revisit the topic I covered in "The Myth of the Intelligent Computer" (essay 1.4, p. 21), the omens seemed to dictate an about-face.

Artificial Intelligence

The term artificial intelligence suffers from many problems beyond the ugliness of its initialism. Hopgood found their nub with his observation "If AI were named 'nifty computer programs,' it would surely be hailed an unqualified success," but treated it as a mere throwaway line.

The term's adoption specifically implies that we see ourselves as creating in machines an intelligence roughly equivalent to *natural* intelligence. The many aspects of natural intelligence that dictionaries define boil down to its being an essential element of successful behavior, especially social behavior.

As computing professionals, we have a moral duty to maintain and promote a distinction between the machines we use as tools and the people whose purposes and well-being we support. People behave or misbehave. Machines function or malfunction. Functioning does not exhibit intelligence. Any inferred intelligence should be credited to the machine's designers.

Society judges our competence as computing professionals by the claims we make for ourselves. If we claim to be creating intelligence, people will assume we claim also to understand what intelligence is. Yet the evidence shows that we don't understand it.

This last point affects three groups of people differently. The computing profession in general, unsuspecting of its self-deceit, will have unrealistic expectations and transmit them to the other groups. People who have not thought much about intelligence will be led into unreasonable hopes and fears. People who have thought deeply about intelligence will consider the computing profession to be both arrogant and ignorant.

In the computing world, the phrase artificial intelligence has a long history, quite untinged with arrogance. But I can't help feeling that a great deal of ignorance has sustained its use.

Natural Intelligence

The misunderstanding of intelligence among computing people springs from the grossly simplified model we use. Hopgood opens his survey with a section titled "A Spectrum of Intelligent Behavior." The text bases this supposed spectrum on "level of understanding involved," while the accompanying figure shows the range, with reaction at one end and expertise at the other. This widely adopted model is uncompromisingly unidimensional. AI people measure its success by how far along that spectrum research has advanced.

But intelligence is not unidimensional. Harvard neuropsychologist Howard Gardner put forth a far more realistic, multidimensional view of intelligence 20 years ago in his book, *Frames of Mind.*[15] His model remains widely accepted, if sometimes misunderstood. In the preface to his book's 1985 paperback edition, Gardner defined an intelligence as "the ability to solve problems, or to create products, that are valued within one or more cultural settings."

Using a variety of evidence, Gardner proposed seven relatively independent dimensions of intelligence, although he has since adopted an eighth and contemplates a ninth. On the basis of rich evidence, he concludes that "all human beings possess not just a single intelligence (often called 'g' for general intelligence). Rather, as a species we human beings are better described as having a set of relatively autonomous intelligences."[16] The seven original intelligences comprise three "object-related" dimensions—spatial, logical-mathematical, and bodily-kinesthetic; two "object-free" dimensions—linguistic and musical; and two cultural dimensions—intrapersonal and interpersonal. The eighth is naturalist, which I would take to be object-related, although it might be considered cultural in that it focuses particularly on relations with animals.

IQ tests usually measure spatial and logical-mathematical intelligences. Artificial intelligence is primarily logical-mathematical.

Intelligent Machines?

Cellary reviews the imminent global information society in terms of the preceding industrial and agrarian societies. We can extend this approach by looking at the different societies in terms of the intelligences most significant to them:

• The agrarian society exploits naturalist intelligence and concentrates on the production of food by workers using their bodily-kinesthetic intelligence. The adoption of agricultural machinery greatly diminished the role of agrarian workers.

• The industrial society exploits spatial intelligence and concentrates on the production of physical artifacts by workers using their bodily-kinesthetic intelligence. The adoption of digitally controlled machinery greatly diminished the role of industrial workers.

• The information society exploits logical-mathematical intelligence and concentrates on the production of representational artifacts by clerical and other office workers using their bodily-kinesthetic intelligence. The adoption of digital computers and telecommunications has already diminished the role of information workers.

These generalizations display a pattern in which successive reformations of society change the role that many of its members play within it. These reformations hinge on the increasing importance of the artifacts that new technology enables the new society to produce.

Two kinds of representational artifacts characterize the information society: those for sale as goods and those used in the production of goods. This is why the commercial world so eagerly seeks and defends copyright and patent monopolies in our information age.

Thus, all the most significant intelligences in the pageant of societies are of the object-related kind. When, in one society, many workers need to use such intelligences, in the next society machinery and technology hugely amplify the object-related capabilities of such workers. For example, it once took hundreds of agrarian workers to do by hand what one driver can do now with a tractor and harvester. Likewise, it once took hundreds of industrial workers to machine the engine block castings that one machine supervised by two or three people can now do. Today, machines built with credit card, barcode, and related technologies have already taken over many of the information workers' tasks.

Although it's appropriate to use machines in this way simply because they're more effective, this doesn't make the machines intelligent. Cellary disagrees, defining human intelligence "as the ability to use accrued knowledge to make correct decisions." This leads him to the following observations regarding the information society: "Computers deprived humans of their monopoly on intelligence. Although they can only capture a fraction of their programmers' real intelligence, computers make correct decisions based on the knowledge encapsulated in the programs they run."

I contend that computers don't make decisions, they compute results by deterministic logical-mathematical means. Deep Blue could play chess better than almost everyone, but it didn't make decisions, it computed moves. Granted, this is only a technical point, but Colwell makes a more fundamental point about logical decisions, computer-aided or otherwise: "Do not apply your outstanding logic deduction talents to a problem involving other people and expect to be thanked for it. Personal relationships are in a special category in which your hard-won engineering skills are a severe liability."

Social Machines?

We benefit from applying our object-related intelligences. Machines can carry out many object-related tasks much better than we can, but that doesn't make the machines intelligent.

What about the other intelligences that characterize humans? The two object-free intelligences, linguistic and musical, are especially interesting because they focus on representations—as does digital technology. The success of digital speech recognition and digital music might suggest that computers have object-free intelligences. But the roles of humans and machines in these areas differ markedly. People use language and music to communicate their beliefs, ideas, and emotions; machines can't communicate beliefs, ideas, or emotions because they don't have any. They have only digital representations, that is, data.

The two cultural dimensions, intrapersonal and interpersonal, lie at the heart of human intelligence because they play the most important role in our being effective members of society and interacting beneficially with other people. Where in this picture does Kismet, the sociable robot, fit?

Kismet consists of a head covered by something that looks a bit like a face. A computer can move the face's features to make "eye contact" and display a variety of emotions, its developers claim. Yet Kismet can't have emotions, so its display is mere mimicry. This is not to say that such robots might not be useful to us. Robotic pets of various kinds are already popular, and social mimicry can be highly effective. For example, during artificial intelligence's early days, a program called Eliza became popular. A Teletype terminal served as Eliza's interface, and the program appeared to engage in conversation by giving simple greetings and asking extremely simple questions, based on keywords selected from what the user typed in. Back then, some people found "talking" to Eliza a compelling experience.

Yet decades later, machines still have far to go before they truly can interact with people intelligently. Our intelligence reflects our cultural and social experiences and the events that shape our daily lives. Machines belong to people and don't have lives. Maybe in a century or two we will craft Asimov-style androids that truly deserve the adjective *intelligent*. But why would we want them?

Whether the computing profession is ill-informed about *natural intelligence* or not, there are good arguments for dropping the term *artificial intelligence* as a name for the nifty programming field. *The Oxford English Dictionary* defines *algorist* as a descriptor for a nifty programmer, but deems the word obsolete.

Here, then, we have a word ripe for reanimation. The derived term, *algoristics*, would make a highly suitable replacement for *artificial intelligence*, being more correct historically than the corrupt *algorithmics*.

Placing this renamed field alongside statistics and logistics, as a branch of mathematics, would benefit the computing profession greatly. Given that algoristic techniques are highly mathematical and require a much greater degree of mathematical knowledge than ordinary programming, they should be taught and studied primarily by mathematicians.

Further, a detailed knowledge of algoristics offers no particular benefit to the computing profession at large: the advanced and intricate algorithms professional algorists will discover could easily be coded into software as calls to library subprograms or, in the Java jargon, classes. We should, therefore, bequeath algoristics to the mathematicians and be done with it.

4.6   In Defense of PowerPoint

(2004 July)

Some minor computing issues become major when repeatedly made public. The denigration of PowerPoint is such an issue, one that, like influenza, seems to come in seasonal waves.

The most recent wave started in the US as "PowerPoint Is Evil,"[28] spread to Australia as "Death by Slides,"[10] to the UK as "How Power Point Can Fatally Weaken Your Argument,"[21] and back to the US as "Does PowerPoint Make Us Stupid?"[5] Further, a *Non Sequitur* cartoon this past April 29th showed a fully equipped Environmental Protection Agency squad storming triumphantly into a PowerPoint presentation.

This kind of story is not a joke. Although the authors of such post hoc arguments show occasional appreciation that the user should bear a little of the blame, they convey the overall impression that vile PowerPoint corrupts minds.

Yet it is their argument that's corrupt. PowerPoint is no more responsible for bad presentations than chainsaws are responsible for the clear-felling of oldgrowth forests. Technology is not itself responsible for the uses to which it is put—technology's users must shoulder the blame.

Computing professionals who blame their machinery for their failures set a bad example for computer users already prone to using the computer as a scapegoat. Countering silly arguments about PowerPoint requires a full appreciation of presentation technology and of the uses to which it might be put. PowerPoint is just presentation technology's latest iteration and will eventually be replaced by something else.

History Lesson

Presentation technology first took a *direct* form. In Europe more than two millennia ago, presenters developed mnemonic techniques. For centuries, early books served only as a reference for presentations, the idea of reading silently being considered strange when first introduced.

Later, chalk and blackboards served as standard equipment in classrooms, with fancy blackboards being used in lecture rooms to record up to an hour or two of lecturing. Then came felt-tip or marker pens, flip charts, and the whiteboard.

The first machine I remember being used for *indirect* presentation, apart from the movie projector, was the *epidiascope*, a rather cumbersome machine that projected by reflected light.   The development of robust transparent foolscap sheets made the overhead projector popular, although it could also be used with transparent scrolls.   Presenters also occasionally used 35-mm photographic slides, particularly at conferences, but the projectors needed an operator and thus were rather "accident prone."

In the early 1970s, the availability of television sets brought computers into use for presentations. The first such machine I used—the 5100, IBM's second-generation personal computer—had a video socket at the back for use in connecting it by coaxial cable to a classroom TV. Later versions of the PC required more complex connections to display the panels that replaced the traditional transparencies sitting atop the overhead projector.   Nowadays, PCs usually are connected to more powerful machines that double as video projectors.

As technology has advanced and the market expanded, developers have crafted a great variety of software. Early on, I found that I could easily use a debug script for DOS to place text anywhere I wanted on the screen, and I used batch files to put together and control presentations overall. I only switched to PowerPoint, which I found very difficult to make do what I wanted, when projectors could no longer be relied on to properly project 40-column DOS screens.

Uses

Although presentations take many forms, they all combine three independent motivations, much as hues can be depicted as located within a color triangle according to their three basic components. Presentations can be used to

- convey information,
- collect information, and
- persuade an audience.

Currently, presenters most neglect the persuasive aspect, yet in olden times, knowledge of rhetorical principles was considered one of a classical education's more important benefits. The persuasive aspect is also the most significant for professionals, who must use facts and reasoning to help their clients and audiences make good decisions.

Informing

Education at all levels focuses in part on getting facts and ideas across to people. The professional issue involves determining what combination of technology and technique will do this best. Some teachers see PowerPoint as a splendid tool to help them convey ideas. Others prefer to use browser-driven HTML.

With the digital technology now available, we must ask if face-to-face presentation offers the best way to inform students. In the classroom at least, students learn better by doing than by merely listening or reading. I still remember a time early in my schooling when I spent hours and hours writing answers to sums on a slate. Thanks to this instruction, I can still sometimes astonish young shop assistants by giving them the correct sum long before their cash register tells them what the total is.

Our digital technology would be better used in the classroom by administering drill and practice as a foundation for literacy and numeracy so that teachers can concentrate on the more important job of inculcating and encouraging social capability, which they must do personally. Using computer-based academic gaming to create social situations could greatly help them in accomplishing this task.

But none of this involves PowerPoint. PowerPoint does, however, reign supreme at conferences—although conference presenters who merely recapitulate the contents of their paper place themselves in danger of putting their audience to sleep, particularly straight after lunch. A more effective approach uses the presentation to persuade the majority of the audience to actually read the paper, then devotes the question time to those few who have *already* read it. All of which puts conference presentations much more in the third class· persuasion.

Gathering data

Presentations are given in person—which means a successful presentation must be interactive. A good presenter will maintain eye contact and will, even in the absence of questions from his listeners, pick up their reactions and modify the presentation accordingly. A canned presentation, however, is hard to modify, whatever the software used. The more intricate the data, the harder the modification.

Many computing professionals focus on data gathering, which can often be done most effectively by taking a group of key informants away from their day-to-day activities to quiz them. These sessions need skilled management. The lead computing professional will typically start off with a presentation that gradually merges into a controlled group discussion. PowerPoint would be inappropriate here.

Although many professionals now prefer using electronic whiteboards in brainstorming and similar activities, I find it difficult to believe that the traditional marker pen and flip chart approach wouldn't be better. The atmosphere in a room with scribbled flip charts hung up around the walls, with new charts being added, old ones being revised and re-sorted, and people moving around and discussing them, can be exhilarating and highly productive.

Persuading

The most important events in a computing professional's career involve the formal presentations given to persuade clients to accept a proposal or the results of work done. Here PowerPoint comes into its own.

Although some data must be shown, the focus stays on the presenter, not the PowerPoint slides. The slides should be as simple and undistracting as possible. Presenters need two kinds of slides for persuasive presentations: bullet-point slides and data slides.

Long ago, I used my DOS batch files with one overhead projector for the bullet points and used transparencies on another overhead projector for the data slides, with a screen for each. This proved more effective than would using PowerPoint on a single projector today.

Data slides must be simplified so that their meaning becomes apparent only as the presenter explains them. Too much detail usually distracts audience members from the presenter and annoys them with difficult-to-read fine print. If presenters plan to show a lot of fancy graphics, they would probably be safer and better off simply showing them all from a videotape or DVD.

Bullet points—PowerPoint's most vilified aspect—are the most misunderstood of presentation techniques. As far as the audience is concerned, bullet points only serve to remind them of the presentation's general context. As far as the presenter is concerned, bullet points replace the mnemonic techniques handed down from the Greeks and the more recent prompt cards hidden in the hand of a formal debater.

Bullet-point slides should be as simple as possible, especially in content. This simplicity provides two important benefits: it lessens the distraction to the audience and supports spontaneity in the presenter—which is even more important than maintaining eye contact. Simple text lets presenters more easily lengthen or shorten the presentation to fit the time allowed, and it also lets them use larger letters.

Spontaneity can be achieved by rehearsing what might be said in respect to each bullet point so that when the point turns up in the presentation, the audience will see that the presenter is actively choosing what to say. The only thing that makes a worse impression on an audience than reciting from memory is reading from the screen—especially because the audience can read the text faster silently than the presenter can read it aloud. If a presenter must put up a long quotation, it should be a data slide that's easy for the audience to read.

A sans serif font is more legible on-screen than a serif one. I also suggest white letters on a black background.

For a computing professional, being able to give a good presentation is essential. Professional training should thus include instruction and practice in making presentations of all kinds, with the objective not so much to constrain the budding professional to any particular set of rules as to emphasize the importance of skill in presentations and purposeful thought in preparing for them.

Students should be trained in determining whether presentations are appropriate in different professional situations and in designing different kinds of presentations for different circumstances. In many situations, simple face-to-face discussions offer the best approach.

Presentations raise a much broader issue for all computing professionals, however. All too often, commentators and authors outside the profession— and sadly some within—take an irrational stand on digital technology, blaming it for all kinds of social and economic ills. The condemnation of PowerPoint is only an obvious example. We must be sensitive to errors of this kind in ourselves and loud in counteracting public errors of this kind in others.

4.7 Notions

The notions are given here partly as a rough summary, but more particularly as topics and issues for students to study and debate. They are in the sequence of their *key word* or *phrase*. The page number to the right of each notion points to its context.

1. The computing profession is preferentially connected
   to any *activity* in which digital technology plays a prominent role 167

2. By the time the PC binge began, computing people
   in the business and government worlds saw themselves
   as *answerable* only to upper management's needs 161

3. Behind every *argument* somewhere sits an axiom, a dogma 169

4. *Artificial intelligence* is primarily logical-mathematical 172

5. People use language and music to communicate their *beliefs*,
   ideas, and emotions; machines can't communicate beliefs,
   ideas, or emotions because they don't have any 174

6. Always double or triple *check* what you actually write
   when you record a recollection or opinion 157

7. Frankenstein systems are a long-standing and widespread
   professional failure that has resulted from *complexity* worship 163

8. Much *computerization* is applied
   to an existing process to make it manageable 164

9. *Computing courses* should include instruction
   in professional ethics and basic management 162

10. A profession has a primary responsibility to the *community*
    that the profession's effect upon it be a benevolent one 153

11. Computers don't make *decisions*,
    they compute results by deterministic logical-mathematical means 174

12. Professional *disagreements*
    must be handled in a professional manner 157

13. The main *duty* of a professional is to put the needs of a client and
    of society at large above those of an employer or of a government 148

14. If a country depends on immigrant professionals then
    there are grave deficiencies in its *education* system and culture 148

15. *Education* at all levels focuses
                              on getting facts and ideas across to people   177
16. To be most *effective*, computing professionals should work
                      as closely as possible with the workers they support   164
17. Professional societies have codes of *ethics* and behavior
                      which require their members to act in the public interest   149
18. People behave or misbehave; machines function or malfunction;
                      such *functioning* does not exhibit intelligence   171
19. As our *global society* becomes more complex and
              more threatened more and more professional people are needed   148
20. *Immigrant professionals* often come from countries
                      where the need for their services is much greater   148
21. The misunderstanding of *intelligence* among computing people
                      springs from the grossly simplified model we use   172
22. Feeling guilty about professional *issues* implies a very personal
                      identification with the profession very close to vanity   158
23. Computers are only *justified* if they help the people
              who use them and the people whose lives are affected by them   165
24. Our intelligence reflects our cultural and social experiences
                      and the events that shape our daily *lives*;
                      machines belong to people and don't have *lives*   175
25. Professionals have an important responsibility
              to inform *management* when potential technical problems or
              opportunities arise, even if their counsel might fall on deaf ears   162
26. Getting technical solutions accepted is a *marketing* task
                      that professionals must take responsibility for   151
27. Artificial intelligence should be renamed algoristics
                      and handed back to the *mathematicians*   175
28. The problem with the term "professional"
                      is that it has two main contrasting *meanings*   166
29. If our profession is to gain the community's respect
                      its *members* must respect one another   157
30. The *opinions* and judgments developed by
              a profession's members distinguish that profession from a trade   157
31. The word *political* is ambiguous   167
32. A distinction must be made between *political activity*
                      on a community's behalf and on a profession's behalf   149
33. For a computing professional,
                      being able to give a good *presentation* is essential   180

4.8   Bibliography

The entries are in order of the first or only author's name. Where no personal author is known, as for popular news items, an indicative name is used. Where there is a page number or two in *italics* at the beginning of the annotation, they point back to where the item was cited. Where some of the annotation is given in quotes it has been taken from the item itself or from some of its publicity.

Because this chapter relates mainly to the computing profession, many of the items here are articles published in *Computer*, which is also where most of the essays in this book first appeared.

1. *APESMA* (2006). *Home Page*, The Association of Professional Engineers, Scientists and Managers, Australia (*p. 150*; apesma.asn.au; "Our mission: To protect and advance the employment, social and economic interests of members").

2. Jane Austen (1813). *Pride and Prejudice.* Harmondsworth, Middlesex: Penguin Books Ltd., ISBN 0 14 043.072 5, 399 pp. (*p. 152*; online in several formats at gutenberg.org/etext/1342).

3. Sara Baase (2003). *A Gift of Fire: Social, legal, and ethical issues for computers and the Internet.* Upper Saddle River, N.J.: Pearson Education, Inc., 2nd edition, ISBN 0-13-008215-5, xvi+464 pp. (a very rich textbook, somewhat specific to the US, focusing on controversies and alternative points of view; Instructor's Manual at www-rohan.sdsu.edu/faculty/giftfire).

4. George W. Bush (2002, Sept.). *The National Security Strategy of the United States of America* (*p. 169*; whitehouse.gov/nsc/nssall.html).

5. David Byrne (2003, Dec. 30). "Does PowerPoint make us stupid?," *CNN* (*p. 176*; "PowerPoint's 'subtle set of biases' indoctrinate users to speak—and think—simply."; cnn.com/2003/ptech/12/30/byrne.powerpoint.ap).

6. Simon Caulkin (2001, Sept. 13). "Make Computers Our Servants, Not Our Masters," *Guardian Weekly*, p. 16 in the Sydney edition (*p. 160*; first appeared in *The Observer* of August 19 as "A bubble we need to burst," online at observer.guardian.co.uk/business/story/0,,538934,.html or text-free at same domain as /print/0,,4241636-102771,.html).

7. Wojciech Cellary (2003, September). "The Profession's Role in the Global Information Society," *Computer*, Vol. 36, No. 9, pp. 124, 122–123 (*p. 171*).

8. Robert N. Charette (2005, Sept.). "Why Software Fails," *IEEE Spectrum*, Vol. 42, No. 9, pp. 36–43 (*p. 150*; "We spend billions of dollars each year

on entirely preventable mistakes"; includes an impressive *Software Hall of Shame*).

9. Robert P. Colwell (2003, August). "Engineering Decisions," *Computer*, Vol. 36, No. 8, pp. 9–11 (*p. 171*).

10. Trevor Cook (2003, Nov. 15). "Death by slides: say it, don't show it," *Financial Review* (*p. 176*; "We risk losing [the] ability to summarise our argument in a single memorable sentence as we become more reliant on the intellectually lazy approach offered by the PowerPoint template."; afr.com/articles/2003/11/14/1068674378566.html).

11. Roger Coombs, Rick Siple and Neville Holmes (2003, February). "Inflation, Greed, and Chattels," *Computer*, Vol. 36, No. 2, pp. 6–7 (*p. 167*; two letters about the essay and a response).

12. Kerstin Dautenhahn (2003, May–June). "Face Time," *American Scientist*, Vol. 91, No. 3, p. 278   (*p. 171*; reviewing *Designing Sociable Robots* by Cynthia L. Breazeal).

13. *Engineers Australia* (2006).   *The Engineering centre*,   The Institution of Engineers, Australia (*p. 150*; www.ieaust.org.au; "the national forum for the advancement of engineering and the professional development of our members").

14. Robin Fincham (ed. 1996). *New Relationships in the Organised Professions: Managers, Professionals and Knowledge Workers*. Aldershot, Hampshire: Avebury Publishing Ltd., ISBN 1 85972 451 5, xii+281 pp. (twelve essays of an interesting variety).

15. Howard Earl Gardner (1983).   *Frames of Mind: The Theory of Multiple Intelligences*. BasicBooks, 1985, ISBN 0-465-02509-9, xx+440 pp.   (*p. 172*; a very persuasive argument for the complexity of intelligence).

16. ———— (2003, April 21).   *Multiple Intelligences After Twenty Years*. Cambridge, Massachusetts: Project Zero, 14 pp.   (*p. 172*; an invited address to the American Educational Research Association mostly looking back, and with very good comments on the relevance of MI theory to education; pz.harvard.edu/Pls/HG_MI_after_20_years.pdf).

17. Michael Grunberg (2001, Jan.). "Letter: Is Holmes Out to Get Us?," *Computer*, Vol. 34, No. 1, pp. 10–11 (*p. 158*; there is also a response).

18. W. Neville Holmes (2001, Feb.). "US Electoral Reform: The Obvious Obligation," *Computer*, Vol. 34, No. 2, pp. 128, 126–127 (*pp. 157, 169*; an essay in *The Profession* left out of this book, it dealt with, among other matters, the problem of the dangling chips).

19. Adrian A. Hopgood (2003, May). "Artificial Intelligence: Hype or Reality?," *Computer*, Vol. 36, No. 5, pp. 24–28 (*p. 171*; "any sense that the field is overhyped probably results from a failure to appreciate the incredible complexity of everyday human behavior").

20. *IEEE* (2006). *IEEE Vision & Mission*. Institute of Electrical and Electronics Engineers, Inc. (*p. 170*; ieee.org/web/aboutus/visionmission.html).

21. John Naughton (2003, Dec. 21). "How PowerPoint can fatally weaken your argument," *The Observer* (*p. 176*; starts from the PowerPoint spoof of Abraham Lincoln's Gettysburg address (at norvig.com/Gettysburg) and later "the assembly of a PowerPoint presentation has become a substitute for thought."; observer.guardian.co.uk/business/story/0,,1110963,.html).

22. Peter Naur (1992). *Computing: A Human Activity*. Reading, Mass.: Addison-Wesley for ACM Press, ISBN 0-201-58069-1, xxvi+630 pp. (an anthology by one of computing's pioneers; many items quite technical, many relevant to this book, particularly 1.2 on data and information).

23. David Lorge Parnas (1996, February). "Why Software Jewels Are Rare," *Computer*, Vol. 29, No. 2, pp. 57–60 (*p. 163*; "a real jewel of a program— written in a consistent style and free of kludges, with simple organized components—is hard to find").

24. Eric S. Raymond (ed. 1996). *The New Hacker's Dictionary*. Cambridge, Massachusetts: The MIT Press, 3rd edition, ISBN 0-262-68092-0, 547 pp. (*p. 157*; also, *The Jargon File* at catb.org/~esr/jargon, though dated 2003 Dec. 29).

25. John Rennie (ed. 2003, September). *Better Brains: How Neuroscience Will Enhance You*. New York, NY: Scientific American, 96 pp. (*p. 171*; a special issue of the *Scientific American* monthly magazine with nine neuroscience articles; sciam.com/issue.cfm?issueDate=Sep-03).

26. Jonathan Schaeffer (2003, May–June). "Tangled Up in Blue," *American Scientist*, Vol. 91, No. 3, pp. 276–278 (*p. 171*; reviewing *Behind Deep Blue* by Feng-hsiung Hsu and *Deep Blue: An Artificial Intelligence Milestone* by Monty Newborn).

27. Herman T. Tavani (2004). *Ethics and Technology: Ethical Issues in an Age of Information and Communication Technology*. Hoboken, N.J.: John Wiley & Sons, Inc., ISBN 0-471-24966-1, xxiv+344 pp. (a useful textbook).

28. Edward R. Tufte (2003, Sept.). "PowerPoint Is Evil," *Wired*, Vol. 11, No. 9 (*p. 176*; the subcaption says it all: "Power Corrupts. PowerPoint Corrupts Absolutely."; wired.com/wired/archive/11.09/ppt2_pr.html).

29. Robert Whelchel (2001, Spr.). "Last Word: The Digerati," *IEEE Technology and Society Magazine*, Vol. 20, No. 1, pp. 43–47 (*p. 158*; "I have nothing against computers and nothing against properly functioning software. What I do oppose is the digerati attitude spawned by excessive pride and arrogance which promotes disregard and disrespect for the rest of us.").

30. Niklaus Wirth (1995, Feb.). "A Plea for Lean Software," *Computer*, Vol. 28, No. 2, pp. 64–68 (*p. 163*; "software's girth has surpassed its functionality, largely because hardware advances make this possible").

Chapter 5

The Potential of Computing

Half a century of experience with digital computers has convinced me that electromagnetic digital technology has enormous untapped potential. And, the way things seem to be going with the world, we'll be needing to tap that potential, and soon, as argued in Chapter 6.

One of the greatest areas of potential, and technically one of the easiest to develop, is in education. That's why Chapter 3 is given over to the topic.

From a somewhat broader point of view, modern digital technology is simply a development of earlier digital technologies—spoken, written and printed, and numeric language—the technologies on which our civilization is based. Therefore a study of the potential of computers should start with its potential to extend these prior technologies.

Speech Technology

Speech is the imposition of language, a digital phenomenon, on sound we produce by our subconscious control of air passing through our throat, nose and mouth, our vocal tract. But vocal tracts vary a lot, and so do people's habits of speech.

Now people's handwriting varied a lot, too, though scriptorium bosses and school teachers brought a degree of uniformity. Movable type and typewriters and the related technology brought a great deal more uniformity, a uniformity that made general literacy a lot easier to achieve. But digital technology has made handwriting much rarer in many parts of the world.

Speech will not go the way of handwriting. It's much more personal, and more temporal. Although speech has been able to be recorded and so made fairly permanent for over a century, such recording, was, until quite recently, not digital. On gramophone records, and later on magnetic wire and tape, voice and music was recorded as an analogy of the sound waves reaching a microphone. The time dimension became a physical line, and the sound pressure became a deflection or a magnetic field variation along that line.

Recent technology has turned to converting the analog sound signal to a sequence of digits and, of course, back again. Witness compact disks, now everywhere referred to as CDs but already passé, and mobile phones. Since such sequences of digits can now be computed very rapidly indeed, many interesting possibilities arise and many have already been realized.

With digitized sound, people can be (unreliably) identified by the sound of their voices, and their voices mimicked; speech signals can be compressed, efficiently transmitted and reconstituted; speech can be transcribed to text and text to speech; machinery can be given spoken commands and can give spoken reports. The benefits to schoolchildren and the handicapped can be enormous.

The computations to do these kinds of things are extremely complex, partly because speech is itself extremely complex. We deal with speech in everyday life without thinking about that complexity, but that is because our brains are much more powerful than any artificial processor yet made.

Thus the programs that process speech more or less successfully today will be continually improved, even into simultaneous translation, heading towards something like Douglas Adams' Babel fish?

Attempting to improve intercultural communication has a long and droll history,[11] but modern digital technology holds some promise, as discussed in "Languages and the Computing Profession" (essay 5.1, p. 197).

Text Technology

While speech is difficult to process with digital computers, written language or text has been easy to process. Written language is essentially digital. When we write with pen or keyboard then we are digitally encoding what we think of ourselves as saying.

Text technology evolved and fluctuated. In the many handwriting systems, various styles and quirks were used from time to time, and then developed or discarded. When movable type was adopted for printing, the handwriting styles and conventions of the time were adopted and gradually developed to suit the new technology.

The evolution of the printing industry up till about fifty years ago is quite fascinating, and relevant to later developments. Around the start of the 20th century, two kinds of hot-metal print line composing technologies came into use and persisted until photocomposing took over in the late 1900s. Both were interestingly digital in their mechanism.

The Linotype machines were self-contained. An operator used a keyboard to select from a magazine the moulds or matrices in sequence for each space or character in the line. The line was then cast within the machine, after which each matrix was returned automatically to its proper place in the magazine. This was possible because each matrix had a set of teeth "digitally" encoding its *sort*.

The Monotype technology separated the line setting into two stages. In the first stage a keyboard was used to encode each sort as a pair of holes in a scroll of paper much like a pianola roll. In the second stage the scroll was used to automatically cast type slugs in sequence for the line. The justification required for each line was encoded at its end, so that, by running the scroll in reverse, the variable spacing within the line could be done automatically.

Linotype was simpler to use, producing directly a single slug for each line, and was favored in North America. Monotype, in producing a separate slug for each sort in a line, was easier to correct and could handle kerning, and was favored in Europe. Kerning is the overlapping of characters to improve their appearance in combination, and for the use of accents or diacritics. This is particularly useful for the letters *f* and *j* and is even essential for Dutch, in which language *ij* is considered a distinct letter and should be printed kerned, as in *ij*s and *IJ*sselmeer, rather than as *ijs* and *IJsselmeer*.

As these technologies came into use for industrial printing, typewriters were being developed for producing individual documents like letters. Some machines, like the Varityper, could proportionally space letters and even change fonts.

While these methods for the large– and small-scale production of books, pamphlets, letters and other documents were being developed and improved, the commercial fields of telegraphy and data processing were, for practical reasons, inhibiting any development of text technology in their areas.

In early commercial data processing only numbers were used, and these were encoded decimally on punched cards with one row for each of the ten decimal digits and a couple of extra rows for controls. In IBM, upper case Latin alphabet encoding was introduced around 1932 by using two holes in each column. Later, the extra characters & . ¤ – $ * / , % # @ were added for commercial use, though these greatly complicated the sorting and collating of card files by machinery.

In the telegraphy of a century and a half ago very simple codes were used, not at all like those used in the prior semaphore networks. Morse code, which was very simple, came swiftly into world-wide for manual telegraphy, and only went out of official use at the end of 1997. Morse was not so all conquering for automatic telegraphy, though it was used with paper tape.

Binary coding was simplest for automatic use, in particular when used with media like punched paper tape. The very significant 5–bit Baudot code was developed by Émile Baudot from coding earlier suggested by Wilhelm Weber and Karl Friedrich Gauss. This code, which became an international standard as CCITT#1, used two special codes, a *letter shift* and a *figure shift*, to provide for the upper case Latin alphabet, the decimal digits, and, as they

became needed, the special characters , .) & : ; " \$? ! / − ′ (
and the control codes: idle, line feed, carrier return, space, and bell. Baudot
code was first used officially on a new line between Paris and Rome in 1877.

Encodings in telegraphy and data processing were fairly stable until the
1950s. When binary media such as ferrite cores and magnetic tape came into
use with computers, the punched card code was mapped onto an informal
standard Binary Coded Decimal Interchange Code. Then IBM, in the mid–'60s,
introduced 8-bit encoding, mapping 6-bit BCDIC onto EBCDIC, providing for
upper and lower case latters of the Latin alphabet. This coding was popular
on mainfame computers.

Similarly, paper tape went from five channel to six and then to seven, and
Baudot code was replaced by a 7-bit code, eventually called ASCII, American
Standard Code for Information Interchange. ASCII was intended for use with
teletypewriters, and was also used by mincomputers, which typically used
Teletypes as their consoles. Then personal computers came to the fore, also
using ASCII, so that it has nowadays largely displaced EBCDIC.

Because computers used very basic text encoding, designed only for quite
primitive textual uses, and because computing technology and technologists
now prevail in the world of text storage and presentation, document design
and production have been very poorly served. Some of the issues are reviewed
in "Toward Decent Text Encoding" (essay 5.2, p.202). This was one of the
earliest essays of this book, but matters have, if anything, worsened since.

One source of difficulty is that candidate encoding systems are directed
solely to solving the storage of text for the world's different languages in one
chaotic mode. This is unfortunate for two reasons. Firstly, text *encoding* is only
part of the deal. Secondly, text is about *writing systems*, not *languages*.

Consider the following points.
• A device such as a keyboard is needed to encode the text in the first place.
• The text needs to be encoded and stored in such a way that processes such
as indexing, searching, sequencing, and marking up can be easily carried out
on it.
• The display of text, whether plain or marked up, by screen or printer needs
to be easily controllable in style and format.
• The text has a great variety, from e-mail messages and blogs to business and
government records to catalogs and books.

The basic issue is that almost all documents use a single writing system,
and require that writing system to be *easily* adaptable to new circumstances,
such as the introduction of foreign words or new symbols, and to the encoding
or transliteration of new languages. The possibilities for encoding the Chinese
writing system, and for encoding alphabetic and syllabic writing systems, in
such fashion are sketched out in the Technical Details appendix, starting on
page 278. The Chinese writing system is only briefly considered, though the

issues treated are very important. The Latin alphabet-based writing system is considered in more detail, and some suggestions are made for how it might be subsumed in a broader encoding scheme, one encompassing all alphabetic and some syllabic writing systems.

Exploiting a standard encoding of this kind for a writing system would need:

- keyboards able to easily take in *any* code in a standard way, even if tailored to a specific language;
- plain text display conventions that show the effect of graphic operations as they are entered;
- mark-up conventions specific to the writing system, and independent of any language;
- composing programs that would handle all the graphic operations of the encoding standard in a consistent way while allowing special combinations to be handled specially.

The development and staged adoption of such code standards would bring huge commercial, social and cultural benefits. This is extremely unlikely to happen unless some politically powerful body like the United Nations brings it about, because the computing industry itself stands to benefit much more in the short-term from the present chaos (see also essay 3.6, p.133) which is so much like the aftermath of the famous incident at the Tower of Babel.

Text Retrieval

Details of how text might be encoded are quite fundamental but somewhat distant from everyday life. More commonplace is what we do with text, and what we do with text is basically cultural.

In everyday life there is a competition between contemplative culture and sensual culture, as discussed in "Digital Technology, Age, and Gaming" (essay 3.2, p.112). With the dominance in the developed world of entertainment, that is, of sensual artefacts like television and videogaming, there is a need to provide more support for contemplative culture (see p.116).

Sensual culture is about images and perceptual immersion. Contemplative culture is about text and contemplative thought.

Digital technology is the basis for video gaming, DVD recording, and, more recently, digital television, all of which immerse their viewers perceptually, or at least try to do so. To achieve more of a balance between the sensual and the contemplative cultures, digital technology needs to be swung more behind text, in particular towards making text more accessible.

The sortemic text encoding suggested in the appendix on *Technical Details* (p.278) would be good support. The ease of transliteration would encourage exchange of ideas between different societies with the same writing system.

At the same time, the code separation of major writing systems would make text translation between the systems easier because it would bring out the contrasts more clearly. A clustering and extension of literary cultures within major writing groups would also support the richer development of contemplative culture. Thus, each cultural group could benefit from having its own World Wide Web, and its own style of browsers and search engines, by having separate Domain Name Server systems operating independently above the Internet Protocol address system and the Internet governance (p.135).

It's quite ridiculous not to have separate Webs for the cultures that use an alphabet and the cultures that use logograms. Maybe the syllabic writing systems need a separate sortemic text encoding system, in which case they would also need their own DNS system, browsers and search engines.

The idea of a browser is a very useful one. Partly, its usefulness depends on the World Wide Web that it "browses" around, and this aspect is explored in another chapter (essay 3.6, p.133). But there are problems other than Web chaos.

There are language problems, even with English. For example, when I Google for *preantepenultimate* I get 386 hits, for *antepenultimate* 44,600 hits, for both 228, for either 45,300, for the shorter without the longer 43,100, for the longer without the shorter 1,500. Very strange, though maybe not a language problem. Nevertheless, the question remains whether a simple request for *antepenultimate* should also return cases of *preantepenultimate*, or for *adequate* cases of *inadequacy*, even if only as an option.

There is a variety of metasearch engines,[5] engines that use ordinary search engines' results, that attempt some form of linguistic analysis, and KartOO[4] shows networks of popular neighboring terms. But these are all superficial structures, and the end result is that of a simple search engine, a list of the "hits" given as a highlighted search word surrounded by some identification and the URL text, "snippets", and links to other versions and to related sites. The Web is vast so the list is sequenced by some form of ranking, a ranking that advertisers seek to exploit with so-called Web spam.

The search engines are really splendid if you're looking for something quite specific, but if you're just browsing then they tend to bewilder. In Google, the hits come in batches of ten, only half of which fit in an ordinary screen window, so you don't get any general feel for what's been found.

For true browsing, a different interface to search engine results is needed, an interface that focuses more on the context of the words of interest and less on identifying the source and nature of the hit. The essay "The KWIC and the Dead" (essay 5.3, p.206), after reviewing some of the history of document indexing, briefly describes such an interface, calling the process *hyperindexing*, though that term has found other uses. This interface extends the KWIC index idea by making words in the contexts hyperlinks to other hyperindexes.

The kind of hyperindex described in the essay displays one line of text for each hit, a line displaying the word of current interest highlighted and aligned centrally. Each line would have a hyperlink, but this would be of only occasional use because mostly the user would be moving from keyword to keyword, imposing conditions, selecting combinations, exploring associations prompted by the rich text on the screen. Orthogonal directions could provide displays of synonyms and prefixed versions of keywords.

The possibilities are many. One possibility of interest is to provide such an interface to individual documents, which would be of great value in reviewing style in ordinary writings, and checking for contradictions in legal documents. Another is to allow two documents to be hyperindexed together, somewhat in the manner originally proposed for Project Xanadu,[21] to allow them to be compared for content and style.

Using Computers

To be able to browse the Web, whether through link lists or hyperindexes, a program is needed. That program determines just what the user can or cannot do with any text that can be brought in. The computer is less than a tool, really a metatool, because it's useless without that program.

The importance of programs and the history of programming, are reviewed above in a subsection of Chapter 2 entitled "The Use of Computers" (p. 45), which leads up to "Computers, Programming, and People" (essay 2.5, p. 69).

What needs to be clearly understood is that however digital technology develops, there will be two ways that computers will be used: *embedded* and *exposed*.

The increasing majority will be embedded, meaning they will be simply components of other machinery, such as mobile telephones, and their users, when the machines aren't completely automatic, will simply be users of that other machinery. Even so, the usability of that machinery will often depend on a user interface provided by a computer.

Exposed programs will be more obvious because they interact with a user, but they will also be more difficult to design and for the same reason. People are much less predictable and uniform than machines.

There have been two approaches to designing interactive programs, that of the *autocrat* and that of the *haut chef*.

The autocrat approach, favoured by government and business, seeks to define all the processes to be carried out and to specify precisely how they are to be carried out. The purpose is to have as many decisions as possible made by the program and to permit as little initiative as possible by the user.

The profit in this approach is expected to come from elimination of labor, firstly by outsourcing but ultimately by complete automation. The problem with this approach is that setting up such a system seems always to cost much more than anticipated, to be much more difficult to maintain and adapt, and almost impossible to replace.

The alternative to this approach is its opposite—to empower the workers to exploit the computer in supporting and improving their work, to provide them with programs that they can modify and amplify if not by themselves then with a minimum of help from application programmers. This possibility and its background are briefly outlined in Blunder 4 (p.61) of the seven given in Chapter 2 (essay 2.3, p.59).

The haut chef approach, favored by the developers of personal computer software, seeks similarly to define all the processes that might be carried out in a general area, but to make them accessible to the user through icons and menus. The purpose is to save the user from having to remember names to key in. The haut chef designs the menu, selects the ingredients, says how they shall be cooked and served, and the user has only to choose.

The profit in the approach is expected to come from its marketability, on the one hand by selling its ease of use and on the other hand by being able to add features willy-nilly so that users can be coerced into buying new versions of the software from time to time.

The problems with this approach and the mind-bending possibilities of its alternative are discussed in "The Case For Perspicuous Programming" (essay 5.4, p.212). Two points about that essay. Firstly, what are referred to there as *batch* programs and *interactive* programs correspond roughly to what are called just above *embedded* programs and *exposed* programs. Secondly, if the essay seems rather grandiose then take note of the month of publication, on the first day of which the essay notionally appeared.

Societal Computers

The Internet—its email, its Web, and all its computers—provides for people to interact commercially and socially. The commercial interaction is between vendor and consumer, unequals in that sense. The social interaction is by and large between equals or near-equals.

The commercial structure of society is hierarchical in the sense that vendors consume the products of their supplier, and digital technology is nowadays essential to that hierarchy.

The social structure of society is also hierarchical in fact, though certain humanistic ideals promote the idea of equality. But even in an fairly equitable society its structure requires separation of responsibilities and delegation of duties. These define social roles, and, while digital computers and networking play an important part in supporting people in different roles, this support is primarily administrative, that is, from the top down.

In a stable society, the hierarchy strives to sustain itself; at least its upper levels do. With digital technology, the ability of the upper levels of society to maintain, even strengthen, their hierarchy is greatly helped because of the ability to transmit rules and regulations down through the hierarchy, and to collect data about conformity to those rules and regulations in the lower levels.

But digital technology is neutral, like all technologies. Any bias comes from the technologists or their employers. The question then arises of how digital technology might be used to close the loop, to allow the lower levels of the social hierarchy to exert some kind of control on the upper levels.

There are many possibilities. Now, *The Oxford English Dictionary* defines *democracy* as "A state or community in which the government is vested in the people as a whole" where *to vest* means "To put, place, or establish ... in full or legal possession ... ," so the most obvious possibility is to use technology to support democracy.

The objective, then, is to find a way to use digital technology to properly effect the vesting of government in the people as a whole. An easy place to start is in the area of "Representative Democracy," and this area is explored in an essay of that name (essay 5.5, p.218).

System Engineering

Perhaps the most unfortunate aspect of digital technology is that using it tends to become an end in itself. The computing profession, and the community at large, often seem to regard digital technology as the magic elixir of the modern age. Indeed the descriptions in this chapter so far could seem to encourage this line of thought.

It is essential to always clearly distinguish between the problem to be solved and the technology most familiar to the solvers. Indeed, problem solvers should not have any fixed ideas about what they are going to solve a problem with before they have found out what the problem actually is.

Professional people solve people's problems. There are certain principles behind the professional solving of problems. To put it very simply, problem solving has three phases:
1. determine what the problem is,
2. design a solution, and
3. implement the solution.

The complications are that the phases both overlap and repeat. Usually the less they overlap and the more they repeat the better the solution.

Overlap is best avoided because, firstly, thinking about the solution too soon muddies thinking about the problem, and secondly, thinking about the implementation too soon conflates the client's problem and the implementor's problem.

Repetition is good because of the importance of checking, and checking the checking, and so on. A short pause for checking now can save hours of backtracking later.

Before the problem can be considered to be determined, the question must be asked "Is this really the problem?" Usually, different people are involved and they see the problem differently since they are people, not machines. An outsider should an advantage in not having preconceptions and allegiances. An outsider will also have to be very careful and skilful in selling a particular problem definition to the people involved.

Before the design can be considered to be completed, the question must be asked "Will this solution really solve the problem?" Sometimes a simulation or prototype of the solution is needed to allow the question to be answered. If the answer is "No!" then the next question is "Why not?" The answer will sometimes be "Because the problem definition is wrong in some way."

Before the solution can be considered successful, the question must be asked "Does this implementation really solve the problem?" This question needs to be asked at various stages of implementation, in particular during testing, and after the implementation has settled into use. If the answer is "No!" at any stage then the solution may have to redesigned, or the problem may even have to be redetermined.

This description should suggest that, at the strategic level, there is little need for expertise in the technology of the implementation. Problem solving is much more a management task than a technological task. That's why it's important to distinguish between trades and professions, as discussed above in "Jobs, Trades, Skills, and the Profession" (essay 3.5, p. 128).

For computing and other professionals, the broad and strategic field of problem solving is often called *system engineering*, and is not only useful in solving technological problems, as is illustrated in the essay "Olympic Games Reform" (essay 5.6, p. 223).

5.1 Languages and the Computing Profession

(2004 March)

Around Christmas, feeling the need for some light technical reading and having long been interested in languages, I turned to a story in *Computer's* Technology News department: "Statistical Language Approach Translates into Success."[28] Toward the end of the story, the following paragraph startled me:

> Nonetheless, the grammatical systems of some languages are difficult to analyze statistically. For example, Chinese uses pictographs, and thus is harder to analyze than languages with grammatical signifiers such as spaces between words.

First, the Chinese writing system uses relatively few pictographs, and those few are highly abstracted. The Chinese writing system uses logographs— conventional representations of words or morphemes. Characters of the most common kind have two parts, one suggesting the general area of meaning, the other pronunciation.

Second, most Chinese characters are words in themselves, so the space between two characters is a space between words. True, many words in modern Chinese need two and sometimes more characters, but these are compounds, much like English words such as *password, output,* and *software*.

Third, Chinese does have grammatical signifiers. Pointing a browser equipped to show Chinese characters at a URL such as ausdaily.net.au will immediately show a wealth of what are plainly punctuation marks [provided your browser can show the characters properly].

Fourth, Chinese is an isolating language with invariant words. This should make it very easy to analyze statistically. English is full of prefixes and suffixes—the word *prefixes* itself has one of each—which leads to more difficult statistics.

I do not mean these observations to disparage the journalist who wrote the story—but they do suggest that some computing professionals may know less than they should about language.

Language Analysis

The news story contrasted two approaches to machine translation.

> Knowledge-based systems rely on programmers to enter various languages' vocabulary and syntax information into databases. The programmers then write lists of rules that describe the possible relationships between a language's parts of speech.
>
> Rather than using the knowledge-based system's direct word-by-word translation techniques, statistical approaches translate documents by statistically analyzing entire phrases and, over time, 'learning' how various languages work.

The superficial difference seems to be that one technique translates word by word, the other phrase by phrase. But what one language deems to be words another deems to be phrases—agglutinative languages mildly so and synthetic languages drastically so—compared to relatively uninflected languages like English. Also, the components of a phrase can be contiguous in one language and dispersed in another—as in the case of German versus English as Samuel Langhorne Clemens described?[26]

The underlying difference seems to be that the knowledge-based systems' data for each language comes from grammarians, while the statistical systems' data comes from a mechanical comparison of corresponding documents, the one a professional translation of the other.

Language Translation

Looking at translation generally, the problem with the statistical approach is that it requires two translation programs for every pair of languages: one going each way. Ab initio, the same is true of the grammatical approach.

The number of different languages is such that complete coverage requires numerous programs—101 languages would require 10,100 translation programs. Daunting when we consider the thousands of different languages still in popular use.

The knowledge-based or grammatical approach provides a way around this. If all translations use a single intermediate language, adding an extra language to the repertoire would require only two extra translation programs.

The news story does describe a similar approach, a *transfer system*, but this uses a lingua franca as the intermediate language, which in part is probably why it has been found unsatisfactory. The other unsatisfactory aspect is commercial—the extra stage when the commercial enterprise seeks merely to translate between two written languages adds extra complexity and execution time.

To cope with the variety of and within natural languages, a completely unnatural language must serve as the intermediary. Designing this intermediate language would be a huge and difficult task, but it would reap equally huge benefits.

Without this approach to machine translation, it would be difficult and expensive to cater for minor languages, to make incremental improvements as individual languages change or become better understood, and to add parameters that allow selection of styles, periods, regionalities, and other variations. When the translation adds conversion between speech and text at either end, adopting the intermediary approach will become more important, if not essential.

Intermediate Language

The intermediate language must be like a semipermeable membrane that lets the meaning pass through freely while blocking idiosyncrasies. Although designing and managing the intermediary would be a nearly overwhelming task, certain necessary characteristics suggest a starting point.

• *Specificity.* Every primary meaning must have only one code, and every primary code must have only one meaning. The difficulty here is deciding which meanings are primary.

• *Precision.* A rich range of qualifying codes must derive secondary meanings from primary meanings and assign roles to meanings within their context.

• *Regularity.* The rules for combining and ordering codes, and for systematic codes such as those for colors, must be free from exceptions and variations.

• *Literality.* The intermediate language must exclude idioms, clichés, hackneyed phrases, puns, and the like, although punctuational codes could be used to mark their presence.

• *Neutrality.* Proper names, most technical terms, monocultural words, explicit words such as *inkjet* when used as shown here, and possibly many other classes of words must pass through the intermediate language without change other than, when needed, transliteration.

My use of the term "code" in these suggested characteristics, rather than *morpheme* or *word*, is deliberate. Designing the intermediate language to be spoken as words and thus to serve as an auxiliary language would be a mistake.

First, designing the intermediate language for general auxiliary use would unnecessarily and possibly severely impair its function as an intermediary. Second, a global auxiliary language's desirable properties differ markedly from those needed for an intermediary in translation, as the auxiliary language Esperanto's failure in the intermediary role demonstrates.

Indeed, given the possibility of general machine translation, it is possible to make an argument against the very idea of a global auxiliary language. Natural languages—the essence of individual cultures—are disappearing much faster than they are appearing. Global acceptance of an auxiliary language would foster such disappearances. Versatile machine translation, particularly when speech-to-speech translation becomes practical, would lessen the threat to minor languages.

Work To Be Done

Defining the intermediate language requires developing and verifying its vocabulary and grammar as suitable for mediating translation between all classes and kinds of natural language.

The *vocabulary*—the semantic structure, specifically the semes and their relationships—will in effect provide a universal semantic taxonomy.   The semes would be of many different kinds, both abstract and concrete. A major challenge will be deciding which meanings are distinct and universal enough to warrant their own seme and where to place them in the seme hierarchy. The key professionals doing such work will be philosophers and semanticists.

The rules for associating and separating semes and seme clusters, the *grammar*, would encompass the work of punctuation, although much of the meaning found in natural-language punctuation could be coded in the intermediate language's semes, unless implied by the language's grammar. The intermediary grammar might need to designate some semes—for example, some of the two dozen or so meanings given for the term "the" in *The Oxford English Dictionary*—as required to be inferred if they are not present in the source language. The key professionals in this work will be translators, interpreters, and linguists.

When involved in a project to develop an intermediate language, these two groups of professionals will need to work closely together, as grammar and vocabulary are closely interdependent. In this case, both must cope with the translation of many hundreds of wildly different languages.

What role would computing professionals play in such a team? Given the project's purpose—to make general machine translation possible—computing professionals would be of vital importance, but in a supporting role. Using different approaches to evaluate the intermediate language and its use for a variety of languages would require a succession of translation programs.

Those involved in this project will need to consider how to keep Web pages in both their original language and the intermediary so that browsers could, if necessary, translate the page easily into any user's preferred language. Allied to this requirement would be consideration of how to index the intermediary text so that all of the Web's content would be available to searchers. Indeed, the qualities of an intermediate language could make search engines much more effective.

Translation of SMS messages and email should also be studied; ultimately, use of the intermediate language in telephones for speech translation should become possible. Users would select the natural language to use on their phone. The translation might then be through text, staged with speech-to-text conversion, or the processor might convert speech directly to or from the intermediate language. In any case, intermediary codes would be transmitted between users' phones and thus the language of one user would be independent of another user's.

General use of such speech translation would trail text translation by a long way, but even general text translation would promote global cooperation, providing an excellent return on investment in the project.

I began this essay when reports from the UN Forum on the Digital Divide in Geneva first became public. The failure of this beanfeast was both predictable (essay 6.2, p. 250), and a scandalous waste of money given the number of poor in the world dying daily of hunger or cheaply curable illnesses.

Strategically, a much better way to use digital technology to help the poor and counter global inequity and its symptomatic digital divide would be for the UN to take responsibility for the development and use of a global intermediate translation language. International support would be essential, both to make swift development possible and, more importantly, to protect the work from intellectual-property predators.

Success would make truly global use of the Internet possible. Ultimately, with translation and speech-to-text conversion built into telephones, UN and other aid workers could talk to the economically disadvantaged without human interpreters.

However, an intermediate language project such as this could not be contemplated without the strong and active support of various professional bodies, particularly those from the fields of computing, philosophy, and language. Computing professionals should work with others to get public attention for this project and ensure that the needed professional support is made available.

5.2   Toward Decent Text Encoding

(1998 August)

Text is composed of characters; we get different kinds of text from different kinds of characters. So character sets are very important. And if there are contending views about whether we are well-served by our character-set standards, these views should be exposed and discussed.

It's strange that the computing industry has for so long stuck to poor and impoverished character sets for text encoding. Now, without much public discussion or dispute, the computing industry seems to be moving to an equally poor but contrastingly obese character set called Unicode.

Traditional Character Sets

The development of writing technology—and, relatively recently, of print technology—has been more a story of the gradual development of standards than a story of the development of machinery. The widespread acceptance of the roman and italic forms of the Latin alphabet—which have become the dominant alphabetic forms in countries such as Germany and Turkey only within living memory—has added an important interlingual aspect to the use of character sets and to international use of print technology.

The early development of automatic data processing mainly in English-speaking countries led to English versions of the Latin alphabet being used in associated machinery, particularly in printers. In the 1950s, the typical line printer sported 26 letters (uppercase roman), 10 decimal digits, and a few special characters added mainly for commercial use. If Fortran programmers wanted to see their additions normally then they had to order their machines with a special feature to replace the ampersands with + signs. And they were forced to use the asterisk as a multiplication symbol.

In the 1960s, two expanded character sets came into wide use. When IBM introduced the 8–bit System/360 computers, it introduced an 8–bit character set called EBCDIC (Extended Binary Coded Decimal Interchange Code) to go with it. A particular desire for compatibility with prior punched-card codings gave a quite bizarre structure to this de facto standard![18]

At the same time, a formal effort resulted in a 7–bit standard character set called ASCII (American Standard Code for Information Interchange), which was particularly designed for the telegraphy of the time.

EBCDIC and ASCII

Both EBCDIC and ASCII were put together with a great deal of thoughtful effort and are still widely used. They included upper- and lowercase Latin alphabets, the 10 decimal digits, a slightly enhanced but still inadequate set of special characters, and a set of noncharacters intended to be used for controlling recording machinery in various ways.

Having two character sets in concurrent widespread use has been problem enough, but there have been many other problems. Both EBCDIC and ASCII provided users with a + symbol as standard, but (with breathtaking arrogance) the developers of both sets refused to provide the traditional multiplication and division symbols. The control characters not only proved inadequate but were used inconsistently. For example, both Unix and IBM PC operating systems have traditionally used the ASCII character set, but in encoding text Unix has used a single line feed control character to separate lines of text, while IBM PCs have used a carrier return/line feed control character pair.

Both character sets became grossly distorted when they were adapted to encoding text in languages other than English. ASCII had a problem anyway in being a 7–bit coding typically running on 8–bit machinery, which led to peculiar and inconsistent uses of the eighth bit. But the way in which versions of ASCII were accreted for new languages was grotesque in the extreme.

Unicode Character Set

Little wonder, therefore, that the computing industry should wish to replace EBCDIC and ASCII with a new improved character set called Unicode, particularly when computing has become so international. What is amazing is that it has taken this long. What is disappointing, if not tragic, is that the replacement is so unsuitable for text encoding.

There has been relatively little popular discussion of Unicode. A recent exception is the complementary proposal by Muhammad Mudawwar [called Multicode[20]]. Unicode seems to be trying to provide a single character set to represent documents in any language or writing system or mixture thereof.

A large part of the difficulty with Unicode, though, is that it is most suitable for—even aimed at—presenting text, not for encoding it. But presentation of text is one technology, while the encoding, storage, and transmission of text is quite another.

Unicode is intended primarily to allow the computing and telecommunications industry to get by with only one character set for the entire world[27] One result is that everyone has to use 16 bits for every character. Surely it would be sadistic to suggest that the great redundancy involved in a 16–bit character set would allow the effective use of data compression techniques. Or to suggest that everyone's equipment should support all the world's writing systems, past and present, at the same time. But with Unicode it's either that or back to proliferating versions.

Mudawwar's Multicode aims to counter the 16–bit drawback and several others that he describes in some detail. But Multicode is essentially a compromise; Mudawwar's article emphasizes in its very last sentence that "both approaches can coexist—Multicode for programming ease and Unicode to support unified fonts." But in international communication, the necessary variety of Multicodes would be much more complex than the single Unicode.

Encoding Text

Most traffic in text is raw text—messages, identifiers, business records—and the vast majority of this traffic is monolingual. Indeed, the vast majority of presented documents are also monolingual. Much of this monolingual text needs only an 8–bit encoding system to be encoded as plain text.

Mudawwar's Multicode scheme recognizes this and therefore provides for a separate character set for every "official language."[10] Most of these languages can be accommodated within an 8–bit coding scheme. In this case Multicode provides for great data compression, but in any case it separates languages from one another, which is no longer the way of the world, if it ever was.

There are two aspects of language interchange. First, languages borrow words and phrases from one another so that, for example, English uses French and German words and takes their diacritical marks with them. Readers are often better served when the markings are kept as they are, showing how words like "café," "cliché" and "façade" should be pronounced.

Second, in this international society it is important to be able to name people and organizations in their own language. Indeed, to many cultures it is insulting not to use their names properly. In Western text, Chinese names are stripped of the tone marks provided in their Pīnyīn spelling system, which would be equivalent to English usage stripping French or German names of all their vowels. Most unfriendly behavior.

The world is divided into writing system zones. For languages that use the same writing system—the system based on the Latin alphabet, for example—a good text-encoding standard would completely support the exchange of names. I should be able to read all Swedish names in plain-text e-mail messages, but at present many are garbled. On the other hand, writing system cultural zones expect to transliterate words and names from other zones, which seems to be a quite amenable approach, provided it can be done well.

Necessary Standards

For text encoding, the world needs a standard for each writing system that suits each and every language using that system. These standards should be in accord with each other so that basic processing—such as distinguishing letters from punctuation and numerals from words—is the same for each system and also so that text using one writing system can be practically encoded or viewed on equipment designed for another writing system.

Text encoded by these systems could be marked up for presentation within the writing system that encodes it. Using markup would surely provide a logical, effective, and efficient separation of function and would make it easy to combine text from different writing systems.

Most of the world's writing systems could probably be encoded using an 8–bit scheme. The one exception is the traditional Chinese writing system, which encompasses thousands of distinct characters. But it could be argued that this rich and time-honored character system is more properly regarded as a reading system because it is more efficient for reading than the various alphabetic systems but it is much less effective for writing/encoding.

There is evidence that languages that use Chinese characters could be encoded under an 8–bit scheme. For example, two articles in *Computer*'s last special issue on such matters[9] proposed encoding the Chinese official spoken language, Pūtōnghuà, using its Pīnyīn alphabetic system. As recently as last year, an 8–bit encoding system has been introduced in South Korea in which the Korean alphabet is used to encode the Chinese characters they use. This system is being adopted in many circles.

There is some reason to hope that a family of 8–bit text encoding standards could be designed to suit all the world's writing systems, a family that would provide for cheap, efficient, and effective machinery for encoding, storing, and transmitting the world's text. The most important gain from adopting text encoding standards for each writing system (concordant between writing systems) is that simple and effective equipment, and text processing software such as plaintext editors, e-mailers, and Internet search engines, could be largely independent of the language within any writing system.

Also, text could be compatibly handled across writing systems by such software even if the equipment wouldn't display or print the text "correctly." Words would still look like words, numerals like numerals, and punctuation like punctuation.

5.3   The KWIC and the Dead:
A Lesson in Computing History

(2001 January)

A culture can be defined as "the sum total of ways of living built up by a group of human beings, which is transmitted from one generation to another" (*The Macquarie Dictionary*). In this sense, a profession is a culture, or at least a subculture, defined by its purpose and responsibilities. To fulfill that purpose better, the profession should cultivate its history.

The computing profession's purpose is to promote, for the greater community's benefit, the use of formal representations of facts or ideas and of machines and processes for the storage and transformation of such representations. Thus, our profession's history originated in the culture of the printers and scribes who promoted the use of the written languages from which our present binary representations developed.

George Santayana wrote that those who cannot remember the past are condemned to repeat it. We can derive two warnings from his observation. First, what we think to be innovations will often be mere repetitions. Second, our profession can develop faster and better through cumulative innovation, building on its past instead of ignoring it.

Repetitive Innovation

About six months ago, British Telecom discovered it had previously been granted worldwide patents with claims that could be considered to cover the use of hyperlinks. Of these, BT cited US patent 4,873,662—which grants a monopoly until 2006—to seek license fees from Internet service providers in the US.

Hyperlinks, included in the body of electromagnetically encoded documents, refer to other electromagnetically encoded documents. Many commentators observed publicly that hyperlinks very closely resemble the endnotes and footnotes long used by scholars. BT's ambitions seem to have softly and suddenly vanished away thanks to this publicity.

Yet even if we disagree that the electromagnetic encoding of index markings follows obviously from the tradition of footnotes and endnotes, or from the allied tradition of embedded scholastic citation, more recent history gives a more specific precedent.

In his very famous article, "As We May Think," Vannevar Bush described in some detail a conceptual machine called the *memex*.[6] According to Bush, an essential feature of the memex, a personal library machine, was that it could perform "associative indexing, the basic idea of which is a provision whereby any item may be caused at will to select immediately and automatically another."

The memex plainly foreshadowed BT's patent, which presumably would not have been granted if the "inventor" or patent examiner had read Bush's article. That article was neither obscurely published nor ignored. It inspired many developments, such as Theodor Nelson's early Project Xanadu,[21] which in turn inspired Tim Berners-Lee's World Wide Web.

Cumulative Innovation

We cannot use the hyperlinks in memex documents, or in the items stored on the Web, without a mechanism for moving from item to item along a trail of links, and they are of only limited use without a means of sharing trails and their items.

Bush envisaged making microfilm updateable in situ through dry photography, which would allow not only the insertion of links at will, but also of marginal notes and comments. The memex would encode each item with an identifier that photoelectric cells could swiftly locate. Two items to be linked would be brought up in separate "viewing positions"—1945's version of Windows. The user could then cross-copy the links from the item identifiers and later use the memex to track along either link between the items. Links became visible for selection as the name of a trail, allowing an item to have more than one link. Following a memex trail strongly resembled the way browser software jumps from URL to URL today.

Although much cruder, Bush's item and trail sharing—in which the user "sets a reproducer in action, photographs the whole trail out, and passes it to his friend for insertion in his own memex, there to be linked into the more general trail"—clearly anticipated the Internet hypertext transfer protocol's support for browser software using URLs.

The misnamed browser

Thus, browsers do with modern techniques what Bush's memex was to have done with microforms. But browsers, however useful, are poorly named: they do not allow true free-association browsing, only page display and link-and-trail tracking.

A drawback to such trail following is that it strictly confines users to existing trails. Using a browser is like shuttling from clearing to clearing in a forest. At any clearing you can only choose from established paths marked by signposts that bear cryptically brief descriptions. Chancing upon an interesting trail remains difficult. Although Bush foresaw "a new profession of trailblazers," a memex user had to rely on a "code book" to find a trail by name.

Link trails hold the Web together. Browsers allow us to wander along them, viewing items as we go. But the Web's trails remain weaker than the trails Bush envisioned. Formed from inherently one-way links, the Web's trails are unlabeled, typically short and highly branched, often very localized, and usually adventitious and unreliable.

Searching for Xanadu

Limitations like these motivate the continuation of Project Xanadu. Started in 1960, Xanadu and various subsequent "virtual library" projects seek to follow Bush's lead.. Such projects strive to build a disciplined nook in the Web, even though most Web material remains woefully undisciplined.

Search engines help us pluck trails from among the Web's general chaos. Playing the role of Bush's code book, search engines usually provide three services: index building, hierarchical classification, and index querying. Commercial search engines index client organization Web sites, while sites such as Yahoo offer general Web users an index to the entire Web—an ever more ambitious task. By the end of last year, for example, the Google Web site claimed to have indexed 1.3 billion Web pages.

These information retrieval services have evolved from decades-old innovations. The index building programs, now often called Web crawlers, build inverted files, pioneered largely by Gerard Salton and first used for text retrieval in the 1960s [but see p. 282]. Hans Peter Luhn introduced automatic hierarchical classification, while index inquiry sprang from Luhn's work on selective dissemination of information, started in the 1950s.

Modern search engines—the products of cumulative innovation—have applied techniques from the past 40 years to Web-based text. As such, these engines suffer from inherent limitations: Those who use their results can either work their way through a hierarchical tree of topics with link lists at the end of branches or can submit search requests that return a list of links. Link lists serve many purposes well, but generally cannot be used for deep research or even to satisfy everyday curiosity. Further, users cannot browse searched text itself, unless they download and display the entire Web page that contains the text.

Historical Innovation

Many researchers still frequent traditional libraries because browsing works best when it takes you down trails you didn't expect or leads to trails others might never have found. Such trails come into being when unanticipated associations occur among ideas through the act of browsing itself.

Query results from search engines provide a limited kind of text browsing, somewhat like using a book index or traditional concordance. In such an index, keywords appear in lexical sequence with a page number or other locator. Figure 1 shows the style of a traditional concordance, which provides only a page and item number for each entry.

> profess   231:26, 389:16
> professes   276:8
> profession   25:14, 99:33, 154:14,
>   181:24, 304:40, 389:36, 437:5,
>   480:29, 489:23
> professionally   178:3
> professions   489:20, 546:40

*Figure 1. Sample index in traditional concordance format,
showing only page and item numbers for each word indexed.*

Lists such as this one lack local context, a shortcoming that has been overcome by expanding the concordance, as shown in Figure 2, drawn from the index of *The Oxford Dictionary of Quotations*.[23] Such indexes resemble the link result list of a Web search query and serve many purposes. They work even better with more context than shown here.

In his work on automatic indexing by computer in the 1950s and later, Luhn proposed two kinds of indexes: keyword out of context (KWOC), which resembled Figure 2's example but gave more context, and keyword in context (KWIC), which provided a rearrangement of KWOC.

The KWIC index, also known as the permuted title index when used for indexing article titles, proved the more enduring. Some search engines still offer a KWIC formatting option for their results, and Lexis has even been able to register KWIC as a trademark for its implementation of this option, implying an understandable historical ignorance on the trademarks registrar's part and a naïve cupidity on the registrant's part.

Yet even with extra local context, the KWIC index offers only a marginal improvement over the more familiar search-result link list. The innovation that would make the index much more effective for true browsing must do for KWIC what hyperlinks did for footnotes: make their text active in what might be called a hyperindex. In a hyperindex the individual words can be used,

Profess: politics like ours p.	231:26
p. and call themselves	389:16
Professes to flatter	276:8
Profession: Adam's p.	437:5
charmed me from my p.	480:29
contrary to their p.	389:36
debtor to his p.	25:14
head of the literary p.	181:24
most ancient p.	304:40
ornament to her p.	99:33
panted for a liberal p.	154:14
parentage is a very important p.	489:23
Professionally he declines and falls	178:3
Professions: all p. are conspiracies	489:20
p. which are full	546:40

Figure 2. Excerpt from The Oxford Dictionary of Quotations *index,
showing an expanded format that gives readers more context for each entry.*

for example, to augment or refine the index being viewed or to view another
section. I believe that a KWIC hyperindex, such as that hinted at in Figure 3—
while an obvious development of the prior art and thus not patentable—has
yet to be adopted anywhere. For further description of how such a hyperindex
might work, see www.comp.utas.edu.au/users/nholmes/hyperindex [at which
is a suggestion about how color might be used to help with navigation, and in
logical selection by clicking on individual words].

Why have KWIC hyperindexes not been implemented or, if implemented,
why have they not been widely adopted? Why do word processor programs
not offer a KWIC hyperindex option for a document in progress so that authors
can check their style as they go? Quite simply, the computing profession
at large remains largely unaware of the history of automatic information retrieval. This oversight has important repercussions not only for our profession,
but for the communities we serve.

The KWIC hyperindex offers a much easier interface for executing any but
the most basic queries. Ordinary users do not readily grasp query expressions,
so the availability of a more usable query interface that also provides a true
browsing capability would undoubtedly boost the value of textual material
stored informally on the Web.

Many groups are striving to build organized, Web-based collections of educational and cultural text. Yet we face the very real danger that the Web's im-

Christians. // All who	profess and call themselves	389:16
less. // They politics like ours	profess, / The greater prey upon the	231:26
of a dedication is flattery: it	professes to flatter. // The known sty-	276:8
-makers; they hold up Adam's	profession. // There is no ancient ge-	437:5
that are contrary to their	profession. // Those things	389:36
man a debtor to his	profession. // I hold every	25:14
-buttons—I panted for a liberal	profession. // My father was an emi-	154:14
the head of the literary	profession. // Your Majesty is	181:24
An ornament to her	profession.	99:33
almost charmed me from my	profession, by persuading me to it.	480:29
Parentage is a very important	profession; but no test of fitness for	489:23
a member of the most ancient	profession in the world. // Lalun is	304:40
friend he drops into poetry. //	Professionally he declines and falls,	178:3
against the laity. // All	professions are conspiracies	489:20
Doing-good, that is one of the	professions which are full. Moreover	546:40

Figure 3. Possible hyperindex application that would enable true browsing, built around Hans Peter Luhn's keyword-in-context automated indexing techniques.

minent commercialization will swamp these collections, which could rapidly make obsolete or altogether block such content. Effective hyperindexes could enhance the usefulness of these altruistic and culturally invaluable collections, making it more difficult for commercial and government interests to overwhelm the Web with e-commerce and video-on-demand content.

The field covered by this essay has often been referred to as information retrieval or IR. Its history can be pushed back in very interesting ways to much earlier than Vannevar Bush, as recounted in a book[24] I discovered after I had written this essay.

5.4   The Case for Perspicuous Programming

(2003 April)

The development of techniques for improving the quality of program code is an important responsibility of computing professionals. There are two aspects of quality: the quality of the code as it affects the computer, and the quality of the code as it affects the various people who interact in some way with the code.

Enigmatic Programming

Throughout programming's development, there has been a persistent struggle between the needs of the computer, which are the main concern of those employed to do original coding, and the contrasting needs of the user and the programmers responsible for repairing and adapting existing programs. Programmers tend to code for the computer, and this can be quite enigmatic, even for other coders.

One early technique used to counter this tendency—important when assemblers and compilers did not support data structures and long data names—added comments to symbolic code.   However, because these comments had no effect on the machine code produced, they were often ineffectual, typically only re-expressing each symbolic code statement. Once long names were allowed, in some circles the presence of comments was said to show the absence of skill in naming.

From time to time, programmers used many other techniques to document their code.

Template programming

In *template programming*, the tools provided a standard structure for the program and came with coding sheets that documented this structure.   This approach to making code more understandable was used by systems such as IBM's 1401 Automatic Report Generating Operation and [its] Report Program Generator, which were popular in the early 1960s.   Most of the code's significance appeared only as headings for the fields laid out on the coding sheets and preprinted on the punch cards for the code.

Highly condensed, template coding was productive because the coder was simply filling out forms. Of course, programs that didn't fall into the standard pattern were difficult if not impossible to write. Yet the pattern remained widely applicable, and the program code was easily understood because its template was always the same.

Prose coding

In the late 1950s, several coding schemes took the opposite approach to implicit documentation. *Explicit documentation* aimed to use conventions close enough to English that programmers could understand the code with very little training, as could their managers and collaborators. These various schemes promptly coalesced into Cobol, a splendid example of professional cooperation and compromise in the interests of standardization.[25]

Cobol's conventions encouraged expressiveness in the code. The provision for defining data structures using lengthy names was particularly important. An experienced Cobol programmer could easily produce code that needed few if any comments.

Unfortunately, Cobol's widespread adoption coincided with the rise of large organizations' mighty data processing departments, for only they could afford the expensive computers of the time. These departments showed more interest in their own progress and status than in looking after users, who were typically involved only in the investigative stages of a project. That users could read the code ultimately produced thus became irrelevant. Further, these organizations attempted only huge projects, which ill-suited Cobol's strengths and for which project documentation loomed much larger than program documentation.

Literate programming

With industrial programming, program documentation divided into external and internal parts. Developers generated external documentation during the system analysis and design phases and, theoretically, also during the coding and testing phases. The normal Pareto distribution of effort meant, however, that developers usually abandoned documentation during these later phases, along with the internal documentation, which typically consisted of comments within the code.

One way around this problem combined external and internal documentation. Donald Knuth introduced this *literate programming* approach in 1984![15] Literate code can be processed either by a compiler to produce machine code or by a formatter to produce a formal document that incorporates and documents the program.

Code Dimorphism

There are two kinds of programs: the traditional batch program with little or no direct user interaction, and the more recent kind that spends most of its time in wait state pending the next click of a button or tap of a key. This interactive kind of program has become practical thanks to faster processors, and it is popular thanks to operating system support for full-screen control and graphical triggering.

The problem is that programmers use the same methods to develop these two quite different program types. Documentation done during development supports only the design and coding of the program: directly executable or algorithmic code is the focus, and traditional documentation supports that focus. Developers view the code as driving the computer and any attached device it uses.

This is fine for a batch program that only works on data extracted from or fed to relatively simple and predictable attached devices. An interactive program developed this way similarly drives the keyboard, mouse, and display screen. But the user feels driven as well by the typical modern interactive program, trundled along predestinate grooves that fight back when the user tries to get out of them. My acronym for this experience is WYSINWYW: What You See Is Not What You Want.

Software producers usually mitigate this unfriendly experience by providing a so-called Help Facility, which in theory helps users get what they want. Searching for some idea of how to get these answers often brings frustration, however, both because the key words used in the facilitator differ from what most naïve users expect and because they must search extensively to find what they need to know—if they can find it at all.

Perspicuous Programming

Traditional approaches to coding interactive programs, even literate programming, suffer from the problem of focusing on what the computer will do, not what the user wants it to do. The algorithmic code is primary and any documentation secondary, especially user documentation. Help facilities appear to be added as an almost independent exercise.

We can solve this problem by focusing on the user documentation and regarding the algorithmic code as a mere adjunct. The production of an interactive program should start with the user documentation, with the majority of effort spent on developing and refining that documentation and its structure. Developers should add algorithmic code for any program module only after its documentation is complete and all parties have tested and agreed to it.

This *perspicuous programming* approach seeks to produce programs for the user that are as unenigmatic as possible. With a touch of blithely false etymology, we could call this *igmatic programming* instead. Take your pick.

The document as program

The popular use of highly interactive programs has been accompanied by much larger main and secondary data stores. Larger main stores, supported by virtual addressing and data caching, mean that program size now has little effect on performance as experienced by the user. Thus, it is quite practical now to package user documentation as an integral part of the program, administered through the operating system.

Developers create a perspicuous program's documentation before adding the algorithmic code to it. It remains with the program when distributed to users and run by them. In perspicuous programming, the documentation provides a model for the designer, a logbook for the manager, a notebook for the programmer, a specification for the coding technician, and an instruction manual and reference book for the user.

As perspicuous techniques develop further, an interactive program can also become a notebook for the user, who can tailor the documentation, and even the algorithmic code itself, to specific needs or applications. We can anticipate that groups sharing use of a perspicuous program could adapt it to their common purpose and even share a common adaptation with remote users across the Internet.

The program as document

The user's needs, not the computer's, determine a perspicuous program's structure. Developers must decide what structure will suit the user, rather than what structure will suit the computer. Thus, the algorithmic code in some modules might be extremely simple but extremely complex in others, depending on what the user needs to know.

The perspicuous programmer also needs to design the module documentation hierarchy so that an unskilled user can select the most detailed level while a skilled user can avoid superfluous explanation. At the same time, the documentation should hide very technical details from the unskilled user but leave them easily accessible to the skilled user.

For the unskilled user, modules should be designed so that parametric values display in the context of their explanation and, if appropriate, are set up so that the user can change their values. The documentation should also let the user see the current values of working variables in their context as the perspicuous program runs.

The perspicuous operating system

Developing a perspicuous operating system presents a nontrivial challenge. Perspicuous programs consist largely of text controlled by some kind of markup, an endeavor better handled interpretively. Not only must the operating system's interactive modules be perspicuous, the system must provide thorough support for running perspicuous application programs as well.

The operating system manages the hierarchy of documentation for each user. Expert users might see menus and toolbars much as they do now, but gain the ability to drill down into the hierarchy as needed. The novice user would start at an opening page that explains the overall program structure, be able to explore the hierarchy, experiment, then back off when an experiment goes wrong. In a well-designed perspicuous program, users should not encounter any difficulty in working out what to do because the learning takes place in the context of the full relevant documentation.

When the operating system supports shared use of perspicuous programs, users can store and manage their own notes and modifications. More generally, especially for countries with more than one official language, the operating system will support simultaneous use of the documentation in various languages. This might be done eventually by translation, although the different cultures implicit in the various languages might demand different program structures entirely.

The perspicuous programmer

The training of perspicuous programmers will differ markedly from that of batch programmers. Developing major perspicuous programs involves applied psychology more than algorithmics. Perspicuous programmers need to be skilled in document design and writing, and they must make their design decisions based on persistent and incremental user testing.

Although perspicuous programmers still need education in computer and operating system architectures, their need for studies in grammar, literature, and cognitive and behavioral psychology will predominate. These programmers would also benefit from practical experience in cross-disciplinary projects.

The recognition that interactive programs are different from traditional batch programs has been slow in coming. This sluggishness may be the major reason behind the frequently expressed dissatisfaction with widely used generic programs.

We cannot simply expect the software industry to change its ways when there is no assured profit in doing so. To start with, developing a perspicuous operating system would be very expensive. Rather, the computing profession must take the lead. A good place to start would be to re-examine the moves toward the certification of software engineers so that we could formally define the different role and skills of perspicuous software engineers as an encouragement for the academic world to train and educate such engineers sooner rather than later.

This essay is not intensely technical, but it does ask any programmers who read it to very drastically overturn their ideas about what they do. That's why I scheduled this rather fanciful piece for April, so that some would take it as a joke instead of being grossly upset.

5.5 Representative Democracy

(2002 February)

A year ago, I considered the now all but forgotten fiasco of the 2000 US Presidential election and suggested ways that digital technology might help make elections to an office such as the presidency more democratic[12] The election of democratic representatives, on the other hand, presents a far more complex issue that offers more significant possibilities for exploiting digital technology.

Ochlocracy and Economocracy

Democracy means rule by the people, and the term refers in an abstract way to a process or institution under which government openly solicits, preserves, and fosters information about its citizens' interests. At the heart of a typical democratic government lies a chamber of representatives that decides issues by vote.

We must not confuse democracy with ochlocracy—or mob rule—the nightmare outcome likely to occur if those who advocate using the marvels of digital technology to give everyone voting rights on every issue have their way. Anyone who doubts the hideous dangers of this approach should read Naomi Klein's description in *No Logo* of how effectively branding can influence public attitudes[14] In an online ochlocracy, branding would be a superb technique for enabling special interest groups to become mobsters.

Economocracy lies near the end of the political spectrum opposite ochlocracy, and is alleged by many to be the creed of Australia's two largest political parties, which contested the federal elections this past November. The main opposition party, the Australian Labor Party, promised that if elected it would implement an elaborately planned "KnowledgeEconomy."

Meanwhile, the incumbent Liberal Party based its campaign on claims of superior economic management. The Liberals had ousted the Labor Party from office in 1996 by condemning its economic management, citing increased foreign debt as "the final indictment." Yet under Liberal Party rule, Australia's foreign debt rose from 38.2 percent of gross domestic product in June 1996 to 46.7 percent in June 2001![16]

The tenor of these campaign tactics indicates that the Australian government—and by extension the governments of similar countries—is more concerned with the economy than with its citizenry, regardless of how that citizenry voted.

The new Federal Minister for Education's post-election proclamation underlined this theme. The minister accused the university sector of being reluctant to embrace change, then promised to "consult with business over what changes are necessary to ensure the universities better meet the community's needs."[17]

Whether justified or not, the perception of incipient economocracy must be reversed. For, to paraphrase a much admired judicial maxim, democracy must not only be done, it must also be seen to be done.

Making elected representatives more democratic and responsive to those represented, or at least less liable to accusations of moving in the opposite direction, seems an obvious measure. The computing profession has a responsibility to take part in publicly discussing democratic reform, and in particular to make suggestions about how such reform could employ digital technology.

The need for reform extends beyond Australia, given that many of the Organization for Economic Cooperation and Development's 29 other members appear just as economocratically inclined.   The organization's very name suggests that tendency.

One Citizen, One Vote

Democracy in its purest form demands that each citizen be able to exert the same influence as do all others. Following this principle, every voter's ballot counts as exactly one vote in democratic elections.

In present-day chambers of representatives, however, it's not the voters who count equally, but the representatives. Representatives' votes thus carry the same weight whether they represent 100,000 citizens or 1,000,000. Three clearly undemocratic consequences arise from this system.

First, there is a restraint on allowing a sparse rural electorate to have fewer citizens than a compact urban electorate. Imbalance in electorate populations has been accepted in many countries to counter the city dwellers' advantage of easier access to their representative, but this practice soon leads to an abuse called malapportionment.[3] Governments usually counter malapportionment with equal-population electorates, but in Australia federal electoral areas range from 26 square kilometers to far more than 2 million square kilometers. Maintaining the democratically necessary personal presence in these larger areas presents representatives with a staggering challenge.

Second, equalizing the number of citizens within established electoral boundaries makes it difficult to have such boundaries match the community's natural borders. This approach undemocratically fractures some electorates' communities, leading to poor coordination and disparities between electorates. These artificial boundaries also mix parts of different natural communities within electorates, leading to conflicts of interest and difficulties in providing clear and forceful representation of community interests.

Third, when the population in a region fluctuates, redrawing electoral boundaries to keep the electorates equal in population can confound representatives with a continually shifting constituency, making it hard for them to press effectively for recognition of their constituent's interests.

Digital technology can enable reforms that would greatly lessen these difficulties. It could, for example, support the principle of "one voter, one vote." With fairly simple identification and voting equipment installed in its debating chamber, a legislative body could give every elected representative one vote for every voter in their electorate.

Each representative would thus cast a different number of votes, and although rules would be needed to prevent a gross imbalance between electorates, mild imbalance could be quite acceptable in improving quality of representation. Australia currently aims to achieve a limit of 3.5 percent imbalance, a very low figure that leads to electoral boundaries that writhe like screen savers.

Allowing mild imbalances, say up to one third, would also eliminate the need to continually redraw electoral boundaries. Better still, on those rare occasions when gross imbalance develops, redrawing the boundaries would be much simpler because the allowed mild imbalance would permit more natural electorate coalescing and splitting.

A digital voting system would offer an additional advantage to electoral systems that do not make registration and voting compulsory. representatives would need to be responsive to their voters if they wanted to increase voter turnout and, in turn, their own influence. Likewise, ignoring voters would likely cause a representative's influence to dwindle.

The Two-Party Vote

A digital voting system could also eliminate the classical gerrymander. This maneuver, often made possible by weak or corrupt electoral administrations, aims to draw electoral boundaries so that the ruling party wins its electorates by a small margin, but crowds the opposition party's voters together into fewer but more populous districts. This tactic makes it possible for a party to have a majority of representatives elected with much less than a majority of votes overall.

To quash gerrymandering, an electoral administration could create much larger electorates, each of which would have two representatives from different political parties. When voting as representatives, each would cast as many votes as they received in the election.

For example, if an electorate's representative A took office with 256,000 votes, and representative B with 199,000, then A would cast 256,000 votes on any issue, while B could cast only 199,000. Digital technology would make administering such a system easy.

Simple variations on this scheme could make direct representation of minor-party voters possible, even across multiple electorates. In federal governments that have a chamber, such as the US Senate, in which states of the federation have equal representation, digital technology could support the sharing of any state's voting power between representatives in proportion to the votes they are elected by. This approach would be simpler and fairer than the proportional representation schemes now adopted in some countries?

Having two representatives for an electorate provides the significant additional advantage of helping voters avoid the feelings of despair and apathy that often occur under typical, single-winner election systems. When their preferred candidate loses, or when a candidate they strongly object to wins, voters in such systems feel unrepresented, diminishing their faith in the democratic process.

Continuous Elections

The voting schemes I've suggested leave intact one great perceived failing of present systems: the great brouhaha surrounding the periodic general election of representatives.

In the time leading up to an election, candidates barrage the populace with bombast, promises, and ads, while marginal but key electorates often receive lavish bribes—usually in the form of lucrative government contracts—in exchange for votes. Many voters feel that their representatives only really care about them at election time. At other times, those representatives pay more attention to the interests of those who supported their election campaigns financially in the past or might do so in the future.

We could employ digital technology to implement continuous elections, thereby reducing this problem greatly. This radical and apparently impractical solution has advantages so profound we should not dismiss it out of hand. Continuous elections would require a computer-based electoral system and an administration under which citizens could enter an electoral office, either physically or electronically, and cast a vote at any time, with certain restrictions.

The electoral administration would set the voting entitlement of representatives for any sitting of a legislative chamber at some statutory time shortly before the sitting. Electoral voting figures would be published regularly— say weekly—so that representatives would get frequent and direct feedback on how the electorate viewed their performance. This system would also eliminate the posturing and rhetoric that comes with opinion polling.

Avoiding instability is a system engineering principle usually applied by smoothing inputs. In a continuous election, system inputs could be smoothed by forbidding change of any vote within six months of it being cast. Another smoothing technique would call for old votes to lapse after a strict three years unless recast.

We could eliminate another source of instability by providing an orderly transition from a retiring representative to a new one, allowing them to split their party's vote for a transition period. The continuous election system could even allow the electorate to choose between candidates for replacement.

Instability could still occur if we apply continuous elections to a parliamentary system in which governments form from the elected representatives of the majority party or from the majority coalition of parties. But rapid changes in such governments could be prevented by applying a honeymoon bias for the voting entitlements of a new government's members, a bias that would gradually diminish to zero, or even beyond. For example, digital technology could apply a 10 percent honeymoon bias upon change of government, making each normal vote worth 1.1, and diminish that bias for each subsequent legislative sitting at a rate that would bring the bias to zero after eighteen months. If occasional changes of government were thought worth encouraging, the bias could continue to be diminished until it reached –5 percent.

Stable governments consist of politicians who see their own interests tightly bound up in the political system's stability. Thus, keeping the system unchanged provides the only issue short of a national emergency likely to attract overt and enthusiastic cross-party support.

To achieve any democratic reform in stable countries, the electorate must first be clearly aware of the nature and benefits of potential practical reforms, then must press strongly for such reforms. The necessary reforms can be envisioned clearly only after careful and detailed consideration of reform measures, a process in which computing professionals can play an important role. As technologists, governments need our support to ensure that reformers make the best possible use of digital machinery, and to ensure that the public clearly understands any such use. As system engineers, governments need our support to ensure that any reforms proposed are, as a system, practical and reliable, and to anticipate and counter the inevitable politically motivated criticisms. This last task presents an especially daunting challenge because of the many loopholes and pitfalls that must be avoided.

Countries with unstable governments face a much more complex situation. Divisiveness, chaos, and uncertainty present at best a moving target for reform, and they may make implementing digital technology irrelevant.

Any computing professional who feels doubt about the directions a government is taking has a duty to air those doubts, as I have done here. If that professional sees a need for democratic reform that would benefit the community, duty also demands that the professional advise the community about how to best use digital technology and system engineering in pursuit of that reform.

5.6 Olympic Games Reform: A Study in System Engineering

(2000 September)

Central to the overall computing profession is the design and implementation of systems. Insofar as our profession looks to the public for recognition, the public should be able to get advice about its systems from us. We should not be slow to give such advice, and should even volunteer it on occasion, as I am about to do.

Our professional responsibility extends beyond a system's computing or communications aspects. Fifty years ago, before the term "automation" became fashionable, a wise saying in the data processing profession warned, "Don't mechanize a mess!" This saying recognized that a professional owes more responsibility to the prospective user than to the equipment supplier.

Many public systems are clearly in the throes of failure, either because they fail to meet their objectives or—and these are big messes—their objectives are ignored, subverted, or inappropriate. Some such systems are local to a neighborhood, to a province or state, to a nation, or to a region. At each level, professional advice most properly should come from members of the profession local to the failure.

The readership of *Computer* is international, however, so for our purposes a case study of a clearly troubled international system will serve best. In September 2000, the Olympic Movement provides an obvious example of such a system. As I write this column, it is unclear just what crises or controversies will arise at the Sydney 2000 Games, although use of performance-enhancing drugs and certain swimsuit designs present clear candidates. Problems like these, together with the prolonged scandals over the selection of sites for holding the Olympic Games, have brought the Olympic Movement into miserable disrepute.

Some might say that the Olympic Movement is simply a branch of the global entertainment industry, and as such owes at least part of its lucrative success to such scandals. But the Olympic Movement itself formally professes different ideals, and Item 6 of the [year 2000 version of the] Fundamental Principles of the Olympic Charter reads as follows[13]:

> The goal of the Olympic Movement is to contribute to building a
> peaceful and better world by educating youth through sport prac-
> tised without discrimination *of any kind* [my emphasis] and in the
> Olympic spirit, which requires mutual understanding with a spirit
> of fairness, solidarity and fair play.

Although the Olympic Movement pursues its agenda mainly through the
Olympic Games, the Games have shifted way out of line with the ideals of
its only professed goal. Instead of exemplifying the Olympic spirit, the Games
exhibit ruthless commercialism combined with a spirit of frenetic partisanship,
unrelenting competitiveness, and a willingness to bend if not break the rules.

Toward the Olympic Goal

If the Olympic Movement is failing to meet its goal through its Games
system, professional system designers should as a matter of professional
responsibility—given the Games' global importance—consider how the
Games system could be improved. Two practical aspects, of a kind familiar
to professional system engineers, must constrain such a system redesign.

First, changes to a system should be introduced gradually; otherwise, we
risk instability and possibly catastrophe. This fact of engineering life is often
overlooked in political circles.

Second, it is proper to expect a complex system of any kind, particularly a
social system such as the Olympic Games, to move toward its goal, but foolish
to expect it to completely attain that goal.

Reforming the Olympic Movement in its entirety would be a vast under-
taking. We can begin, however, with some practical suggestions for a staged
redesign of the Games. In making the following suggestions for reform of the
Olympic Games, I am trying to

• show that the principles of computer system engineering can usefully be
applied to broader systems, though my application of them must be taken as
very tentative; and

• emphasize that professional system engineers have both the capacity and
the duty to take a lead in pressing for needful reform of social systems such as
the Games.

I propose a three-step, system engineering approach to reforming the
Olympic Games.

Modular Programming

Perhaps the oldest principle in system engineering is to split the system into
parts—the "divide and conquer" technique. The Games are such a large system that the first step in fixing them is to split them into several independent

modules—or maybe that should be objects: "The OO Olympics" has a certain wry charm. Fortunately, there is a precedent for such division: The Winter Games already take place separately from the summer events because they require distinctive venues.

In addition to winter events, then, the next group we could split off might be those based on water, giving us the Aquatic Games, which would include swimming, diving, and various boating contests. As it is, these events' distinctive venues require that they must often be held in a different part of the host country from other Summer Olympics events.

If we can achieve an aquatic separation, we need only one further split to allow four different yearly Games modules, which would let us run one module each year of the four-year Olympic Games cycle. For that split, we could use the fairly clear distinction between events that have a finishing sequence and those that don't: matches of the win-or-lose binary-result kind. This split would separate the Olympic Sports—composed of events like track and field, cycling, archery, and gymnastics—from the Olympic Matches, composed of events like hockey, fencing, badminton, and wrestling.

With four independent smaller modules running across a four-year cycle, more cities and countries could afford to host what would then be yearly festivals, spreading the direct benefits to more parts of the world. Moreover, with a Games module every year, the Olympic Movement could reasonably set up its own permanent professional staff to supervise directly the organization and management of all modules. Doing so would ease the cost to the host cities and reduce the opportunity for corruption.

Interfaces and Information Hiding

With the modules limned out, the professional system engineer will typically focus on the second step of development: the design and implementation of the modules themselves—in particular how they should appear to users. For the Olympic Games modules, this step means deciding how the Games should appear to the spectators, in particular the youth of the world toward whom the Olympic Movement should direct its efforts. Controlling the Games' appearance means controlling or at least guiding the Games information that the public receives from the media.

Reducing commercialism and partisanship

The two public aspects of the Olympic Games that are probably most at odds with the Olympic Movement's proclaimed goal are commercialism and partisanship. Splitting the Games into yearly modules could reduce the commercialism somewhat because the costs per module would be lower, thus lessening the dependence on large-scale commercial sponsorship.

Reducing partisanship is possible, but trying to eliminate it would be point-less. After all, Olympic events are promoted and staged as competitions, and spectators both present and distant expect to cheer on those competitors with whom they identify. Unfortunately, as things stand, the representational spread of both competitors and their successes is very lopsided. The playing of national anthems and tabulating by nation the medals won only draws attention to this imbalance.

An exercise in information hiding

We can solve the partisanship problem not by censoring information about competitors' nationalities, but rather by hiding it behind other information. A good way to achieve this objective would be to have competitors represent supranational regions, not nations themselves, and to have each region repre-sented by equal numbers of competitors. The Olympic Movement should then require that all public information about the Games, as far as its organizers can negotiate it, should identify regional affiliations and ignore nationalities.

This solution would not keep participants' nationalities secret, but would hide them as much as possible behind other information. Partisanship could then focus on equally represented regions, which might well foster cooperation within them. Rules ensuring that all regions got to share the hosting of Games modules equally among them would further reduce parti-sanship.

Computing professionals would probably consider it best to divide the world either octally or hexadecimally, with eight regions the better choice for simplicity. Figure 1 shows how the world could be divided into such regions and provides a symbol for each region. Having 8 or 16 regions would also suit the event administrators responsible for scheduling heats and matches, given equal regional representation.

Agreeing on a regional approach would be politically challenging, but sharing the Games' hosting evenly between regions should make the proposal easier for smaller nations to accept.

Designing With Patterns

The third step in my redesign of the Olympic Games relies on using pat-terns to simplify structures and procedures. One aspect of patterns—their symbolism—is sometimes overlooked. In the Olympic Movement, the pattern of five has a powerful appeal—as in the Olympic rings symbol.

The five rings could continue to stand for the five continents, but the introduction of a regional competition structure would certainly weaken that connection. The new structure might well be strongly opposed unless some new application of the five-ring symbolism accompanies it. This concern

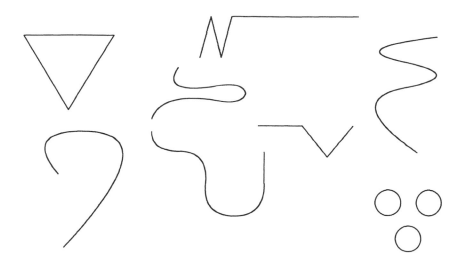

Figure 1. To reduce the obsession with national medal tallies—which invariably favors a few powerful nations—Olympics participants could be grouped into eight regional entities. The eight regions, represented by my suggested symbols for them, are (reading roughly from left to right) North America, South America, the Mediterranean Nations, Sub-Saharan Africa, North Eurasia, South Asia, East Asia, and the Island Nations.

provides a good example of the need to take user psychology into account when designing systems.

Thus, we could use the symbolism of the five rings to reduce another significant Olympic Games blight—the unrelenting competitiveness that, given the media's depiction of the Games, overwhelms what cooperation and comradeship there is. Television, the press, and advertisers all focus on *the* winner of any event. The only relief from coverage of these anointed celebrities occurs when the occasional accident or scandal flares up.

From competition to cooperation

To those less competitively inclined, the most interesting events of any Olympic Games are those that require all-round excellence, either by individuals, as in the heptathlon or decathlon, or by teams, as in the various relay events. Thus, we can use the Olympic rings symbol to shift the Games' emphasis toward versatility and cooperation—a development congruent with the Olympic Movement's goal—by focusing on events and teams in sets of five.

We could reduce the focus on specialized individual achievements simply by introducing an extra class of awards—say gold, silver, and bronze crowns or wreaths—that would be more prestigious and fewer in number than medals. We would give these new awards to individuals and teams of five that excelled in groups of five events–in other words, generalized individual and team pentathlons. Medals would still be awarded for each specific event, but the appearance of competitiveness would be reduced, and the role of versatility highlighted, by awarding crowns for groupings of those same events.

Five by five

To show how we might implement this new award system, consider those Olympic Sports events primarily concerned with using the human body—gymnastics and track and field—in contrast to those primarily concerned with equipment such as cycles, horses, and weapons. The following five groups could encompass most of these events:

- sprints: 100 m, 200 m, 400 m, 800 m, 1,500 m
- endurance: 3,000 m, 5,000 m, 10 km, 20 km, marathon
- throws: pole vault, shot put, hammer, discus, javelin
- jumps: high jump, long jump, triple jump, high and low hurdles
- gymnastics: vault, floor, parallel bars, and two others

The judges could award individual and team crowns for each five-event group. Further, we could increase the emphasis on versatility by providing separate awards and events for, say, two different selections of sports across each group of five. The awards could focus on themes such as brevity and length, augmenting present events like the decathlon.

The arrangement for teams of five to best emphasize cooperation and leadership would perhaps have two competitors from each team for each event, with each such competitor pairing used only once. One member of each team would serve as captain and be permitted to substitute for any injured or ill member, but would otherwise be required to compete only in the last event.

These speculations show how thoroughly we could apply designing by patterns to the problem of controlling competitiveness. We couldn't configure all Olympic events in this fashion, but—given that there are many other promising patterns of five—we could work on going in that direction if the Olympic Movement accepted the design principle.

Engineering Social Reform

Redesigning and reforming the Olympic Games presents a huge exercise in system engineering. I've explored the design of such a social system to demonstrate that, as computing professionals, we possess professional skills and knowledge appropriate to assist in social reform. Further, as professionals we have a duty to involve ourselves in reforms wherever our particular skills and techniques are useful.

This professional duty extends beyond being willing to act if asked. If a social system is failing to meet its objectives, as the Olympic Movement quite clearly is, then professional system engineers, such as the Computer Society's members, must engage in and even lead public discussion and consideration of the failing system's redesign. Should the community decide to proceed with such reform, professionals also have a duty to take part in implementing the redesigned system.

In the case of the Olympic Games, the Computer Society's nearly 100,000 members, spread through so many countries, could bring about meaningful changes if they take the lead in discussing reform. Doing so requires only a willingness to take part and some idea of the direction to be taken. The final outcome of the Olympic Games' reform would be different, possibly very different, from what I've hinted at here. What's important is not the redesign itself, but getting the reform process under way. Once under way, the participation of professionals like ourselves will be more important in ensuring that the process is not hijacked by special interests than in ensuring an ideal design. Such is the nature of social systems.

The attention the Sydney 2000 Olympics are receiving provides an opportunity to promote consideration of Olympic reform. Most likely, the Games will be a huge commercial success. Indeed, to continue as they have, the Games must always be a commercial success in the broad sense. The motivation for reform, on the other hand, must come from the desire to make the Games a success in other terms, particularly those expressed in the Olympic Movement's charter and goal. Alas, on those terms, the Sydney 2000 Olympics could result in abject failure.

5.7   Notions

The notions are given here partly as a rough summary, but more particularly
as topics and issues for students to study and debate. They are in the sequence
of their *key word* or *phrase*. The page number to the right of each notion points
to its context.

1. To *balance* the sensual and the contemplative cultures better,
digital technology needs to be swung more behind text   191

2. *Browsers* are poorly named: they do not allow free-association
browsing, only page display and link-and-trail tracking   207

3. If you're looking for something quite specific, *browsers* are great,
but if you're just browsing then they tend to bewilder   192

4. Changes to a system should be introduced gradually,
otherwise we risk instability and possibly *catastrophe*   224

5. A short pause for *checking* now saves hours of backtracking later   195

6. The adoption of writing system *code standards*
would bring huge commercial, social and cultural benefits   191

7. In some programming circles the presence of *comments*
was said to show the absence of skill in naming   212

8. Encoded text could be *compatibly* handled across writing systems
even if the computer wouldn't display the text "correctly"   205

9. Natural languages—the essence of individual *cultures*—
are disappearing much faster than they are appearing   199

10. *Democracy* must not only be done, it must also be seen to be done   219

11. Documentation done during traditional *development*
supports only the design and coding of the program   214

12. The oldest principle in system engineering is to split
the system into parts—the *divide and conquer* technique   224

13. Almost all *documents* use a single writing system,
which needs to be easily adaptable to new circumstances   190

14. Continuous elections through digital technology
could end *election* frenzy and funding scandals   221

15. A good text *encoding* standard would support name and word
exchange between languages that use the same writing system   204

16. Programmers tend to code for the computer,
                and this can be quite *enigmatic*, even for other coders   212

17. A digital voting system could end the classical *gerrymander*   220

18. A complex system of any kind may be expected to move toward
                its *goal*, but it's foolish to expect it to completely attain that *goal*   224

19. Digital technology might be used to allow the lower levels
                of the social *hierarchy* to exert some kind of control on the upper   195

20. The computing profession's *history* came from the culture of
                the printers and scribes who developed the written languages
                        from which our present binary representations developed   206

21. The KWIC index would be much more effective for true browsing
                if its words were active in what might be called a *hyperindex*   209

22. Avoiding *instability* is a system engineering objective
                        usually achieved by smoothing inputs   221

23. There have been two approaches to designing *interactive*
                programs, that of the "autocrat" and that of the "haut chef"   193

24. The majority of effort in the production
                of an *interactive* program should go to developing
                        and refining the user documentation and its structure   214

25. Separating *languages* from one another
                        is no longer the way of the world, if it ever was   204

26. Traditional *libraries* are useful because browsing works best
                when it takes you down trails you didn't expect
                        or leads to trails others might never have found   209

27. Problem solving is much more a *management* task
                                than a technological task   196

28. Don't *mechanize* a mess!   223

29. *Ochlocracy* is likely if those who advocate using digital technology
                to give everyone voting rights on every issue have their way   218

30. The motivation for reform of the *Olympic Games* must come from
                the desire for them to succeed in other than commercial terms   229

31. Larger main stores mean that program size
                now has little effect on *performance* as experienced by the user   215

32. Stable governments consist of *politicians* who see their own
                interests tightly bound up in the political system's stability   222

33. It is essential to always clearly distinguish between the *problem*
                to be solved and the technology most familiar to the solvers   195

5.8 Bibliography

The entries are in order of the first or only author's name. Where no personal author is known, as for popular news items, an indicative name is used. Where there is a page number or two in *italics* at the beginning of the annotation, they point back to where the item was cited. Where some of the annotation is given in quotes it has been taken from the item itself or from some of its publicity.

1. Mark Abley (2005). *Spoken Here: Travels Among Threatened Languages.* London: Arrow Books, ISBN 0 09 946022 X, 322 pp. (personal visits to areas of threatened languages, with commentary).

2. Douglas Adams (1995). *The Hitchhiker's Guide to the Galaxy.* Ballantine Books, ISBN 0 34 5319802, 224 pp. (*p. 188*; for an explanation of Babel fish translation: en.wikipedia.org/wiki/Babel_fish).

3. Thomas G. Alexander (1995). *Utah, the Right Place: The Official Centennial History.* Layton, Utah: Gibbs Smith, ISBN 0-87905-690-8, ca. 480 pp. (*p. 219*; the original citation was to an excerpt headed "Legislative Malapportionment and Rural Domination" which was then to be found at www.utahhistorytogo.org/lemalapport.shtml).

4. Laurent Baleydier and Nicholas Baleydier (fdrr. 2001). *KartOO: Home Page.* KartOO S.A., also KartOO Technologies (*p. 192*; kartoo.net with meta-search engines at kartoo.com and, more recently, ujiko.com).

5. Joe Barker (2005, August 23). "Meta-Search Engines," in *Finding Information on the Internet: A Tutorial.* UC Berkeley Library (*p. 192*; online at lib.berkeley.edu/TeachingLib/Guides/Internet/MetaSearch.html).

6. Vannevar Bush (1945, July). "As We May Think," *The Atlantic Monthly.* Vol. 176, No. 1, pp. 101–108 (*p. 207*; describes a forerunner of hyperlinks; theatlantic.com/doc/194507/bush).

7. *The Center for Voting and Democracy* (2006, March 6). *FairVote Archives: Links.* (*p. 221*; fairvote.org/links.htm gives many links, quite a few for proportional representation; the original citation *was* to Illinois Citizens For Proportional Representation at prarienet.org/icpr/links.html).

8. Chao Yuen Ren (1968). *Language and Symbolic Systems.* Cambridge University Press, xv+240 pp. (a very learned review of the wide field of linguistics, broader and more intense than most texts nowadays).

9. Chu Yaohan (ed. 1985, Jan.). "Chinese/Kanji Text and Data Processing," *Computer*, Vol. 18, No. 1, pp. 11–66 (*p. 205*; a special issue with seven articles and an introduction).

10. James Do and Muhammad Mudawwar (1997, June). "Unicode Misunderstood," *Computer*, Vol. 30, No. 6, pp. 6, 9 (*p. 204*; a letter and a response).

11. Umberto Eco (1993). *The Search for the Perfect Language*. London: Fontana Press, 1997, ISBN 0 00 6863787, xii+385 pp. (*p. 188*; translated by James Fentress; "aims ... at delineating, with large brushstrokes and selected examples, the principal episodes of the story of a dream that has run now for almost two thousand years").

12. W. Neville Holmes (2001, Feb.). "US Electoral Reform: The Obvious Obligation," *Computer*, Vol. 34, No. 2, pp. 128, 126–127 (*p. 218*; an essay in *The Profession* left out of this book, it dealt with, among other matters, the problem of the dangling chips).

13. *International Olympic Committee* (2006). *The Olympic Charter: Fundamental Principles of Olympism*, p. 9. (*p. 223*; in the year 2006 version at multimedia.olympic.org/pdf/en_report_122.pdf, Item 5 is now specific to condemning discrimination in the Olympic Movement, and Item 4 includes a more general condemnation).

14. Naomi Klein (2000). *No Logo: Taking Aim at the Brand Bullies*. London: Flamingo, HarperCollins*Publishers*, 2001, ISBN 0 00 6530400, xxiv+547 pp. (*p. 218*; about marketing; the subtitle does not appear in the British edition; the website nologo.org goes beyond the book).

15. Donald Ervin Knuth (1984, May). "Literate Programming," *The Computer Journal*. Vol. 27, No. 2, pp. 97–111 (*p. 213*; the first formal article; PDF at comjnl.oxfordjournals.org/cgi/reprint/27/2/97; there is a rich website at literateprogramming.org for an approach to program coding that should be much better known).

16. Stephen Koukoulas (2001, October 29). "Burden of rising foreign debt," *Australian Financial Review*, p. 56 (*p. 218*).

17. Steve Lewis and Katharine Murphy (2001, Dec. 17). "New minister feels universities have a lot to learn," *Australian Financial Review*, p. 3 (*p. 219*).

18. Charles E. Mackenzie (1980). *Coded Character Sets: History and Development*. Reading, Massachusetts: Addison-Wesley Publishing Company, ISBN 0-201-14460-3, xxii+513 pp. (*p. 202*; a very detailed description and history focused on mid–20th century codes, particularly ASCII).

19. Ved Mehta (1971). *John Is Easy to Please: Encounters with the Written and the Spoken Word*. New York: Farrar, Straus & Giroux, SBN 374.1.7986.7, viii+241 pp. (six essays on language and its people; for example the first

essay focuses on George Sherry and the rise of simultaneous translation, and the last on Noam Chomsky and generative grammar).

20. Muhammad Mudawwar (1997, April). "Multicode: A Truly Multilingual Approach to Text Encoding," *Computer*, Vol. 30, No. 4, pp. 37–43 (*p. 203*; "Multicode allows 8-bit representations—adequate for most languages—as well as 16-bit representations for languages with more characters . . . . Through switch characters, Multicode can support files that incorporate more than one language").

21. Theodor Holm Nelson et al. (2006, March 11). *Project Xanadu.* (*pp. 193, 207*; the home page for this noble endeavor is at xanadu.com).

22. Donald A. Norman (1999). *The Invisible Computer: Why Good Products Can Fail, the Personal Computer Is So Complex, and Information Appliances Are the Solution.* Cambridge, Massachusetts: The MIT Press, ISBN 0-262-14065-9, xii+302 pp. (5pp. references; p.x: "A basic goal of this book is to help companies make the transition from being technology centered to being human centered.").

23. *OUP* (1941). *The Oxford Dictionary of Quotations.* London: Oxford University Press, second edition, 1953, rev. to 1974, ISBN 0 19 211523 5, xx+1003 pp. (*p. 209*).

24. Neil Rhodes and Jonathan Sawday (edd. 2000). *The Renaissance Computer: Knowledge Technology in the First Age of Print.* London: Routledge, ISBN 0-415-22064-5, xii+212 pp. (*p. 211*; ". . . looks at the fascinating development of new methods of information storage and retrieval which took place with the arrival of the printed page"; 12 essays, 51 illustrations, 14 pp. further reading and index).

25. Jean E. Sammet (1985, Oct.–Dec.). "Brief Summary of the Early History of COBOL," *IEEE Annals of the History of Computing*, Vol. 7, No. 4, pp. 288–303 (*p. 213*; in a special issue for the 25th anniversary of COBOL, PDF at csdl2.computer.org/dl/mags/an/1985/04/a4288.pdf).

26. Mark Twain (1880). "Appendix D: The Awful German Language," in *A Tramp Abroad*. Harmondsworth, Middlesex, England: Penguin Books, 1998, ISBN 0 14 04.36081, 448 pp. (*p. 198*; this humorous piece can be read online at ccat.cat.upenn.edu/jod/texts/twain.german.html, for example, or the whole book from gutenberg.org/files/119).

27. *The Unicode Consortium* (2006). *Unicode Home Page.* (*p. 203*; the gateway to the incredible world of Unicode is unicode.org).

28. Steven J. Vaughan-Nichols (2003, November). "Technology News: Statistical Language Approach Translates into Success," *Computer*, Vol. 36, No. 11, pp. 14–16 (*p. 197*).

Chapter 6

Facing the Future

Digital technology, as Chapter 1 strove to show, is the basis of civilization. However, the people who live and die in it are the substance of civilization, the people who talk, speak, write, draw, figure, and toil in it make it what it is. The buildings, machinery and goods are mere artefacts of civilization.

Human civilization has been very productive of artefacts and population. This productivity, its bulk and distribution, is now threatening civilization's continuing development (see p. 242). When the world starts trying to counter this threat much more seriously than it has yet done, and as it will very soon be forced to do, then technology, particularly digital technology, will be central to whether and how we survive.

The degree of success in the struggle to survive will depend on how soon and how purposefully civilization can turn its human and material resources to the task. Only people who can convincingly predict where civilization is now heading, and show how our future prosperity, even survival, depends on human collaboration, can persuade civilization to face up to its the future, and to start working together rather than fighting and competing. Prominent among these forecasters are the professionals of various kinds, but particularly scientists and system engineers, with computing professionals in support of all of them.

As the need for drastic action slowly becomes accepted by communities and their governments, more professionals and technicians of many kinds will be needed. The need to greatly enhance education systems and bring forward the contemplative culture that will produce more people able to be trained and educated as technicians and professionals will become obvious (see p. 116), though it will be slow to achieve. Also the education level of all communities will need to be raised so that everybody will understand why changes are being made and why collaboration is needed on many scales.

The problems of the future are not only material and environmental, they are also social and cultural. Thus professionals and technicians in all fields will be needed, and their education will need to be focused on the forecasts of the times to come.

I'm quite sure that many readers will consider what I have just written above to be ridiculously apocalyptic. If I seem so it is because I have become convinced that the future is extraordinarily dangerous. There seems to me to be a very real possibility of a global *tipping point*, of reaching a point beyond which return is impossible. James Lovelock fears, even expects, the same thing as described in his book *The Revenge of Gaia*.[31]

Nonetheless I hope and believe that the prospective future is only bleak if the rational observations and modeling are politically ignored for too long, but I remain conscious that the longer action is postponed the more difficult the task will be.

The essays that follow were written to capture the interest and to provoke the involvement of computing professionals. Their messages are universal, however, because the issues they canvass are of global importance.

Social Systems Analysis

The computing profession doesn't have a very clear view of itself. The popular academic view has been encapsulated in the popular label of *computer science*, though the weakness of this is starting to be seen.

Peter Denning and Andrew McGettrick, in their "Recentering Computer Science,"[16] write that "Along with analysis of algorithms and complexity theory, many of us take programming as the heart and soul of computing." This is in an interesting article outlining three measures the Association for Computing Machinery is taking to reverse the dramatic decline in enrolments in computer science courses in the US by moving away from this traditional viewpoint to one more aligned with the computing industry's. This decline is also seen in other developed countries.

The ACM wants computer science courses to broaden. "Programming is one of four core practices; the other three are systems thinking, modeling, and innovating." These three encompass more or less what has long been called systems analysis within the computing industry. Certainly by the early 1960s DP departments had separated their programmers and their systems analysts. However, because programming and systems analysis training was only to be had within the computing industry, systems analysts were usually promoted programmers.

A systems analyst was and is a person who studies a problem and designs a system to solve that problem. Although this sounds simple, problems usually aren't simple to identify and to solve, especially if the system involves people as its users, and solutions need to be very innovative.

Systems analysts in the computing industry were given problems where a computer was expected to be part of the solution. Clearly systems analysis, or, more descriptively, system engineering, doesn't have to involve computers. Indeed, given the broad definition of systems analysis, all professionals who design systems of any kind are systems analysts.

Of course, everyone solves minor problems all the time, but well-trained, educated and experienced professionals are needed to solve major problems. There are two main reasons for this. The first is that big problems are usually costly to solve and very costly if the solution fails to solve the problem. The second is that the best solutions come from a deep understanding of what the problem *really* is, and this deep understanding usually takes an experienced person to discover.

Civilization is a system. Civilization faces severe problems. Professionals who analyse systems could and should contribute to the search for solutions to civilization's problems. This postulate is elucidated in "The Professional and the World" (essay 6.1, p. 245).

Global Digital Technology

Civilization is based on digital technology, as was outlined in a section on its history in Chapter 2 (p. 40) that introduces an essay on the history of data processing (essay 2.2, p. 54). The processing of data by digital computers of many kinds now plays a huge part in present-day civilization.

In the 1950s electronic computers numbered only in the thousands. "In contrast, 1993 alone saw over one billion processors shipped."[18] "There are 1 billion [personal?] computers in use" said Bill Gates in 2005.[39] Given the popularity of devices with embedded computers—devices like cars, mobile phones, sewing machines, iPods, videogame consoles, CD players and even automatic milking machines[30]—there must be many billions of computers scattered around the world.

However, the scattering is far from uniform socially. There are two reasons for this.

Firstly, computers and the devices that they go into need electricity to run them. Billions of people don't have electricity laid on and can't afford batteries. These are much the same people who don't have water that's safe to drink, or medicines to cure common illnesses, or enough food to build strength and vigor, or homes to live in, or enough education to be able to understand how to use such devices.

Secondly, computers and the devices that they go into need money to buy them. Billions of people live on less than $2 a day. There are others, many living in developed countries, who have only enough income to stay alive and not enough even to rent a room to live in.

Often seen statements like "The average home has two or more computers with broadband access to the internet . . ."[4] and "The average home now has many invisible small computers . . ."[34] come across as very sick jokes seen in this light.

These tragic facts are acknowledged in some circles. At government levels this has resulted mainly in rhetoric and promises that have done nothing to slow down the widening of this divide.

Part of the rhetoric has focused on digital technology. This is the all too familiar government approach of solving problems by throwing computers at them. They are going to help poor people by giving them computers. Some day or other.

The inequality in respect of digital machinery is commonly referred to as the *digital divide*. Governments of developed countries would like have the digital divide seen as a problem mainly in poor countries.

The abysmal fatuity of the approach to the digital divide by governments is reflected in their "support" of the United Nations' efforts to close the divide, as reviewed in "The Digital Divide, the UN and the Computing Profession" (essay 6.2, p. 250).

When there is a global body, in this case the UNDP, and a persistent and clear set of symptoms, then the global problem of growing, even accelerating, inequity both international and intranational can be studied, measured, and modeled by professionals of the appropriate backgrounds.

That nothing effective is actually done about solving the problem is most likely because the problem can be ignored by those who have the economic and political power to tackle the problem. For various reasons the political will does not exist, and the community will is not nearly informed or strong enough to create the political will.

Most of the time inequity gradually increases the social isolation of those who are less fortunate. This allows the political discussion of inequity to be indefinitely extended, where it is discussed at all.

Global Problem Solving

When there is a catastrophe, such as the 2004 tsunami in the Indian Ocean or Hurricane Katrina or the 2005 earthquake in Kashmir, then it's rather hard for the fortunate to completely ignore it because the plight of the afflicted is shown explicitly on the television screens of the fortunate. However, such catastrophes soon become less newsworthy and then it doesn't seem to matter much if the initial help is largely wasted, or if the promised aid never arrives, or if continued aid is not even offered.

Inequity hurts the poor very much more than the rich when they suffer such catastrophes. The vast majority of the poor affected by those three recent ones are still suffering, and will for years to come, possibly for generations.

The relatively rich have the resources to rescue themselves, or the influence to succeed in getting help.

This is the picture I have formed of recent events, but I hasten to emphasize that I have also read of, and seen on television, a lot of very praiseworthy help for the recent victims of catastrophe, but much of it from non-government organizations.

This seems to me to contrast weirdly with the assistance being given to the people of Iran and Afghanistan which, when it gets through, is mainly from governments.

The weirdnesses that I see are several. Firstly, the aid is being violently discouraged by insurgents. Secondly, the aid does not seem, so far at least, to even be balancing, much less exceeding, the continuing damage being done by some at least of the donor governments. Moreover, the spending on the war, $226 billion to early 2006 by the US, greatly exceeds the roughly $60 billion "pegged for reconstruction"[41] which is way below what is needed[37] Thirdly, the damage of the Iraqi catastrophe, and of the other three mentioned above, is much greater than that of the event that seems to have caused the invasions of Afghanistan and Iraq, namely the terrorist attacks on eastern United States of 2001 September 11.

But the ironic aspect is that the attack of September 11 was answered by an intense, very costly, and highly technological offensive against the shadowy terrorist organizations deemed to be responsible for those attacks, an attack which "Terrorism, Technology, and the Profession" (essay 6.3, p.255) argues is directed at the symptoms of the real problem, which is inequity.

This circumstance brings out the necessity of carefully working out what the cause of any problem is before designing and implementing a solution, particularly when the problem primarily involves people.

When there is a "natural" disaster like an earthquake then the cause is fairly plain, at least plain enough and abrupt enough for the world to concentrate on humanitarian aid. The aid will not provoke another earthquake.

When there is an "unnatural" disaster like a terrorist attack, the cause should be looked for behind the attack, and behind the terrorists. The cause suggested in essay 6.3 seems to have been borne out by the way things have gone since it was written.

It seems likely, according to Misha Glenny, that inequity also causes the growth in the shadow economy of "the corrupt and criminal networks that now account for up to 20 per cent of global GDP."[21] Glenny writes further that "the imbalances between developed and developing nations ... might leave the latter with no option but to go down the illicit route. ... The job of traffickers in women and economic migrants is made easy by high levels of unemployment and poverty in the countries of origin."

Rationality and the Maxiproblem

Glenny, who is writing a book on the shadow economy, holds that "it runs a close second to global warming and poses a much more serious threat than terrorism."[21]

From an overall point of view, all three of these phenomena are symptoms of the one basic problem, the *maxiproblem*. The inequity behind both terrorism and the shadow economy is caused by *the particular style in which the Earth's resources are being exploited*. So too is the atmospheric change behind global warming, or, as it is perhaps better termed, climate change.

However, terrorism and the shadow economy are human activities, social phenomena that affect different people in different ways and to very different degrees. Not so climate change. Climate change threatens life on Earth, all life and all people.

The main argument against this threat has been that climate change is *only* a theory. This shows a deep ignorance of the nature of a scientific theory which is, in the words of *The Oxford English Dictionary*, "a hypothesis that has been confirmed or established by observation or experiment, and is propounded or accepted as accounting for the known facts."

A scientific theory accounts for a phenomenon of nature. The value of such a theory is that it allows predictions to be made with confidence about effects of the phenomenon. Furthermore, scientific method requires a theory to be continually and thoroughly tested so that its predictions may be taken with the utmost confidence.

Isaac Newton came up with a theory of gravitational attraction, the inverse square law. It accounted very well for the motion of the planets around the Sun. Newton's theory, it turned out, is not completely exact. The inexactness can only be detected under extreme conditions, such as predicting the orbit of Mercury, because Albert Einstein's theory of relativity then comes into play. But this does not invalidate Newton's theory, only modifies it; observation tells us it's not the absolute truth, but it's very close to it.

Even if investigations of the anomalies in the trajectories of the Pioneer spacecraft 10 and 11 lead to further refining of the theory of gravity,[24] this will not invalidate the theory. It will just make it more precise.

A quantitative scientific theory can be seen as a model that can be used in a digital computer to simulate the phenomenon explained by the theory. The trajectories of meteors and spacecraft can be predicted very well in this way. So can the Earth's climate, but less well because the climatic system is much more complex.

Ideally, the development of scientific theories is quintessential rationalism. Of course, rationality has its limits, as discussed in "Rationalism and Digital Technology" (essay 3.3, p.117), but these limits are philosophical rather than practical.

The learned professions are learned because their members are experienced in their calling and rational in getting that experience, and their members are professional because their profession imposes a duty to apply their experience and rationality to matters of public interest, even outside their calling, as is reviewed in the essay "Should Professionals Be Political?" (essay 4.4, p. 166).

Thus, in a matter as much in the public interest as is climate change, all professionals have a duty to apply their experience and rationality to issues in the public debate, as argued in more detail in "The Profession and the Big Picture" (essay 6.4, p. 261).

Climate change modeling is very complex, and so not a topic to which a professional outside the sciences involved can *directly* contribute. What such a professional can and should do, however, is to look closely and rationally at the public argumentation.

To me, the public debate seems to oppose professional climate scientists and their colleagues to what have come to be called *contrarians*. Most of the contrarians seem to be irrational, ill-informed, emotive and persistent. A very few argue so quietly and rationally that refutation or acceptance must be left to the professionals directly involved, though typically any such refutation seems to be concertedly attacked by the more rabid contrarians. One public forum for such debate is realclimate.org.[42]

One of the peculiarities of the public debate is that, now the Arctic ice has shrunk so much that the Russian ship Akademik Fyodorov, not an ice-breaker, was able to reach the North Pole, and now the US Geological Survey has said that a quarter of the world's undiscovered oil reserves are under the Arctic Ocean, the oil companies, historically prominent contrarians, are rushing to find and claim those reserves.[2]

But even if the contrarians are right, and I don't believe for a moment that they are, there remains the maxiproblem behind not only the possible climate change but the undoubted shadow economy and the pervasive and increasing social inequity, namely the accelerating exploitation of the Earth's resources.

The world's major governments and commercial organizations have an openly expressed and unconditionally espoused belief in economic growth as an indisputible and universal good. This economic growth is a rate, so that the larger the economy the more it must increase to sustain the desired rate. This is called exponential growth, and is well understood by most professionals as persistent acceleration. Think how well you could control a car if it never ever stopped accelerating.

Accelerating economic growth must be, for the foreseeable future, fed by accelerating consumption of energy and material. Sooner or later this must lead to utter environmental destruction, unless the present acceleration of global inequity continues, in which case social destruction will precede and might mitigate the environmental destruction.

For a system analyst, the difficulty is clear. Governments never look very far beyond the next election, and corporations never look very far beyond the next accounting period. Professionals have an ability to look further and a duty to do so. Thus the future of our civilization will be determined by the professions.

Where do computers come into all this? Well, firstly, improved and more extensive use of digital technology will be absolutely essential to the study of these problems, and to the design and implementation of solutions to them. Secondly, improved and extensive use of digital technology will be absolutely essential to the basic education and subsequent training and education (see Chapter 5) of the many more technicians, technologists and other professionals who will be absolutely essential to this problem solving.

6.1 The Profession and the World

(2002 November)

Late this August, the *Guardian Weekly* included a 16-page supplement simply titled *Earth*, which bore the caption "Health check for a planet and its people under pressure."[22] Compiled in association with ActionAid, the supplement "examines some of the most pressing issues of our time" in the leadup to the Earth Summit in Johannesburg, held 26 August to 4 September.

The contents of *Earth* would startle and perturb anyone, and deserve a much wider readership than the *Guardian*'s normal circulation. For a computing professional, it carries, or should carry, much greater significance. Professionals have a responsibility to use their skills and experience where relevant to judge the nature and reality of problems facing their community and to promote and support solutions to those problems. This responsibility distinguishes professionals from people who ply a trade.

A computing professional's skills and experience are particularly relevant to the community. We can apply traditional systems analysis to the global problems we encounter, and digital technology has undoubted potential for supporting good solutions to many of these problems.

Rich and Poor

The *Earth* report's opening article, "Look at the Progress We've Already Made,"[13] provides its most provocative element. Written by Diane Coyle, who runs the Enlightenment Economics consultancy, the article's first paragraph reads: "Here's a familiar and terrible story. It says we live in a world where poverty and inequality are increasing, where powerful corporations are ravaging the environment on a global scale, and technology is out of control. And it's all nonsense." With this article, Coyle plainly seeks to contradict the rest of the supplement.

In an article entitled "European Cows Are Better Off than Half the World,"[17] Charlotte Denny notes that an average European cow brings in $2.20 a day in subsidies and other government aid, while 2.8 billion people live on less than $2 a day in developing countries around the world.

The contrast between these two articles can only be deliberate—chosen, perhaps, to encourage further thought and study. Obviously then, the concerned reader must find what the facts really are. Many individuals and institutions—especially the United Nations Development Programme—affirm affirm that the gap between rich and poor countries, and between rich and poor *within* countries, is not only widening but, according to some economists, is doing so at an accelerating rate. On the other hand, many economists offer detailed statistics that show the gap is narrowing.

At this point, systems analysis skills become relevant. First, we must determine the real problem. Having been trained to see the bigger picture, a skilled systems analyst looks below the surface to determine a system's purpose.

System and Purpose

In this case the system being studied is the world itself, primarily from the human population's viewpoint. For humans, the disagreement implicit in the *Guardian*'s supplement relates to the poverty of people and the inequality of nations. To resolve this disagreement, we must determine the human purpose of the world system.

The two focuses usually suggested are the economy and the general community. One school of thought, which I'll call *materialist*, holds that the economy is the end and the community merely one means to that end. The other school, which I'll call *demotic*, holds that the *community* is the end and the economy merely one means to that end.

How a systems analyst will look professionally at the world's purpose will depend on who she sees as having the problem. As the employee of a client, the systems analyst will take a materialist approach. But as a professional primarily responsible to the community, that same systems analyst will take a demotic approach.

The entirely quantitative materialist approach looks at economic aspects—factors such as incomes, prices, interest rates, exchange rates, employment rates, and economic growth—to discover relationships between these factors so that the controllable aspects can be manipulated to benefit the economy. Materialism offers the advantage that it *is* quantitative and, superficially at least, objective. Present-day First World governments favor this philosophy.

The demotic approach looks at the welfare of the overall population and considers personal benefits—factors such as health, education, security, and full employment—as primary goals. The difficulty with social welfare is its subjectivity, which makes it more difficult to measure and defend. Many post-World War II, First World governments favored, at least theoretically, social welfare.

The two approaches need not conflict directly. The global systems analyst might suggest that we should consider material and social welfare together, and recent research on economics and happiness supports this view. Much of the apparent conflict derives from the materialists' tendency to cite averages of indicators such as incomes and productivity, whereas the demoticists cite extremes of poverty and inequality. For materialist facts and arguments, the systems analyst can seek the help of economists. For demotic facts and arguments, however, the social scientists' help alone is insufficient because the analysis involves moral issues.

Poverty and Inequality

One frequently cited poverty statistic asserts that 2.8 billion of the world's people live on less than $2 a day. On the surface, this figure should shame any prosperous person. But the systems analyst will take a closer look.

Is a person who lives on less than $2 a day poor? In places such as the Amazon basin, some "primitive" people live off the land and outside any monetary system. They are mainly healthy and happy, except where the outside world has started interfering.

On the other hand, is a person who earns an official minimum wage happy and healthy? Not according to two recent books, which depict the utter misery and degradation of living on a wage of $7 an hour in the US and $6 an hour in the UK.[11]

Poverty arises from social context and represents a moral issue, not an economic one. How can we justify the persistence—some would claim the increase—of widespread misery in most if not all nations? How can we leave 1.1 billion people without clean drinking water, and 2.4 billion people without sanitation?

Inequality, often mentioned alongside poverty, presents a slightly different issue, one that suggests conflict: the have-nots envy the haves, and the greater the disparity in property, the greater the envy. A little systems analysis can clarify this highly confused issue.

Inequality in property differs from inequality in income. People can only acquire property if their income regularly stays above that required for their subsistence. Further, property comes from the accumulation of income surplus, so, at the margins of subsistence, few if any can own anything at all.

Equality is a moral ideal for a just and civilized society, but *what* equality should be sought? Economic historian Richard Tawney provides a good definition when, in the manner of a professional systems analyst, he distinguishes social inequality from individual differences: "While natural endowments differ profoundly, it is the mark of a civilised society to aim at eliminating such inequalities as have their source, not in individual differences, but in its own organisation. Individual differences that are the source of social energy are likely to ripen and find expression if social inequalities are, as far as practical, diminished."[45]

Unemployment and Inflation

In modern developed societies, unemployment causes the greatest social inequality. The most objectionable idea in modern economics is the "natural rate of unemployment," which directly opposes Tawney's ideal by implying the desirability of unemployment—often at the rate of 6 percent. It's significant that postwar governments in several developed countries, such as Australia and New Zealand, successfully adopted a policy of full employment for 10 to 15 years. Unemployment as an economic benefit only came into vogue in the early 1970s with the monetarist economists, led by Milton Friedman.[33]

Its formal name reveals the true significance of "natural" unemployment: Non-Accelerating Inflation Rate of Unemployment. NAIRU works from the theory that inflation can be controlled by manipulating unemployment rates. If you want inflation to go up, push unemployment down; if you want inflation to go down, push unemployment up. Clearly, this theory primarily concerns itself with the economy, not the community. It's far from clear that the theory works.[8]

Inflation, which refers to increased prices, amounts to diminishing the value of money. Over this hallowed territory supposedly none but economists can tread. Yet the economy is a system, and a systems analyst might see a bigger picture here than the economist can.

Nowadays, economists consider inflation normal, deflation—its opposite— abnormal. Eminent economist Roy Harrod wrote in 1969, "It is a strange fact that after so many centuries of experience in so many countries, man has not yet succeeded in providing for himself a money with a stable value."[23]

Part of the problem is that we now use "money" as a *store of value* rather than as a *medium of exchange*. When money mainly consisted of precious-metal coins, the value of a coin remained as stable as the value of its metal. For example, in England after William the Conqueror one pound of silver was generally minted into 240 silver pennies. Harrod notes that "It is a remarkable thing that for more than two centuries the British monetary unit suffered no depreciation at all."

Inflation arises from money's use as a store of value because people can acquire money without exchanging it for commensurate value. In effect, this means that greedy people can draw more value out of society than they put into it and thus depreciate the value that other people have stored.

One of data processing's finest developments ever—double entry bookkeeping—makes a simple explanation of inflation possible. Such bookkeeping—usually considered a 15th century Venetian development—works on the principle that every transaction involves a balanced exchange of value. Thus, if I buy a cow for $100, I formally gain $100 worth of cow in exchange for $100 worth of money. I therefore record the transaction in my books as a positive $100 of stock and a negative $100 of cash.

In such bookkeeping, all transactions are neutral: Adding up all entries, positive and negative, always totals zero. That the books balance proves the arithmetic correct. Within the system, different classes of values allow calculation of nominal worth. Thus, if I now sell the cow for $90, I gain the $90 cash in exchange for a cow nominally worth $100, so that a balancing entry of $10 must be made to represent the loss of value to me. Where has the $10 gone? To the cow's original vendor.

I seek to make two points with this example. First, my loss consists of money I originally paid to someone else. Thus, when we read of enormous losses made by a company like Enron, those losses balance with money paid to someone else. Second, in any transaction, someone pays money for goods or services. Thus, there will be no inflation in the overall commercial system as long as the value of all money paid balances with the value of all goods and services received.

Inflation is evidence of greed—people taking out more value than they put in, the difference necessarily diminishing the value of money because the missing value must come from people's monetary savings.

Looking at the global picture is risky and difficult—risky because we must work with the often confused and confusing "facts" on record, difficult because of the world's complexity. The world situation is arguably out of balance in many ways and highly dangerous. All people with professional skills have a clear duty to study the problem from their own point of view and to join in constructive discussion and planning. Given their particular training in systems analysis, I especially urge computing professionals to undertake such efforts.

This essay attracted quite a few responses from readers, many criticizing my grasp of economic theory. The following is a published clarification.[12]

I wrote the article as a systems analyst, not as an economist. The example of the cow was meant to illustrate double-entry bookkeeping, not to explain inflation. An explanation of inflation might have described how, if I sold the cow's milk for $50, and if the value I put in to providing feed and labor was $40 (remember the $10 capital depreciation), this would be neither inflationary nor deflationary. If, on the other hand, I sold the milk for $500, this would be inflationary—and greedy. The point I subsequently made was that, in the inflationary case, the books would still balance, but the value and money would not.

I had no intention of implying that the greed was solely that of capitalists, nor that greed was the only cause of inflation. Capitalism itself is neutral, just like technology or, for that matter, socialism. If such –isms express greed or other selfish aims, this is the responsibility of the –ists, not the –isms. And it's not just the greedy who take more out of society than they put in. The unemployed and, more modernly, the underemployed are prevented socially from putting in as much as they take out, as another paragraph in my article was intended to imply. Unfortunately, the typical response of many governments to this last problem is to reduce social welfare payouts, which then increases the inequity and misery.

6.2   The Digital Divide, the UN, and the Computing Profession

(2003 December)

The term *digital divide* usually refers to the great disparities between and within societies in the use of digital technology. This month, the United Nations is holding a World Summit on the Information Society[29] (WSIS) to adopt a declaration that embodies, in its draft form at least, "the ambitious vision" of "bridging the Digital Divide." The declaration's hopes focus on

> the rapid pace of development of ICTs [information and communi-
> cation technologies]—unprecedented in history—which allows for
> the development of applications that make it possible that no one is
> left behind and that those who were left marginalised in previous
> development cycles can have a real opportunity to attain higher
> levels of development without having to follow the traditional path
> nor its time requirements.

The Computing Profession

We might think that a UN summit focused on the application of digital technology would enjoy the participation of professional bodies, particularly those representing engineers and computing professionals. The list of "entities involved" does include the International Federation for Information Processing and the International Institute for Applied Systems Analysis. But, considering that the list contains more than 2,000 entities of bewildering variety, the participation of engineers and computing professionals seems purely nominal.

More significant is the shorter list of the partner organizations of the United Nations Information and Communication Technologies Task Force, the main—or at least professionally most relevant—body behind the summit.[20] My classification of these organizations yields 15 political bodies, divided into eight UN and seven national government bodies; 13 commercial bodies, of which eight are corporations like Cisco and Hewlett Packard; and seven or eight miscellaneous minor organizations.

This line-up makes it no surprise that the draft declaration embodies a bizarre farrago of largely ideological and often contradictory platitudes. The draft action plan isn't much better. Thus, I consider it highly unlikely that the outcome of this UN summit will be any more effective than the outcome of recent World Trade Organization meetings.

The Professional Approach

The UNICTTF list's most significant feature, however, is the complete absence of professional bodies of any kind. Perhaps this absence stems from professional organizations' disinclination to either take part in an apparent boondoggle or to appear to support the most likely outcome of such an event.

Whatever the reason, their absence is deplorable. Professional people, dissociated from business and politics, are best qualified to thump the table, insist on purposeful and effective approaches to solving problems, inform the decision makers of the nature and significance of technical realities, and advise them of different solutions' relative feasibility and benefits.

When solving problems professionally, we must first define each problem's scope and nature. The "ambitious vision" makes it clear that the people behind WSIS take the problem to be the digital divide. A moment's informed thought should confirm that the digital divide represents only one symptom of the chasms that increasingly divide rich nations from poor and the rich within nations from their poor, as the United Nations Development Programme has long persistently and fruitlessly documented.[46] The draft declaration states, "We are aware that technology alone cannot solve any political and social problems. ICTs should therefore be regarded as a tool and not an end in themselves." But the declaration shows no awareness that the basic problem's severity might spring at least partly from the use of digital technologies, or even that digital technologies might be completely irrelevant in many circumstances—as they must be, for example, to the 24,000 people who die of hunger daily.[26]

Another principle of problem solving dictates that we understand the problem's causes. In understanding gross social inequity, a system analyst's skills become relevant. One common economic argument denies the existence of the problem on the grounds that per capita gross domestic product or average annual income is increasing everywhere. This may be true. But a system analyst could point out that

• the subjective inequity is in wealth, not productivity or income;

• the ability to acquire wealth in a monetary society depends on an excess of income over living costs;

• wealth once acquired accelerates its own growth; and

• this results in a dumbbell effect—the wealthy naturally get wealthier while the poor get relatively poorer.

Once defined, a problem must be placed in its full context. The UN WSIS declaration repeatedly places overriding importance on increased economic development. Yet we have reason to doubt that global conditions will let us sustain present levels of economic production much longer, much less support increased production levels.[35]

Digital Technology

When tackling the problem of sustained economic production, we can— whether we agree with him or not—consider eminent capitalist George Soros' views on the global capitalist system's deficiencies.[43] Soros puts these deficiencies into five classes, thereby providing an analytical structure for examining the close links between digital technology and global capitalism:

• *The benefits of global capitalism are unevenly distributed.* Digital technology makes capital and profits much more mobile than labor and goods, providing perhaps the most important of those factors that "combine to attract capital to the financial center [of the global economy] and account for the ever increasing size and importance of financial markets."

• *Financial markets are inherently unstable, and international financial markets are especially so.* Soros makes many comments regarding market equilibrium and economic theory. But apart from this, we should note that digital technology has both enabled the formation of a global financial system more complex than the national ones it replaced and greatly reduced the system's reaction time to disturbances. Complex systems with small time constants are inherently less stable, as the recent catastrophic failures of integrated electricity distribution systems—such as those that have repeatedly blacked out much of northeast North America—show.

• *Instability is not confined to the financial system, however. The goal of competitors is to prevail, not to preserve competition in the market.* Digital technology provides an effective tool for avid competitors. Successful companies typically become more successful by reducing their costs, and large companies are much more able than small companies to reduce costs by exploiting digital technology. If it's only stability we're after, monopolies or oligopolies might be the best result, except that some think they make a much bigger mess when they do eventually crash.

• *Since the end of the Second World War the state has played an increasing role in maintaining economic stability, striving to ensure equality of opportunity, and providing a social safety net, particularly in the highly industrialized countries of Europe and North America. But the capacity of the state to look after the welfare of its citizens has been severely impaired by the globalization of the capitalist system.* Digital technology has made global private enterprises spectacularly successful. Yet corporations and a few private citizens in developed countries own or control most of these enterprises, exerting an influence so profound that governments and major political parties have wholeheartedly adopted an economy-first approach to policy and legislation. This is particularly noticeable here in Australia.

• *Every society needs some shared values to hold it together. Market values on their own cannot serve that purpose . . . . We can have a market economy but we cannot have a market society.* This Soros considers to be "the most nebulous problem area." His concern is also the most relevant to WSIS, given that the IS in WSIS stands for information society—the area in which digital technology has most significance.

Readers who assume Soros argues for abandoning capitalism will be mistaken and should consult the cited paper or soros.org[37]

The Information Society

The WSIS draft declaration's unbridled enthusiasm for the information society depicts it as a new kind of paradise. The computing profession could give this view a more realistic perspective.

Human societies and primates in general have always formed information societies, as delightfully displayed in the last two episodes of David Attenborough's *The Life of Mammals*.[3] Recent digital technologies have given us extremely cheap machines for generating, displaying, storing, and transmitting *data*: representations of the ideas that in the human mind can become information. New, at least in their intensity, are the industries that have arisen to exploit data commercially.

The very cheapness of modern machinery would ordinarily ensure plenty of competition for data-based industries, but global corporations use patent and copyright monopolies to hamper if not completely suppress competition. They also use digital technologies to enforce their monopolies. Indeed, the World Intellectual Property Organization, a UNICTTF partner, "is dedicated to promoting the use and protection of . . . intellectual property."[48]

Thus, when the UN declaration affirms that "In building such an information society, the ability for all to access and contribute their information, ideas and knowledge is essential," this sentiment seems platitudinous indeed in the face of commercial reality. Most disturbingly, this passage and the declaration as a whole give the impression that the world should aim to create a single, uniform, information society by using digital technology to bring the developed world's benefits to "those who were left marginalised in previous development cycles." Two assumptions underpin this statement:

• societies in the developed world have benefited from technological development, and

• what will benefit the developed world will ipso facto benefit the undeveloped world.

We can doubt from a social viewpoint the net benefits of technology, considering the gross social inequities that have developed in the so-called advanced countries since digital technology's widespread adoption. Certainly, we can reasonably doubt that digital technology should be used in the Third World in the same way it has been used in the First World.

The UN declaration properly emphasizes education. Unfortunately, it also implies that the First World's educational system should be brought to the poor world and that digital technology will play a central role in delivering it.

This brings us back to Soros' fifth problem—the shared values that a successful society must have. Education provides the means for maintaining traditional shared values; thus, the family and professional educators, not digital technology, provide education's essential and principal tools. The educational system's failure to maintain traditional social values in a world where, frequently, no family exists to perform that role, provides the most likely reason for the First World's social gaps.

In this vacuum, marketeers choose social values and use media such as television, video games, and, increasingly, the Internet and its Web to instill them.[40] In response, innumeracy and illiteracy increase steadily while inoralcy—the inability to communicate orally—has become a problem in primary schools.[5]

Although I believe the WSIS is doomed to failure, it forms only part of an effort scheduled to go on until at least 2005. This work offers all professionals, and particularly computing professionals, an opportunity to urge their representative bodies to press for a formal role in the WSIS sequels and similarly important international endeavors.

Professionals who can do so should volunteer to support their professional bodies and other organizations in any activities that seek to better both their own and international society. Digital technology has a great potential for supporting such efforts. The difficulty lies in realizing that potential.

6.3   Terrorism, Technology, and the Profession

(2001 November)

When the wireless news woke me with a description of the terrorist mayhem in Manhattan and Washington on September 11, a part of my mind refused to accept it. That part said this must be a spoof in much worse taste than the one Orson Welles broadcast in 1938, when he passed off a radio play of H.G. Wells's *The War of the Worlds* as a real alien invasion.

A few minutes later, when my television showed the unforgettable scene of a large commercial airliner flying into the south World Trade Center tower, that same part of my mind insisted that I must be watching a clip from a Hollywood technothriller. Its repetition and the commentary soon made the truth undeniable. Disbelief became grief, grief became tears, and going on with ordinary life became a struggle—even though the events thus affecting me were taking place on the other side of the world.

Later that morning, as I forced myself along to the lecture room where my students waited, my mind turned to what I should tell them—these young people hoping to join the computing profession—about their responsibility as professionals to a community that had just had technology so publicly used against it. I urged them to look at the tragedy and its circumstances from a professional and personal standpoint, to try as apprentice system analysts to understand what had happened and might yet happen, and to work as professionals toward a world system that would make such tragedies less likely.

Technology and Tragedy

Technology made the scale of this terrorist tragedy possible: It built both the towers and the planes that destroyed them, and it produced the funds and provided the communications the terrorists used to implement their plan. Much of this technology is digital.

The authorities had technology in place to predict and prevent terrorist acts such as this and, because of September 11's events, they will receive calls for much greater use of preventive technologies and systems. Much of this technology will be digital, and members of the computing profession will be heavily involved in its development.

Many computing professionals have great experience in preventive systems, particularly for the Internet, and this experience will surely be relevant to the antiterrorism effort. Their professional judgment should be used to evaluate proposals that, if accepted, will likely have a considerable effect on the conduct of everyday life, our freedom of movement and speech, and our personal privacy and liberties.

Terror As a System

We should recognize and strive to help the public recognize, however, that preventive measures can never be infallible. Fallible people will employ these techniques against clever and determined opponents who can study them at their leisure and who have the patience to wait for loopholes to become evident.

Terrorists—the circumventers of security—only need to achieve one success amid a host of failures to further their agenda. Security enforcers, on the other hand, cannot afford a single failure.

If preventing every possible act of terror is all but impossible, we must seek other measures. One obvious alternative is to wipe out all those who would commit such acts. However, this approach presents many difficulties. To begin with, terrorists, like everyone else, come in a range of shapes and sizes. Indeed, successful terrorists will succeed because they aren't obviously terrorists. The ratbag end of the terrorist spectrum could well be the less dangerous end. So which ones do we wipe out, how do we find them, and how do we stop people from becoming terrorists in reaction to the removal of those who already are?

We must take a broader viewpoint, a system viewpoint. We must determine the components of organized terror and analyze what motivates and sustains terrorists. This project presents a huge challenge, but several important aspects of systematic terrorism can already be seen.

First, the system of international terrorism extends far beyond the network alleged to be responsible for the September 11th tragedy. It extends beyond the US and the Taliban. Moreover, the scale of the Manhattan massacre pales alongside the millions killed by terrorists in Cambodia and, more recently, the many hundreds of thousands killed in Rwanda and Bosnia-Herzegovina.[27]

Second, although terrorists often use religion to justify their actions, religious belief does not provide the basis for terrorism. Richard Dawkins, of meme fame, wrote most eloquently against religion's role in terrorism. "To fill a world with religion, or religions of the Abrahamic kind, is like littering the streets with loaded guns. Do not be surprised if they are used."[15] But his shafts flew wide of the target: atrocities in the name of religion are incited for sociopolitical reasons, not religious ones. Religion, like technology, is inherently neutral. Either can be used for good or evil. If the outcome is evil, it is the user's responsibility, not religion's or technology's.

Third, the terrorist atrocities of September 11 were not acts of mindless anger and hate. The terrorists planned and carried them out deliberately and systematically. Terrorist system projects are purposeful. To understand them, we must understand their purpose. Their perpetrators meant these particular acts to be highly symbolic, a declaration to the world. The people killed in these incidents were not targets, but rather "collateral casualties." That the terrorists targeted the Pentagon and, reportedly, the White House, implies that they meant to attack the US government. That they allocated two planes to the World Trade Center, however, strongly implies that it was their most significant target. They see world trade as their enemy, then, and they targeted the US government because of its perceived role in world trade.

Terror's Context

To effectively counter a terrorist system, we must first understand its context. The sociopolitical system of organized terror forms a subset of all sociopolitical systems. Given that the September 11th attacks targeted world trade, the world's sociopolitical system thus serves as the context for these terrorist incidents.

Undoubtedly, the issues at this level will be discussed and reviewed extensively in other publications. Such discussion will likely be fruitless because a variety of experts will steer it in different directions: political and social scientists, security experts, historians, economists, theologians, militarists, biochemists, financiers, and many more will each approach the issue from their own specialist perspective.

In this event, confusion will likely spring from each specialist perceiving the problem differently. The system professional's role will thus be to evaluate and reconcile these different perceptions and arrive at a problem definition as consistent as possible with all expert viewpoints.

The system analysts and engineers within our profession have an opportunity to make a generalist and convincing contribution to these debates. We face a tremendous problem. Solving problems is the forté of system analysts and engineers, whose traditional problem-solving method starts by determining the problem before designing its solution.

Once the problem is well defined, the system professional can search for and design solutions to it. Digital technology will then play an important role in most, if not all, possible solutions.

The Potential Problem . . .

It is too early to suggest that any particular analysis of the problem is correct, but some general conclusions seem obvious. If world trade was indeed the terrorists' symbolic target, it follows that they see their support as coming from those who feel victimized by world trade as it is now conducted. The most obvious sufferers of the world trade status quo are the inhabitants of the world's poorest countries.

For more than a decade, the United Nations Development Program has been drawing attention to the growing inequity in the world. Chapter One of the UNDP's 2001 report[46] records that one survey found "The richest 10 percent of the US population [0.5 percent of the world's people] (around 25 million people) had a combined income greater than that of the poorest 43 percent of the world's people (around 2 billion people)." Those who point to overall economic growth to justify extended commercialization fail to recognize that, despite such growth, the gap between rich and poor—as the UNDP reported—is widening.

Many of the world's poorest people live in Islamic NorthAfrica and Southwest Asia. At the same time, these locations contain some of the world's largest oil fields and, thus, they are also home to some of the world's richest individuals. These people have become conspicuously rich thanks to the developed world's—and particularly the US's—need for fuel.

The poor see the resulting inequity clearly. Those who wish to make trouble find it easy under these circumstances to depict the US as the villain. The US's own actions in the area further these perceptions, as Deakin University's Scott Burchill noted? [He] describes how several significant incidents from the past 20 years have tarnished the US's reputation in the region. The list includes planes shot down, cities exposed to bombing and naval bombardments, ships sunk, soldiers and civilians killed by "peacekeeping" forces, ongoing military and financial support for Israel, the establishment of US military bases in the Gulf area, and support for corrupt and oppressive Arab régimes.

Burchill gives special emphasis to the 1998 attack on a factory in Khartoum, which was bombed into oblivion without warning and with great loss of life because of its suspected role as a bin Laden chemical weapons factory. Only after the bombing did it become clear that the factory actually produced pharmaceuticals, supplying the Sudan with 60 percent of its medicines.

Incidents such as these help explain why the world's numerous poor so bitterly resent the world's conspicuous rich. Such resentment and such inequity can only serve to sustain extremists and provide them with suicidal volunteers.

We must understand that it is the *perception* of severe inequity and oppression that generates extreme emotions. It would, I believe, be wrong to say that this perception is the only or even most direct cause of organized terror. But it is overwhelmingly obvious that this perception greatly assists organized terror. Likewise, it's highly probable that terrorism cannot be eliminated while this perception persists.

... And the Possible Solution

Although severe inequity and extreme poverty may be the prime motivators of terrorist support, according to the UNDP's 2001 Report, a Robin Hood approach to redistributing the world's wealth will not eliminate them. Instead, we must empower the poor, especially the poorest of the poor, to help themselves—and we must use technology to do so.

Third World poverty is a scandal, and much of the Third World Islamic. Sadly, such poverty is much more visible to its victims than to those of us who hold the power to rescue them from it.

The UNDP supports educating and enhancing communications in the world's poorest regions, while *The Economist* advocates increased education in the developed countries. Both recommendations have merit. But in Britain, for example, spending on education has reached a 40-year low[44] yet the system remains hell-bent on "recruiting the best teachers from classrooms in developing countries." From the system analyst's viewpoint, this approach is global systematic lunacy.

We must make a greater investment in teacher training and the educational use of digital technology, for there can be no education without educators. The use of digital technology in education would be greatly aided if we set aside our marketing and profit priorities and instead manufactured stable, mass-produced machinery, then made it globally and cheaply available.

I doubt that we can look to the Internet to further education, however. As I have detailed elsewhere[25] the commercialization of the Internet will likely render it about as useful for education as television and radio have turned out to be.

The computing profession is based on the study and design of complex systems. We therefore have not merely an opportunity, but a special responsibility, to take part in the discussions and debates that follow from the September 11th incidents. We all must use our particular training and experience to understand the problems involved and help others understand them.

The problem is international, and its solution must be international. The computing profession is international and should work with international organizations to help define and solve the problem. In particular, we should support the UNDP, which advocates using technology to reduce poverty and inequity in the world.

As things stand, we can plausibly condemn using technology—industrial, commercial, or military—to create poverty and inequity. To me it seems obvious that if the poor of the world could see technology as something they can use, and are being helped to use, to alleviate their abject misery and poverty, this more than anything else will remove the perceived need for terrorism.

Whatever the root causes of terrorism, we system professionals must make the facts plain and public. To spend one or two years now using technology to fight the wrong problem will only lengthen the recovery by 10, 20, or even 100 years.

6.4   The Profession and the Big Picture

(2005 February)

This column has on occasion emphasized that the responsibilities of computing professionals—indeed of any learned profession's members—go beyond acquiring and applying technical experience and wisdom and beyond acting in their clients' best interests. The greatest professional responsibility is to act in the best interests of the society to which the profession owes its status.

By definition, human society's greatest interest is its continued existence. It seems the greatest threat to that continuance—climate change—is at last being given credence beyond scientific and environmental circles. The computing profession will play a crucial role in the battle to mitigate the effects of climate change and, if possible, adapt to them.

Therefore, we now share a responsibility to inform ourselves of the facts and press for the strategies and measures that we believe will be most effective in combating this threat.

Climate Change

The term *climate* refers to both the pattern of weather over a typical year and variations from typicality over longer periods. Climate varies from place to place, determining the kind of plants and wildlife that can live in a given location and, to a lesser degree, the kind and quality of life people can have there.

Geological records show quite clearly that climate can change greatly over various time scales. Historically, meteorological records show that the global climate has been gradually warming over the past century, while more recent meteorological records show that extremes of weather are becoming more frequent.

Although these meteorological records build a picture of anthropogenic climate change validated by scientific modeling and accepted by practicing climate scientists[38] some people still deny the facts. As professionals avowing rationality, we should become familiar with these facts and be ready to promptly counter such denials. The most popular denial at the moment is Michael Crichton's deceptive *State of Fear*,[14] authoritively rebutted at realclimate.org.[42]

Geological records show that many of the catastrophic discontinuities that separate major eras coincide with elevated temperatures that result from atmospheric changes. Simple projections of current trends show that a similar, if not worse, elevation in temperature is probable by the end of this century. This strongly implies that human society faces a catastrophe. Yet this impending disaster is still not widely realized. As professionals, we have a duty to spread this information.

The differences between today's climate changes and those of past catastrophes derive from their source: human activity largely drives today's change, primarily through the extraction of huge amounts of carbon—as gas, oil, and coal—from underground. When used, these minerals subsequently convert to atmospheric carbon dioxide, CO_2, presently at double the rate at which the Earth can absorb it. This CO_2 buildup has been accepted at an international level as harmful and man-made, although the acceptance lacks any sense of emergency. Indeed, critics typically advance arguments against doing anything about it because a discounted cash flow analysis suggests that countermeasures would be cheaper if postponed.

An engineer could easily demolish this absurd kind of argument, which is based on a superficial estimate of the costs involved and an assumption that climate has a simple linear behavior. Like all complex systems, Earth has time constants that could well induce dramatically nonlinear behavior, even unto catastrophe, that no delayed action could avoid.

Prediction

Human society must react to climate change. Just how it should react depends on reliable predictions of what will happen and how quickly, and what effect various countermeasures will have. Such predictions will rely heavily on digital technology. The quality of a digital climate model depends on two factors: the data available and the model itself.

Having large amounts of the right kind of data available ensures that the simulation is more reliable and allows refining the model by comparing predictions to outcomes. Digital technology could and should be more widely used to gather, store, and distribute meteorological and geological data.

Global climate models are already tremendously complex, and their development makes them steadily more so. Such models are based on 3D spatial grids, so halving the grid spacing to improve accuracy requires eight times as many data points. Refining the model, as discrepancies between prediction and outcome are explained, leads to the need for more data and computation at each grid point.

Presently, there are two approaches to climate simulation: distributed, as practiced at climateprediction.net[10] and using supercomputers. Both approaches must be improved continually.

This raises the basic problem that prediction cannot simply be a matter of projection. Too many contingencies also need scientific study and modeling: natural contingencies such as methane burps and ocean current changes and human contingencies such as mass migration resulting from the imminent Peruvian parching and the eventual Bangladeshi submersion. As researchers develop a better understanding of these contingencies, they must build the likely effects, singly and in combination, into the overall climate model.

From my reading, I suspect that these computations will require special-purpose multiprocessors with, for example, one processor per grid point. The arithmetic might also need improvement to lessen the accumulation of error in such large calculations. Whatever the case, the computing profession will play a crucial role in developing climate modeling.

Mitigation

The international community already recognizes that the human activity causing global warming must be curbed. The Kyoto Agreement[47] intended just that but seems unlikely to have any nonpolitical effect.

The problem seems to be that key political agents either do not know or do not accept the relevant facts. For example, at the recent two-week UN conference on climate change in Buenos Aires, the US representatives reportedly said that their government wants to concentrate on long-term programs to develop cleaner-burning energy technologies.[50] This statement implies that they do not understand that *dirty* burning has been lessening global warming, while the burning of fossil fuels adds CO_2 to the atmosphere and—perhaps just as seriously in the long run—any burning removes oxygen from it.

There is no doubt that we need to slow the accelerating addition of net CO_2 to the atmosphere, even though it is not the only cause of climate change. Indeed it's possible that soon we will need to actually reduce the CO_2 content to avoid catastrophe. Better modeling would give us a better idea of what's needed and provide a more persuasive argument to make to the politicians.

Because the situation calls for political action, informing the public of the relevant facts and projections might seem a practical activity, one in which computing professionals could use the Web and media as useful conduits. However, this assumes that an effective percentage of the public can understand the relevant scientific evidence and reasoning.

This assumption might well be wrong. For example, *The Nation's Report Card: Mathematics 2000* noted that more than one-third of US high school seniors lack basic proficiency in mathematics.[6] Worse, fewer than one-sixth have better than a basic proficiency.

Clearly, the computing profession should be pushing for the use of computers in schools simply to inculcate such basic skills, not just to ensure that younger people can understand what the climate has in store for them.

If we accept the need for practical and intense mitigation, a boost to education is crucial because of the underlying need for more scientists to analyze and model the climate and for more engineers to design and implement the machinery for mitigation. Further, given digital technology's potential to help educators, scientists, and engineers be more effective, more computing professionals will be needed. And their education must focus on the problems they will face.

Adaptation

Engineers in general, and computing professionals in particular, understand professionally the likely short-term and long-term behavior of complex systems. The Earth's climate is changing now, will change dramatically within a few human generations, and could change catastrophically in the longer term. These changes will drastically affect human society. If this is not soon accepted globally and officially, the world's scientists and engineers must take a large part of the blame.

The greatest danger is that human society will not adapt to the inevitable changes. Both mitigation and adaptation must be technologically based, just as the climate change itself is. In the worst case, the human effects of widespread starvation and thirst brought on by glacier disappearance alone could cause social disruption widespread enough to block the development and use of mitigation technology.

Governments will need to use technology of many kinds, necessarily supported by digital technology, in critically threatened areas in the immediate future simply to keep people there supplied with food and water.

In the medium term, agriculture as we know it might not survive if we cannot stop the spread of deserts. Should this occur, scientists would need to develop ways to industrially manufacture food. The flooding of low-lying coastal areas will require either constructing enormous levee banks or relocating many of the world's largest cities and densest rural populations. Increasing heat will mean that a large proportion of the world's population will depend on air conditioning for its very survival—even now, thousands die of extreme summer heat each year. Extremes of weather will require constructing buildings and the infrastructure more sturdily or even completely redesigning them.

In the long run, if mitigation is unsuccessful, the human race will be forced to live in a completely artificial environment, isolated from Earth's climate. Achieving this will present a huge technological challenge. On the bright side, if we succeed, we should be abler to colonize the Moon and Mars as well.

Motivation

Some readers may view this essay as mere scaremongering. I intend it to scare, but only because my reading has convinced me that the human race faces truly frightening prospects and that we might indeed already be doomed, at least as a civilization.

I ask only that those of you who remain unconvinced of the reality of these threats at least read some of the resources I have found—all directly or indirectly available through our wonderful Web and discoverable using its search engines. George Monbiot's short essay, "Goodbye, Kind World,"[36] shows that I am not alone in my apprehensions. Mark Lynas's book, *High Tide*,[32] is a persuasive and well-documented eyewitness account of some climate change effects already being felt.

More details can be found at government Web sites such as the Intergovernmental Panel on Climate Change,[28] academic Web sites such as that for the American Institute of Physics,[49] and of activists such as the Worldwatch Institute[51] and Climate Ark.[9]

Technology has almost entirely shaped the outward aspects of our civilization, and civilization's use of technology will certainly determine its own fate. Given that digital technology has become the main enabler of other technologies, this issue has undeniable relevance to the computing profession. In this case, we face the real danger that inaction by our profession and others might force us to share the fate of the apocryphal frog who, oblivious to his imminent demise, boiled to death in a gradually warming saucepan.

6.5   Notions

The notions are given here partly as a rough summary, but more particularly as topics and issues for students to study and debate. They are in the sequence of their *key word* or *phrase*. The page number to the right of each notion points to its context.

1. Buildings, machinery and goods are mere *artefacts* of civilization   237

2. *Capitalism* is neutral, just like technology or socialism   249

3. It is the mark of a *civilized* society
    to aim at eliminating such inequalities as have their source,
        not in individual differences, but in their own organization   247

4. *Climate prediction* cannot simply be a matter of projection   263

5. The *community* is the end
        and the economy merely one means to that end   246

6. The goal of competitors is to prevail,
        not to preserve *competition* in the market   252

7. The *computing profession* doesn't have a very clear view of itself   238

8. To effectively counter a terrorist system,
        we must first understand its *context*   257

9. The *digital divide* is only one symptom of the chasms
    that increasingly divide rich nations from poor
        and the rich within nations from their poor   251

10. *Digital technology* should not be used in the Third World
        in the same way it has been used in the First World   254

11. The *economy* is the end
        and the community merely one means to that end   246

12. The family and professional educators, not digital technology,
        provide *education*'s essential and principal tools   254

13. We must *empower* the poor, especially the poorest of the poor,
        to help themselves, and we must use technology to do so   259

14. In the long run, if mitigation of climate change is unsuccessful,
    the human race will be forced to live in a completely
        artificial *environment*, isolated from Earth's climate   264

6.6 Bibliography

The entries are in order of the first or only author's name. Where no personal author is known, as for popular news items, an indicative name is used. Where there is a page number or two in *italics* at the beginning of the annotation, they point back to where the item was cited. Where some of the annotation is given in quotes it has been taken from the item itself or from some of its publicity.

1. *ActionAid International* (2006). *About Us* (*p. 245*; "an international development agency whose aim is to fight poverty worldwide. Formed in 1972 ... today ... helping over 13 million of the world's poorest and most disadvantaged people"; www.actionaid.org/309/about_us.html).

2. David Adam (2006, April 18). "Global warming sparks a scramble for black gold under retreating ice," *The Guardian* (*p. 243*; a similar story on the front page of the *Guardian Weekly* of April 21 declares "British scientists are at loggerheads with US colleagues over a controversial plan to work alongside oil companies to hunt for fossil fuel reserves in the Arctic,"; guardian.co.uk/print/0,,329459327-103681,.html and the other at guardian.co.uk/guardianweekly/story/0,,1756812,.html).

3. David Attenborough (2002). *The Life of Mammals*. London: BBC Books, ISBN 0-563-53423-0, 320 pp. (*p. 253*; the TV series is described at bbc.co.uk/nature/animals/mammals).

4. *Baha Systems* (2006). *Welcome to Baha Systems*. Baton Rouge, Louisiana: BAHA Systems LLC (*p. 240*; just an example thrown up by Google at www.bahasystems.com/index2.htm).

5. *BBC* (2003, Nov. 4). "TV children taught how to talk," *British Broadcasting Corp'n* (*p. 254*; news.bbc.co.uk/2/hi/uk_news/education/3239861.stm).

6. James S. Braswell et al. (2001, August). *The Nation's Report Card: Mathematics 2000*. Washington, DC: National Center for Education Statistics, Institute of Education Sciences, NCES 2001–517, xx+348 pp. (*p. 263*; nces.ed.gov/nationsreportcard/pdf/main2000/2001/2001517.pdf).

7. Scott Burchill (2001, Sept. 21). "What Matters Is Why," *The Australian Financial Review*, Review section, p. 8 (*p. 258*; the author is on the staff of Deakin University and quite a few of his writings are online through scottburchill.net).

8. E. Ray Canterbery (1976). *The Making of Economics*. Belmont, California: Wadsworth Publishing Company, 1987, 3rd edition, ISBN 0-534-06786-7,

xvi+416 pp. (*pp. 248, 272*; a superb introduction to economics in general, in particular see Chapter 13 for a discussion of NAIRU).

9. *Climate Ark 2.0* (2006). *Climate Change and Global Warming Portal: Home Page* (*p. 265*; "... and search engine that promotes public policy that addresses global climate change through reduction in carbon dioxide and other emissions, energy conservation and ending deforestation."; climateark.org).

10. *ClimatePrediction.Net* (2006). *Gateway*, funded by the NERC and DTI e-Science programmes (*p. 262*; a large-scale distributed computing project using the otherwise idle computers of volunteers; climateprediction.net).

11. Matthew Collin (2002, August 31). "Wage slaves," *Guardian Weekly* (*p. 247*; reviews Barbara Ehrenreich's *Nickel and Dimed: Undercover in Low-wage USA* and Fran Abram's *Below the Breadline: Living on the Minimum Wage* as exposing the banality of life on the minimum wage on each side of the Atlantic; books.guardian.co.uk/print/0,,4491062-110738,.html).

12. Roger Coombs, Rick Siple and Neville Holmes (2003, Feb.). "Letters: Inflation, Greed, and Chattels," *Computer*, Vol. 36, No. 2, pp. 6–7 (*p. 249*; another letter was published in the previous month's issue).

13. Diane Coyle (2002, August 22). "For better: look at the progress already made," *Guardian Weekly* (*p. 245*; the author, who runs the *Enlightenment Economics* consultancy (www.enlightenmenteconomics.com), writes, inter alia, "It easy for economists to sound foolishly optimistic, because even if things are getting better, not worse, it's obvious that the pattern of world economic development has been deeply flawed."; online at guardian.co.uk/print/0,,4485127-110922,.html).

14. Michael Crichton (2004). *State of Fear*. HarperCollins, ISBN 0-066-21413-0, 624 pp. (*pp. 261, 273*; highly fictitious fiction).

15. Richard Dawkins (2001, Sept. 15). "Religion's Misguided Missiles," *The Guardian* (*p. 256*; guardian.co.uk/Archive/Article/0,,4257777,.html; "Promise a young man that death is not the end and he will willingly cause disaster").

16. Peter J. Denning and Andrew McGettrick (2005, Nov.). "The profession of IT: Recentering computer science," *Communications of the ACM*, Vol. 48, No. 11, pp. 15–19 (*p. 238*; "The recent decreases of enrollment in computer science programs signal a chasm between our historical emphasis on programming and the contemporary concerns of those choosing careers."; cs.gmu.edu/cne/pjd/PUBS/CACMcols/cacmNov05.pdf).

17. Charlotte Denny (2002, August 22). "Cows are better off than half the world," *Guardian Weekly* (*p. 245*; the subtitle: "The growing chasm between rich and poor is threatening global security."; online at guardian.co.uk/print/0,,4485133-110922,.html).

18. John Devlin (hd. 2006). *Computers, Networks and Architectures.* Latrobe University, Department of Electronic Engineering (*p. 239*; on research at latrobe.edu.au/ee/research/computer.html).

19. Tim Flannery (2005). *The Weathermakers: The History and Future Impact of Climate Change.* Melbourne, Victoria: The Text Publishing Company, ISBN 1 920885 84 6, xx+332 pp. (an authoritive survey of global relevance though with somewhat of an Australian focus).

20. *GAIPG* (2006).   *United Nations Information and Communications Technologies Task Force: Home Page.* Global Alliance for ICT Policy and Development (*p. 250*; unicttf.org).

21. Misha Glenny (2006, January 16). "The dark side of globalisation," *New Statesman.* (*pp. 241, 242*; reviews *Illicit: how smugglers, traffickers and copycats are hijacking the global economy*, by Moisés Naím, editor in chief of *Foreign Policy*; newstatesman.com/Books/200601160040).

22. *The Guardian* (2002, August 22). *Earth: Health check for a planet and its people under pressure.* (*p. 245*; this 16 page supplement to *Guardian Weekly* was prepared just in advance of the 2002 World Summit and is archived at guardian.co.uk/worldsummit2002/earth).

23. Roy Forbes Harrod (1969). *Money: A comprehensive account of the nature of money and of the development of monetary theory and of modern institutions.* London: Macmillan, ISBN 0 33310 506 0, xi+355 pp. (*p. 248*)

24. Alexander Hellemans (2005, October). "A Force to Reckon With: What applied the brakes on Pioneer 10 and 11?," *Scientific American*, Vol. 293, No. 4, pp. 12–13 (*p. 242*; "Especially if the mysterious force points toward the sun, then the explanation might be a deviation from Newtonian dynamics—termed modified Newtonian dynamics, or MOND—an idea originally proposed to explain why rotating galaxies do not fly apart."; sciam.com/article.cfm?articleID=000BB6BE-A7BA-1330-A54583414B7F0000).

25. W. Neville Holmes (2001). "The Net, the Web, and the Children," in *Advances in Computers*, ed. Marvin V. Zelkowitz, Vol. 55, pp. 49–85 (*p. 259*).

26. *The Hunger Site* (2006). *Home Page: Give Food For Free to Hungry People in the World* (*p. 251*; seems to be a well organized charity, despite the .com URL: thehungersite.com).

27. *Institute for the Study of Genocide* (2006).   *Selected Websites on Genocide Studies, State Killings, Groups at Risk, International Law and Past Genocides.* International Association of Genocide Scholars   (*p. 256*; the original citation, at worldhistory.com, has gone, but isg-iags.org/othersites.html has authoritive annotated links, and there's a simple longer link list at webster.edu/~woolflm/genocide.html).

28. *IPCC* (2006). *Intergovernmental Panel on Climate Change: Home Page.* World Meteorological Organization and United Nations Environment Programme (*p.265*; the Panel "has been established by WMO and UNEP to assess scientific, technical and socio- economic information relevant for the understanding of climate change, its potential impacts and options for adaptation and mitigation."; www.ipcc.ch with www.wmo.int and www.unep.org).

29. *ITU* (2006). *World Summit on the Information Society: Home Page.* The International Telecommunications Union (*p.250*; actually two summits, one in Geneva in 2003 and one in Tunis in 2005; their URL is itu.int/wsis).

30. *LinuxDevices.com* (2005, Oct.21). "Device Profile: DeLaval Voluntary Milking System" (*p.239*; "A 122-year-old dairy equipment company has used embedded Linux in a robotic cow-milking system"; a short report at linuxdevices.com/articles/AT8308307720.html).

31. James Lovelock (2006). *The Revenge of Gaia: Why the Earth Is Fighting Back—and How We Can Still Save Humanity.* London: Allen Lane, ISBN 07 13999 144, 192 pp. (*p.238*; a pessimistic book, advocating rapid adoption of nuclear power generation as the only way to save the world; reviewed timesonline.co.uk/article/0,,23114-2008072,.html).

32. Mark Lynas (2004). *High Tide: How Climate Crisis Is Engulfing Our Planet.* London: Harper Perennial, ISBN 0-00-713940-3, 349 pp. (*p.265*; there seems to be a variety of editions and also of subtitles, but the website marklynas.org/books is a good starting point).

33. Damien McCrystal (2002, September 22). "He may have just hit 90, but Milton Friedman should not be allowed to rest on his far from Nobel laurels," *The Observer.* (*p.248*; the title refers to the Bank of Sweden Prize; for more on monetarism's background, see Canterbery[8]; observer.guardian.co.uk/business/story/0,,796373,.html).

34. Peter Manolescue (2000, September). *A new approach to Integrated Security Systems.* Cheltenham, Gloucestershire: securityXML Limited, 3 pp. (*p.240*; a summary paper at securityxml.com/whitepaper.pdf).

35. Michael Meacher (2003, October 25). "The planet's polluters should be put in the dock," *The Guardian* (*p.252*; "Only a world environment court can curb capitalism's excesses"; the author was UK environment minister from 1997 to 2003; guardian.co.uk/print/0,,4782372-103677.html).

36. George Monbiot (2004, August 10). "Goodbye, Kind World," *The Guardian* (*p.265*; concludes "We live in the happiest, healthiest and most peaceful era in human history. And it will not last long"; monbiot.com/archives/2004/08/10/goodbye-kind-world-).

37. *Open Society Institute* (2006). *Iraq Revenue Watch* (*pp.241, 253*; this web

site, an initiative of the Open Society Institute (soros.org), holds links to a remarkable variety of news items; iraqrevenuewatch.org/news).

38. Naomi Oreskes (2004, Dec. 3). "Beyond the Ivory Tower: The Scientific Consensus on Climate Change," *Science*, Vol. 306, No. 5702, p. 1686 (*p. 261*; concludes "there is a scientific consensus on the reality of anthropogenic climate change"; sciencemag.org/cgi/content/full/306/5702/1686).

39. Lindsey Paterson and Kevin Bergqvist (2005, Oct. 17). "Gates encourages students to enter 'amazing' field," *The University Record Online*, University of Michigan (*p. 239*; a report of an address by Bill Gates of Microsoft; umich.edu/~urecord/0506/Oct17.05/00.shtml).

40. Charles Rosen (2003, November 6). "Culture on the Market," *The New York Review of Books*, Vol. 50, No. 17 (*p. 254*; text for subscribers or purchase at nybooks.com/articles/16746).

41. Rowan Scarborough (2006, January 20). "In search of rebuilding billions," *The Washington Times* (*p. 241*; "The World Bank has estimated [Iraq] needs another $40 billion in reconstruction money . . ."; online at washingtontimes.com/national/20060119-114656-2069r.htm).

42. Gavin A. Schmidt (2004, December 13). *Michael Crichton's State of Confusion*, RealClimate (*pp. 243, 261*; an exposure of *State of Fear*[14] on a website "on climate science by working climate scientists for the interested public and journalists"; includes several updates and many comments from readers; realclimate.org/index.php?p=74).

43. George Soros (1998, January). "The Economy: Towards a Global Open Society," *The Atlantic Monthly*, Vol. 281, No. 1 (*p. 252*; "The outspoken financier outlines more sharply a position for which he has been roundly attacked: that the global capitalist system urgently needs to be protected from itself"; the table of contents is at theatlantic.com/issues/98jan and the essay, for subscribers only, is opensoc.htm).

44. Heather Stewart, Charlotte Denny and Will Woodward (2001, Sept. 4). "Labour cut education spending to 40-year low," *The Guardian* (*p. 259*; guardian.co.uk/Archive/Article/0,,4250158,.html).

45. Richard Henry Tawney (1931). *Equality*. London: George Allen & Unwin (*p. 247*; for the author's biography, see infed.org/thinkers/tawney.html).

46. *UNDP* (2006). *United Nations Development Programme: Home Page* (*pp. 251, 258*; undp.org, and the various Human Development Reports are at hdr.undp.org, in particular, Chapter One of the 2001 report is in /reports/global/2001/en/pdf/chapterone.pdf; note that their initialism MDG stands for Millennium Development Goal).

47. *UNFCCC* (2006). *Essential Background: Kyoto Protocol*. United Nations Framework Convention on Climate Change (*p. 263*; the Protocol that,

conspicuously, neither Australia nor the US ratified; unfccc.int/2830.php).

48. *UN ICT Task Force* (2006). *Partner Organizations* (*p. 253*; they have slightly
prettied up the quotation without changing its essence and it is now at
unicttf.org/stakeholders/partnerships.html).

49. Spencer Weart (2005, December). *The Discovery of Global Warming.* The
Centre for the History of Physics, The American Institute of Physics
(*p. 265*; supplements the author's shorter book of the same name, linked
to from aip.org/history/climate; the summary is particularly useful,
though apparently not updated since 2004 July; "A hypertext history
of how scientists came to (partly) understand what people are doing to
cause climate change.").

50. *White House* (2004, November 19). *Fact Sheet: U.S. Climate Change Policy.*
Washington, DC: Office of the Press Secretary (*p. 263*; curiously subtitled
"The Bush Administration's Actions [sic] on Global Climate Change";
state.gov/g/oes/rls/fs/2004/38641.htm).

51. *Worldwatch Institute* (2006). *Home Page* (*p. 265*; "Independent research for
an environmentally sustainable and socially just society"; also put out a
bimonthly magazine; worldwatch.org).

Technical Details

The essays that form the bulk of each chapter of this book were written for members of the IEEE Computer Society, and so assumed some understanding of technical matters in computing.

Although the essays chosen for inclusion above are the less technical ones, those judged to be of more general than technical interest, they do sometimes have technical passages. This appendix is intended for those readers without the background to understand easily the more technical parts but who have an interest in understanding more about them.

The various sections that follow extend particular aspects of computing introduced in the body of the book. Also, at the end of this appendix (p.285) is an early essay published in *The Profession* which itself extends the topic of program coding that follows here.

Program Code

There have been many schemes for coding programs, which are usually called "programming languages" but which I call "coding schemes" (for my reasons, please refer to the essay below starting at p.285), and there are many yet to come.

The code resulting from use of such schemes tends nowadays to look quite similar, whatever the scheme, for three reasons.

Firstly, they are in the form of text and so are encoded using the ASCII character set. This character set, although it provides both upper and lower case letters, is impoverished in its provision for special characters. This leads to abominations such as the use of the asterisk as the symbol for multiplication.

Secondly, they specify operations to be carried out on data. Therefore the coding scheme must provide for both operations and data to be named and given values.

Thirdly, perhaps from unwillingness to use the keyboard's shift key, most programmers use only lower case letters. Actually, there could be a real though subtle reason for this habit, namely that some computing systems use upper and lower case letters dictionary fashion, that is, by treating a lower case letter and its corresponding upper case letter as being interchangeable.

With this background, consider the following code, written in the once popular C coding scheme, and as given on page 125 above.

```
//function to eliminate blanks from a string
   void eatspaces (char * string) {
      int to = 1;
      int from = 1;
      while ('\0' != (*(string + to) =
                         *(string + from++)))
            if (' ' != *(string + to)) to++;
      return;
   }
```

The following description is meant to make it a little clearer to the general reader what kind of ideas go into program code, not to teach anyone how to code programs, or even to explain exactly what the code of the example does.

In reading the description, it will be important to keep in mind that the computer has two roles to play. The first role is to convert the program code to machine instructions, and the second is to carry out the machine instructions. The first role is here distinguished by referring to the *compiler*.

In general terms, the block of code above will make the computer go from left to right along a character string moving only those characters that are not blanks ' ' until an end of string character '\0' is moved. This will almost always shorten the string.

The first line is a called a *remark* because it conveys general information about the code, in particular about its intended use. This has only significance to the human reader, and the coding convention is that the two consecutive / characters require the compiler to ignore any characters beyond them in the same line. Note that C also has the compiler ignore shorter or longer strings of characters if they follow a /* and precede a */ as shown on page 124.

Outside remarks and comments, formal words can be recognized as strings of consecutive letters of the alphabet. These are of two kinds: *keywords*, which are kept by C for its own purposes, and *names*, which the coder can choose to name data to be used within the program. In the example, `void char int while if` and `return` are keywords, but `eatspaces string to` and `from` are names referring to data, names chosen by the coder.

The comments, remarks, keywords and names are really only superficial descriptions. They contribute nothing to the shape or structure of the code. Thus, the overall structure of the code is set up by the outermost pair of braces.

The *header* is all that precedes the leading brace, the *body* is all that the first and last braces enclose.

The header specifies what the program code block is to look like to any coder who wants to use it. The eatspaces is to be the name of the code block (or *function* or *method* in modern parlance). The (char * string) specifies and names the data to be given to the block for it to process; they are to be characters, and the * specifies that string is to be where those characters are stored, not the characters themselves. The keyword void says that no value will be returned to the user by this code.

In general, the body specifies what data are internal to the block, and what process is to be applied to the various data. Each specification ends with a semicolon. The int to = 1 gives the integer value 1 to the name to. The keyword return says that processing by the block is to stop when the computer reaches this point.

The bulk of the processing is done by part of the code that has the form

while (*control*) if (*condition*) *action*

where the importance of the parentheses for defining the structure of the code becomes obvious. The control of the while keeps the if going until the control turns *false*. The action of the if is only carried out if its condition is *true*.

The innermost details are a bit technical, but need to be understood before what actually is meant to happen can be understood. If you are daunted by now, don't feel you have to read on! Programmers might need to understand this kind of thing, but there are less complex coding schemes that aren't so tricksy and that are more suitable for everyday use.

The != that follows each of the ' ' and '\0' characters asks for a comparison to be done that results in *true* if the comparison shows unequal and in *false* otherwise. Because string says where the first character of the string being processed is, (string+to) says where the character at offset to is. (This makes it peculiar that to and from were made to start at one, meaning the character at offset zero is ignored.) The to++ says that the value of to is to be used, but also that it is to be bumped up by one after each use. Finally, the asterisk * (which here does not ask for a multiplication) makes the * (string+to) refer to the character at the location string+to.

With these inner details explained, the nature of the while control

'\0' != (* (string + to) = * (string + from++))

can be described. The comparand to the right of the != is specified within the parentheses, where the = symbol dominates, but it oddly does *not* ask for a comparison to be done. Rather, it asks for the character at string+from to be copied to string+to and only then to be used for the != comparison.

Overall, the while moves the from pointer each time, but the to pointer only when a non-blank character has been copied across. Just how this is done is left for the reader to work out.

One terminological subtlety to notice is my use of the word *blank* and the code's use of the word *space* in eat spaces. While a blank character is always only the character produced by the space bar, the word *space* is sometimes used to include the tabulate, carrier return and line feed characters of the ASCII character set. Careful usage, though, prefers the term *whitespace* for this.

Sortemic Text Encoding

The thesis being argued here is that the most benefit commercially, culturally and socially would come from providing text encoding standards for writing systems based on facilitating the use of each writing system as a graphical instrument. For convenience, I refer to such encoding here as *sortemic*.

The idea of sortemic coding is to go back to the earlier days of the printing industry and encode for a variety of fundamental graphic components plus some operations for combining them. Such components are called *sorts* in the traditional printing industry. Sorts can be combined by operations such as kerning, as explained and illustrated in the section GREEK TYPE of *A New Introduction to Bibliography*.[5] I use the term *sorteme* to name the basic graphical element of a writing system, either a sort or a graphical operation on sorts, by analogy with *grapheme*, which *The Oxford English Dictionary* defines as "a feature of written expression that cannot be analysed into smaller meaningful units."

Sortemic text encoding would allow more fluent encoding of text, more useful plain text display, more expressive marking-up of encoded text, more effective processing of stored text, and more versatile composition of displays and documents.

These properties will be explained more fully after giving an outline of the possibilities for two major and distinct writing systems: the Chinese writing system which aims to represent *meanings* by stringing characters together,[12] and the alphabetic writing systems, primarily the one using the Latin alphabet, which aim to represent *speech* by stringing characters together.[10]

The Chinese Writing System

The various coding systems for the Chinese writing system treat the many thousands of characters as simply a collection of characters. Keying in is often done using a QWERTY keyboard to key in the official Latin alphabet spelling of the official spoken language's word for each character. Because there are many homonyms, these spellings may have to be disambiguated. Keying in by this method is therefore a relatively slow process. Furthermore, this method is specific to only one of the many languages that use the Chinese writing system.

Chinese characters are, however, composed of a strict sequence of parts, typically two, usually called *roots*, the first root being called the *radical*. A keyboarding scheme used in mainland China and called wŭbǐzìxíng maps the roots onto the QWERTY keyboard, using twenty-five keys (the z is used as a "wild card") with about seven different roots on each![1] At most four keystrokes are needed for a character, and a skilled typist can key 160 characters a minute.

The problem with wŭbǐzìxíng is that it's too complex for most people to learn. If a Chinese keyboard were produced with around sixty keys then the commonly used roots could be three to a key allowing shift keys to be used to directly choose any root. This would have several benefits.

• Being so simple, it could be used by anyone who could read the characters.
• It would be much faster than wŭbǐzìxíng with QWERTY, particularly if a radical shift key were used to signal the start of every character.
• Children could be much more easily taught to read and key in characters, as could older learners.

The benefits would be much greater if, instead of storing the text encoded by character as at present, it were encoded by root, that is, by sorteme.

• Less storage space would be needed.
• Processes such as indexing and sequencing would be easier.
• New combinations of roots could be used as characters, freeing the Chinese writing system from its shackles of tradition. The system, being much faster than alphabetic or syllabic systems for both keying and reading, and being relatively independent of any spoken language, could then come into much wider use as an international writing system. The few simplified characters inconsistent with the traditional root system could easily be dropped.

Alphabetic and Syllabic Text Encoding

These benefits for users of the Chinese system would come from recognizing that writing systems embody graphical principles that could be, and could be further, exploited through the use of computers. These graphic principles inhere to the writing system, not to the languages that use the system.

In writing this description, I am able to use accents and ligatures, as in *æsthete ångstrom façade gauß naïve* and *pīnyīn*, because of the genius of Donald Knuth who built the TEX system[7] which is behind the LaTEX software I'm using here.[8] I can even use accents and ligatures unconventionally, as in Ḍōñàḻḏ and ƕ, and, not quite so easily, unusual accents and overlays, as in ⊙ and č̓.

Graphical devices or *constructs* are part and parcel of the writing system that has developed around the Latin alphabet. They go way beyond the needs of any particular language, though some languages are much more dependent on them than others. These constructs are also the basis for the variations used for the International Phonetic Alphabet, and for the initial teaching alphabets used particularly for English.

The barrier to the free use of graphical constructs with the Latin alphabet is the QWERTY keyboard. In TEX Knuth uses mark-up conventions, that is, special sequences of ASCII characters, to encode conventional accents and ligatures. To become general, the *constructors* need to be built into the character set encoding and thence into keyboards and into the programs that compose text for display.

It is essential here to distinguish between plain text and composed text. Plain text is simply sequences of characters at the lowest level, but text that can be seen and read in full without complex processing. Composed text is text such as this, set in a particular font, Palatino, with different size letters in different parts of the text, and with both *italic* and roman styles in use.

Composed text is derived from plain text by placing mark-up, instructions for composition, at places in the plain text where it is to have effect. Thus there are three influences on the composed text: the plain text outside the mark-up, the mark-up itself, and the program that does the composition. If I wanted to have a euro symbol here, which the ASCII character set does not have, then I could combine plain text C= by interposing mark-up of \llap as C\llap= which would be composed to €. Although it's quite clearly a euro symbol, it's not very pretty, but the composing program could be made to pick up the special coding and produce a more handsome version.

In TEX the ASCII character set forces simple graphical construction into the mark-up. But because many of the ASCII ideographic characters can be viewed as combinations, it's feasible to consider using an 8-bit encoding to provide two alphabets, just as Linotype and Monotype once did, and encode graphic constructors to allow creativity. For example, were $η$ to denote a 90° rotation, then $8η$ and $Aηη$ would yield the mathematical symbols ∞ and $\forall$.

However, what can be done for the Latin alphabet can also be done for other alphabetic writing systems, and probably for syllabic ones as well. If these were all, or most of them, done to the same pattern, then transliteration could be almost automatic and switching between these writing systems for display might be made as simple as switching fonts in the mark-up.

What such a coding scheme might look like is suggested in following two diagrams, where the graphic operations are called *constructors*.

The diagram on the left shows a general scheme under which alphabetic and syllabic writing systems might be coalesced. The diagram on the right shows the general scheme as it applies to the Latin alphabet. Other alphabets could very well be fitted into the same specific pattern, so that transliteration could be done merely by using mark-up to change the font. The alphabetic writing systems, like Hanguel, Nāgarī and the Arab system[1] that have syllabic effects might have these effects applied either at the plain text stage or through fonts at the composition stage.

With the Latin alphabet the scheme provides for the following classes of sortemes:

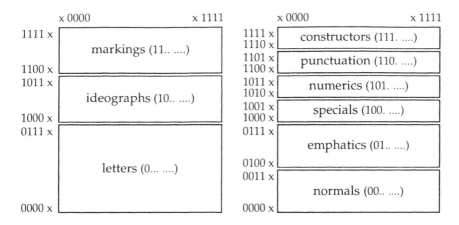

- 32 letters in each of upper and lower case in each of normal or roman and emphatic or italic style,
- 32 basic special characters, basic in not being derivable from other sortemes by simple construction,
- 32 numeric characters allowing for ten decimal digits in each of two styles plus six arithmetic signs and six arithmetic operation symbols (see p. 66),
- 32 punctuation symbols, including normal punctuation symbols that are also basic shapes suitable for graphical use, and format symbols such as blanks and tabulations, and line end and other structural symbols, and
- 32 constructors specifying graphical operations, probably best divided equally between the monadic (a modifier for the sort to its left) and the dyadic (a combiner for the two sorts to its left).

The benefits

The following examples are specific to alphabetic encoding. The benefits of sortemic encoding for the Chinese system are of course different.

More fluent encoding: A universal keyboard for all languages that use the Latin alphabet would have 32 lettered keys. Three shift keys used in combination for each hand would suffice. Extra lettered keys for frequent code sequences could be used on language-specific keyboards. Simpler, much faster and very cheap would be a chordal keyboard (or data gloves) with eight bit keys for the fingers and a complement key for each thumb. Such a design could be useful with mobile telephones.

More useful plain text display: By having constructors apply to the sort or sorts to their left, plain text entry can show the effect of each constructor as it is keyed in, and the effect of backspace deleting when used for correction. By assigning symbols that are not easily constructed to the constructors, and by providing a *stet* constructor to select the symbol rather than the operation for plain text, two modes of display could be provided: one with the constructors in effect, one with their symbols showing.

More expressive mark-up: Because the plain text itself is more expressive, for example in providing superscripts and subscripts, the mark-up can be specific to formatting and structuring. Because some constructor combinations, such as double reflection, are redundant to plain text, these can be used to separate mark-up from body text conveniently.

More effective processing: Because the encoding is more systematic, the classes of symbol can be determined and manipulated in program code by simple use of the leading bits. For example, all letters have a zero leading bit, and can all be folded for lexemic sequencing into lower case normal style letters by changing the following two bits to zero. The sequence of letters within the alphabet would need to be phonetic so that transliteration, for example between the Latin and Cyrillic alphabets, would be automatic. The resulting natural sequencing could be used across languages, though the various and inconsistent traditional sequences of different languages (German treats *ä* and *a* as the same letter, Finnish as distinct; English treats *ll* as two letters, Welsh as one) could be handled by separate program code.

More versatile composition: With two styles and with sort construction built into the plain text encoding, the font program could deal more thoroughly with esthetic details. Fewer fonts would be needed as phonetic and initial teaching sorts, novel sorts and "foreign" names could be handled within an ordinary font.

These are only examples of benefits. Care with the detailed design of sortemic text encoding standards could lead to many more that are hard to foresee. The basic problem, though, is getting such a project going and getting its results into use because the benefits are mainly social and cultural and these have little marketing heft, especially if they aren't brought into the intellectual property fold. Indeed, sortemic text encoding is basically a simplification, and simplifications are notoriously unprofitable in the computing industry.

Inverted Files

When "The KWIC and the Dead" (essay 5.3, p.206) was published, Richard Veith took issue with my statement that inverted files were "pioneered largely by Gerard Salton" (p.208). He was right to do so. Salton was the leader of the pioneering Project SMART at Cornell University which used inverted files, but inverted files or their close relatives were in use long before.

A simple illustration of an inverted file can be appreciated by considering two kinds of punched cards which were in use into the 1960s: *edge-notched* cards[4] (also called needle, McBee and edge-punched cards) and *peek-a-boo* cards[13] (also called aspect, optical coincidence and Batten cards).

Edge-notched cards were used for making a catalog searchable. A typical card would have a few rows of holes just in from one or more edges of the card. A catalog would have a card for each item. Each card would have data about its item written in labelled boxes on the card. A hand tool encoded identification and key data by making notches out of the holes, which were typically labelled to make the notching easier to get right.

Selection was done by lining small batches of the cards being searched up on a stand, putting a needle through the next hole of interest, and carefully lifting and shaking the batch so that all the cards with a notch at the needle would drop down. Suppose the cards were for books and the cards had holes standing for keywords. If there were holes allocated for the keywords *computer* and *library*, then needling those two holes in succession would drop out all cards for books about computers and libraries.

Peek-a-boo cards turned this idea on its head. In the case of a library index, instead of having one card for every book, the peek-a-boo idea was to have one card for every keyword and one hole position on every card allocated to a book. A smallish card having 12 rows and 80 columns for holes would allow each deck to accommodate 960 books.

Selection was done by picking out the cards for the keywords of interest, holding the cards together and looking for light. With the cards for *computer* and *library* in hand, light would shine through all those positions allocated to books about computers and libraries.

If these card files were to be handled by machine, the search time for the edge-notched cards would depend on the number of books, while the search time for the peek-a-boo cards would depend on the number of keywords.

Machinery nowadays uses magnetic or other recording media which allow many more and much larger records, so that the number of items in a catalog or any other collection of data will usually outnumber the distinct words or other search categories. Moreover, a set of distinct words or categories can be arranged so that search is greatly speeded up.

The kind of index implemented by peek-a-boo cards is called an inverted file index. The following example should show why inverted file techniques have been so widely used in searching by machine.

The table below shows short quotations selected from the KWIC index on page 211. There are four quotations, and they are identified here by the letters *a b c* and *d* given to their left. The words in each quotation are lined up by using extra spaces so that their index number can be easily seen. There are thirty one words altogether, so that searching this table for all the occurrences of any particular word would require thirty one comparisons, plus all the time taken to pick the words out of their quotations.

	0	1	2	3	4	5	6	7	8	
a	I	hold	every	man	a	debtor	to	his	profession.	25:14
b	An	ornament	to	her	profession.					99:33
c	Your	Majesty	is	the	head	of	the	literary	profession.	181:24
d	Those	things	that	are	contrary	to	their	profession.		389:36

This table or file can be inverted in the sense that a one-time process can set up a list of the distinct words in the file, and show which quotations each word occurs in. As there are only twenty five distinct words, only thirteen comparisons are needed on average to find any word in the table, and, as the table is in sequence, about the same to find out that a word is not in the table.

a	*a*4	her	*b*3	majesty	*c*1	their	*d*6
an	*b*0	his	*a*7	man	*a*3	things	*d*1
are	*d*3	hold	*a*1	of	*c*5	that	*d*2
contrary	*d*4	i	*a*0	ornament	*b*1	those	*d*0
debtor	*a*5	is	*c*2	profession	*a*8 *b*4 *c*8 *d*7	to	*a*6 *b*2 *d*5
every	*a*2	literary	*c*7	the	*c*3 *c*6	your	*c*0
head	*c*4						

The word numbering in this index is not needed if the task is only to find the quotations with specific words. However, in practical use the number of items being indexed will be very large, enormous in the case of the World Wide Web, so extra data are usually kept to enable more particular selection. Keeping word locations as shown here would allow aspects like adjacency and frequency to affect selection.

One way to lessen the time taken to find particular words in a list is for each word in the list to have two pointers to other words, and use these pointers to impose a fan-like structure on the list. Such a structure is shown below for the example above.

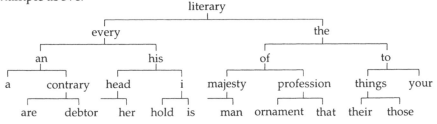

That there are five levels of words here means that at most five comparisons are needed to find any word, or to find that any word is absent. The gain over simple sequential searching is very much greater for very long lists.

Some Comments on the Coding of Programs

(2000 November)

Exactness and accuracy are not the same thing. Compilers require program code to be exact. Computers provide arithmetic that is inexact. Programmers must take particular care with their coding if they wish to ensure that their programs produce accurate results.

Programmers must also take particular care if their compilers are to produce correct results. Coding must be exact, except for the comments, which the compiler ignores. Overlook one inconspicuous mistake in spelling or punctuation and your program may run wildly astray or, much worse, subtly astray. Although compilers, interpreters, and code editors detect many of these mistakes, not all such errors render the code invalid; those that do not will escape automatic detection.

Much could be done to help programmers avoid such coding errors. Unfortunately, more attention seems always to be given to making programs understandable. The two objectives are not contradictory, but there seem to be ingrained attitudes that prevent the use of certain simple coding techniques such as those that I'll describe. Cobol provides a case in point.

Text As Code

In the 1960s, Cobol's designers deliberately made their coding scheme verbose with the laudable objective of making it difficult to code programs that others would have trouble understanding. Not only must Cobol programmers use many required keywords, but the whole system of naming data fields in records was well designed to encourage descriptive naming. A program's most significant components are its data names, so the introduction of Cobol's structured naming scheme provided a great step forward for legible programming.

The downside of verbosity is the coding effort required and the difficulty of exactly coding all the names within the code. Thus, developers created many Cobol preprocessors—programs that filled in the text required by Cobol and greatly abbreviated the data names chosen by the programmer.

ICT's Rapidwrite was such a preprocessor, and it could produce the fully-filled out Cobol program listing that management expected to be able to read.

The Rapidwrite programmer used short names of up to five letters, but could provide a long synonym to be used in the Cobol listing instead of the less meaningful short names that were more convenient in practical coding.

Developers proposed many other schemes for systematic abbreviation of names in program code in those days of small main stores and slow cycle times. The scheme advanced by June Barrett and Mandalay Grems in 1960[2] was based on eliminating English's most frequently occurring letters first, while always retaining a word's first letter. However, this scheme consisted of more than 20 rules—a few too many for the average programmer.

I prefer a simpler, three-rule scheme for abbreviating names:

• Always keep the first letter.
• Shorten double letters to single, treating CK as KK.
• Remove the vowels A, E, I, O, U.

The last rule resembles one adopted by the writing system normally used for languages such as Arabic and Urdu, which omits vowels from normal text.

Consider a program code sample that Ted Lewis included in his November 1998 Binary Critic column[3] shown in Figure 1 with comments removed.

```
Implement Payroll.Update Class{
   With Person.Payroll {
      Write Update(typeof(Name) N,
                   typeof(Gender) G,
                   typeof(Phone) Ph )
                   {
                      Name = N;
                      Gender = G;
                      Phone = Ph;
                   }
   }
}
```

Figure 1. A program code sample, which will be used throughout
to demonstrate the effects of various coding techniques.

I produced the version of this code shown in Figure 2 by applying the three rules. I left the first instance of any data name in full, as a compiler or interpreter using the rules would require.

This example demonstrates that, in English-based coding schemes at least, the significance lies mainly in the consonants. Naturally, this small example only implies the convenience of such an abbreviation system in a large program. However, I find it useful and convenient to use this system in naming files and directories as well.

For greatest benefit, the compiler or interpreter would need to prevent

```
Implmnt Payroll.Update Cls{
    Wth Person.Pyrl {
      Wrt Updt(typf(Name) N,
              typf(Gender) G,
              typf(Phone) Ph
            ) { Nm = N;
                Gndr = G;
                Phn = Ph;
              }
    }
  }
```

Figure 2. The code after application of a three-rule abbreviation scheme.

accidental synonyms, but would tolerate a variety of the more common misspellings. In the 1960s, the Autopromt coding system for numerically controlling machine tools successfully used a similar abbreviation scheme in its compiler. Strangely, this compiler technique failed to achieve widespread adoption. Had it done so, programmers would have gained much-needed relief from having to code programs so exactly.

The Ultimate Challenge: Punctuation

Misspelling is not the greatest challenge to coding exactness, however. That honor goes to punctuation: the various nonalphabetic, nonideographic marks that impinge so little on the eye and so greatly on the program.

For example, enclosure symbols such as quotation marks are much easier to use in prose than in programs. In prose, they suggest how the text should be read out loud more than they prescribe meaning. In programs, punctuation has an enormous effect on how the compiler reads the enclosed text: leave out a quotation mark and error messages flow like water.

Enclosure marks pose two problems in program code. First, telling symbols apart can be difficult because they tend to look similar in most print fonts, on the screen or off, particularly the parentheses and braces of our examples. Second, properly pairing enclosure marks can be challenging. This difficulty leads to the coding practice of bringing the enclosure symbols out where they can be seen more easily, as shown in Figures 1 and 2. Some programmers line up the symbols even more systematically, as shown in Figure 3. A layout such as this makes checking enclosure symbols much easier by lining up the pairs vertically and spacing them away from nearby text.

There are exceptions. There is no point in splitting shortrange enclosures: In Figure 3, (Name) is clearly a single item and should be treated as such.

```
Implmnt Payroll.Update Cls
  { Wth Person.Pyrl
    { Wrt Updt ( typf (Name) N,
                 typf (Gender) G,
                 typf (Phone) Ph
             ) { Nm = N;
                 Gndr = G;
                 Phn = Ph;
  } }                    }
```

Figure 3. The code with enclosure symbols aligned systematically.

Nor can quotation marks, typically used in program code to delimit character strings, be given this treatment.

This example suggests that punctuation marks other than enclosures—especially separators that are easily overlooked, like commas and semicolons—should also be highlighted through code layout. This highlighting can be done in the first instance by spacing out the marks so that they are more easily seen—a practice completely foreign to natural language text, but clarifying to code, as can be seen by comparing Figure 3 and Figure 4.

```
Implmnt Payroll.Update Cls
  { Wth Person.Pyrl .
    { Wrt Updt ( typf (Name) N ,
                 typf (Gender) G ,
                 typf (Phone) Ph
             ) { Nm = N ;
                 Gndr = G ;
                 Phn = Ph ;
  } }                    }
```

Figure 4. The code with separators spaced out to increase their visibility.

But having these separators at the end of lines causes problems. If they are scattered, it's harder to notice that one is missing. Further, when they are at the end of lines it's easy to delete them along with trailing text. So it would really be better to line them up vertically as well, as shown in Figure 5.

Obviously, code laid out this way acquires a tabular flavor. This formatting suggests the possibility of doing away with that pesky punctuation altogether—which is exactly what Rapidwrite did. RPG, arguably the most productive of coding schemes, also makes do with very little punctuation. Still widely used even though it's nearly as ancient as Fortran, RPG is is tarred with the brush of business and thus lacks respectability in academic circles. Perhaps

```
Implmnt Payroll.Update Cls
{ Wth Person.Pyrl
   { Wrt Updt ( typf  (Name)  N
              ,  typf  (Gender)  G
              ,  typf  (Phone)  Ph
              )  { Nm  =  N
                 ;  Gndr  =  G
                 ;  Phn  =  Ph
} }                        }
```

Figure 5. The code with punctuation spaced out and aligned vertically.

it needs a touch from the fairy godmother's OO wand?

Coding Versus Writing

Maybe the layout scheme I've described seems straightforward and thus leaves you at best lukewarm. Experience suggests, however, that some readers might feel strangely disquieted by this scheme, or even stirred to anger.

The problem seems to be psychological and springs from the unfamiliar arrangement of commas and semicolons. In the early 1960s, someone wrote to one of the less formal programming newsletters and suggested that semicolons in program code be aligned vertically at the front of code lines. Many responses to this proposal adopted an irrationally irate and somewhat incoherent tone. Clearly, some programmers' dander was way up, and few readers supported the scheme.

Nevertheless, it seemed like a good idea to me, and I adopted it for the PL/I programming I did at that time and have persisted in the practice. In the early 1980s, I taught a second-year programming course at a tertiary education institution. The Pascal examples I presented in class all had their semicolons up front and vertically aligned. When this news reached my colleagues they reacted swiftly, passionately, and negatively.

Such punctuation alignment was, they solemnly told me in a protest meeting, "not structured programming." After much discussion, they agreed that I should at least inform the class that the practice was rarely followed and generally frowned upon, particularly by my fellow lecturers.

It's hard to explain the heat of such reactions. I can only infer that the literary practice of placing periods, commas, semicolons, and colons strictly at the immediate end of words is so habitual that to suggest doing otherwise stimulates instinctive opposition.

Confusing program code with prose writing—viewing coding as somehow literary—must be deeply ingrained. It's a pity that I. D. Hill's splendid article

"Wouldn't It Be Nice If We Could Write Computer Programs in Ordinary English—Or Would It?"[6] has not been more widely read. It thoroughly demolished the idea that program code proper should have any literary content—although program comments are quite another matter. Indeed, the computing profession would be wise to promote a more considered view of programming that contrasts coding and literary endeavor.

A good start would be to abandon expressions like "programming languages" and "writing programs" in favor of "coding schemes" and "program coding." That's what they really are, and that's what we, or our technicians, really do. Adopting such terminology consistently in our talk and writing would dispel loose thinking about what programmers do, both for programmers themselves and for the profession and its public at large.

Notions

The notions are given here partly as a rough summary, but more particularly as topics and issues for students to study and debate. They are in the sequence of their *key word* or *phrase*. The page number to the right of each notion points to its context. This being an appendix entitled *Technical Details*, the maxims mostly concern technical issues.

Bibliography

The entries are in order of the first or only author's name. Where no personal author is known, as for popular news items, an indicative name is used. Where there is a page number or two in *italics* at the beginning of the annotation, they point back to where the item was cited. Where some of the annotation is given in quotes it has been taken from the item itself or from some of its publicity.

1. Simon Charles Ager (2006). *Omniglot: Writing Systems and Languages of the World.* (*p. 280*; at omniglot.com, this is an absolutely brilliant and thorough compilation).

2. June A. Barrett and Mandalay Grems (1960, May). "Abbreviating words systematically," *Communications of the ACM*, Vol. 3, No. 5, pp. 323–324 (*p. 286*; PDF for ACM members via portal.acm.org/toc.cfm?id=367326).

3. Robert S. Casey, James W. Perry, Madeline M. Berry and Allen Kent (edd. 1958). *Punched Cards: Their Applications to Science and Industry.* New York: Reinhold Publishing Corporation, second edition, x+697 pp. (the classic text of its day; 29 chapters and a large annotated bibliography).

4. Robert S. Casey and James W. Perry (1958). "Elementary Manipulations of Hand-Sorted Punched Cards," Chapter 2 of Casey et al.3 pp. 12–29 (*p. 283*; other chapters describe uses).

5. Philip Gaskell (1972). *A New Introduction to Bibliography.* Delaware: Oak Knoll Press, corrected edition, 1995, ISBN 1-58456-036-3, 438 pp. (*p. 278*; a splendid book, with more on the history of book production than on what is conventionally seen as bibliography).

6. I. D. Hill (1972, June). "Wouldn't It Be Nice If We Could Write Computer Programs in Ordinary English—Or Would It?," *The Computer Bulletin*. Vol. 16, No. 6, pp. 306–312 (*p. 290*).

7. Donald Ervin Knuth (1986). *The TEXbook*. Reading, Mass.: Addison Wesley Publishing Company, ISBN 0-201-13447-0, x+483 pp. (*p. 279*; there is a TEX Users Group website tug.org).

8. Helmut Kopka and Patrick W. Daly (2004). *Guide to LATEX*. Boston, Mass.: Addison Wesley, ISBN 0-321-17385-6, xii+597 pp. (*p. 279*).

9. Ted Lewis (1998, November). "Binary Critic: The Legacy Maturity Model," *Computer*, Vol. 31, No. 11, pp. 128, 125–127 (*p. 286*; available as csdl.computer.org/dl/mags/co/1998/11/ry128.pdf).

10. John Man (2000). *Alpha Beta: How Our Alphabet Shaped the Western World*. London: Headline Book Publishing, ISBN 0-7472-6447-3, 312 pp. (*p. 278*; *New Scientist*: "Crisp, taut and clear as a bell ... It is a fascinating story with many a beguiling subplot along the way").

11. Joe Wicentowski (1996). *Wubuxing For Speakers of English*. Harvard University (*p. 279*; an excellent introduction, if your browser can display the characters: people.fas.harvard.edu/~wicentow/wubixing.html).

12. L. Wieger (1927). *Chinese Characters: Their Origin, Etymology, History, Classification and Signification*. New York: Paragon Book Reprint Corp. and Dover Publications, Inc., second edition, reprinted 1965, LCCCN: 64-18441, 820 pp. (*p. 278*; the classical book on the topic, still informative though not up to date).

13. W. A. Wildhack and Joshua Stern (1958). "The Peek-a-boo System—Optical Coincidence Subject Cards in Information Searching," Chapter 6 of Casey et al.[3] pp. 125–151 (*p. 283*; other chapters describe uses).

Index

Guide to the Index

My main aim for the following index is for it to be a useful resource. This book ranges widely over many topics, so the reader, remembering vaguely about some particular technique or issue, might well wish to get back to it. The more easily this can be done the better, and in particular every personal name mentioned in the book has been indexed.

The index mixes many kinds of entries. Titles of books, serial publications, and named entities such as videogames, are given in *italics*. Sometimes long titles are given on two lines, particularly when there is a title and a subtitle.

Names of people, such as authors, are given as surname followed by name, or initials, depending on what is known. Long organization names may be split onto two lines. While indexing of personal names has been thorough, names of some organizations have been left out, and there are no publishers' names included.

Otherwise entries for ordinary words appear ordinarily, except that plurals are indexed as singular. Topics have been included impulsively, sometimes whimsically, in parallel with the composition of the book.

The essays within each chapter are indexed under the entry of *Profession, The* by their date of publication, and in that sequence. Note particularly that the early essays were not actually published in that column, but they are shown there in the index with the name of their month of publication in *italics*.

Simple citations of the essays are also given there, but they will have a single page number rather than a range. This part of the index can be used to find where such citations have been made, an approach which avoids having to change the original text of the essays included in this book.

Significant initialisms and acronyms are collected under the entry for "initialism" with a page number where some explanation might be given. When the page number is in italics there *is* an explanation on that page. Only sometimes are initialisms indexed under their full name.

Another special entry is that for URL, an initialism of the World Wide Web standing for Uniform Resource Locator. This entry serves as a subindex to where URLs are cited within the book, mostly in the bibliographies. A finer index is provided under *domain name* where the domain names from the URLs are also indexed, in sequence by their reversed components.

Index